Greenhouse Management for Amateurs:

DESCRIPTIONS OF THE BEST GREENHOUSES AND FRAMES, WITH
INSTRUCTIONS FOR BUILDING THEM, AND PARTICULARS OF
THE VARIOUS METHODS OF HEATING;

DICTIONARIES OF THE MOST SUITABLE HARD-WOODED, SOFT-WOODED,
CLIMBING, AND ANNUAL PLANTS, WITH GENERAL AND
SPECIAL CULTURAL DIRECTIONS FOR EACH;

AND

ALL NECESSARY INFORMATION FOR THE GUIDANCE OF
THE AMATEUR.

By W. J. MAY

(Author of " Villa Gardening," " Vine Culture for Amateurs," &c.)

LONDON:
"THE BAZAAR, OFFICE," 170, STRAND, W.C.

LONDON :
PRINTED BY ALFRED BRADLEY, 170, STRAND, W.C.

PREFACE.

WE do not wish to apologise for any part of the hints herein given, as they are all the results of practice, and if followed will not fail to give satisfaction to all amateur growers; but it must be remembered that "an ounce of practice is worth a pound of theory," a maxim particularly applicable to gardening, as all the books in the world will not make a person a good grower of plants unless he has practice in the art. We mention this, as so very many of our correspondents appear to think that there exists a royal road to the gardener's craft; but this is not the case, as patience and perseverance, combined with close observation and practice, are the only paths to success.

We have omitted many plants that are often seen in greenhouses, and inserted others of more rare occurrence, in short, we have given place to such plants as we considered would most recommend themselves to the use of the amateur, and in the lists of varieties of the several plants we have striven to give good rather than new sorts.

Palms, ferns, and succulents we have omitted, as they would require a volume to themselves.

We shall be very happy to answer any queries on subjects respecting gardening, if the queries are directed to *The Bazaar* office, 170, Strand, and generally to assist our readers in all matters horticultural to the utmost of our ability.

W. J. MAY.

Greenhouse Management for Amateurs.

I.—INTRODUCTION AND GENERAL REMARKS.

THE Greenhouse is a structure that is perhaps the most varied in shape, size, style, and appearance, of any structure used for horticultural purposes extant, and the contents are as a rule of the most heterogeneous character. Apart from the house or plants the heating arrangements are generally far from useful, and on this alone much of course depends. As it is our wish to give only useful information combined with practicability, we shall treat the subject from the beginning, describing the way to stock various structures for the use of amateurs; and as we consider frames to be a necessary adjunct to an amateur's house, two or three two-light boxes should be at hand for use. As all our readers probably know, a greenhouse is a rather costly building when put up by a builder, as generally a lot of superfluous ornamentation is added to the erection, which, while giving a rather showy appearance to the house, tends to obstruct the light, and so reduce the value of the house for horticultural purposes. Ventilation is a subject of paramount importance, as on the method of obtaining this a very great deal depends, in fact we may say that more plants are injured from bad ventilation than from any other cause. Ill-placed ventilators, and inaccessible swing sashes, are often sources of continued annoyance and loss, and in a well found house or conservatory should not exist, but still it often happens that for some caprice of the builder the ventilation is "no how;" and as a certain consequence the plants suffer. The heating arrangements are the most troublesome of any, as in hundreds of cases some loudly praised affair is well recommended by the vendor, is purchased by the amateur, and before the season is out breaks down, and consequently entails the whole or partial loss of the stock of plants that has cost so much labour to get together. It is there-

A 2

fore the best plan to have a well constructed affair at first, the cost of which in most cases not being much more than the cheap (?) apparatus.

Stock.—The stock of plants should not be too great at first, as there are always plenty of opportunities to add to it. Indeed, if the house is only about 12ft. square, two or three dozen permanent plants will be ample, as there are plenty of season plants to keep the house gay at all times. A few pots of crocuses, musk, scarlet pelargoniums, &c., serve to give a very bright appearance to what would otherwise be a dull uninteresting mass of green, and if the amateur has a taste for tricolour and bronze pelargoniums, then at no season of the year will the house be devoid of interest. Camellias, azaleas, epacris, chorozemas, solanums, Cape pelargoniums, and genistas, are a host in themselves, while of roses it may truly be said that they are of inestimable value. We would advise our readers to have only a few plants, and do them well, rather than have a large collection and do none of them well. There are many ways of making a house look gay at a far less expense than is generally allowed, so making a greater pleasure of the place than it otherwise would be.

Pots and Sand.—Pots and sand should be selected with care, as they are of some importance in horticultural work. Pots should be of a porous and hard nature, and when suspended and hit with the knuckles should give off a sharp resonant sound. Close smooth-grained pots should be avoided, especially if made of the London clay, as they soon go rotten and crumble away. Coarse sand should be used for all purposes, as it gives far better results than the fine, and has not that tendency to become covered with a green slimy coating that very frequently shows up on dirty fine soft sands.

Soils.—Soils and manures should be of the best quality and suited to the work for which they are required, and cheapness should not be a consideration in laying in a stock of these necessary adjuncts to the greenhouse.

The necessary soils for general use are maiden loam, yellow loam, peat, leaf mould, and sand, and these we will describe in turn. Loams should be laid up for at least six months to become quite rotten and mellow, and to attain that state so necessary to the well-being of the plants.

Maiden loam is the top spit of a pasture, and should be alike free from clay, and, if possible, wireworm. It should also be free from red, rusty looking streaks, as such loams are, as a rule, taken from water-logged pastures, and are generally sour and bad. If the common hard-rush is also found in the herbage it is also a sign that the soil is poor, and, therefore, of course, should be avoided. Our plan is to use turf cut off as for making lawns, and laid up for a year, as it is much richer in fibre, and plants of all kinds do better in it. The price of ordinary loam in London is about 6s. per cubic yard, and the turf about 9s. per 100, and it will be found that the latter is the cheaper in the end.

Yellow loam is, as its name implies, yellow in colour, and is the top 6in. from a common. Wimbledon and Epping loam used to be considered the best near London, but since it has become unobtainable we believe it is brought from much further in the country. The best is full of fibre, and bracken roots, and is quite mellow. It also contains a certain, or rather uncertain, quantity of sand, and no clay. We have found the loam, peat, and sand, supplied by Mr. Kennard, of Old Swan-place, Old Kent-road, to be the best to be obtained in or near London, as Mr. Kennard makes a speciality of such things.

Peat is the top spit of a "dry" bog, and is quite distinct from the peat that is used for fuel, which latter is useless for plant food. Fibrous sandy peat is the best, and can be obtained of Mr. Kennard as above.

Leaf mould is simply thoroughly rotted hard-wood leaves, and the soil is thus full of humus, a very necessary adjunct to primula, and similar plant soils.

Silver sand is a white sand formed principally of pure silica, and free from lime. It should be very coarse and sharp, and also very clean, or it soon becomes covered with a green slimy film, which although very beautiful under the microscope, is almost certain death to cuttings or seedlings that may be surrounded by it. Reigate sand is generally esteemed the best. The fine white scouring sand sold at the oilshops is of very little use for plants.

Manures.—Manures are a matter of importance, and are generally the least thought of. With the majority of greenhouse plants a steady lasting effect is desired, and not a sudden spurt, and then a complete standstill, and to obtain the best effects, thoroughly rotten sound manure must be used. Horse and cow manures are the best, either mixed or separate as occasion may require, and they should be used for all purposes. Guano is a substance that has a great effect in driving the plants up, but they are useless for any purpose afterwards. For quick acting liquid manure we prefer sulphate of ammonia, but for all hard wooded plants, the best liquid manure is made by soaking a quantity of rotten horse manure in water, and using the clear water after the solid portions have settled.

With all soils and manures it is the better plan to have a shed, with compartments in which the soils can be placed and kept free from superfluous moisture.

Sundries.—A good supply of crocks for drainage should also be provided, or the plants will probably suffer for want of the proper means for the exit of superfluous water. A hammer, trowel, water cans, and a few other tools will be required, but of these we will speak in the future. Amongst the sundry requisites of a greenhouse, water-pots both of the ordinary shape and what is known as a strawberry pot, are required, a good syringe, one of Read's 15in., with three roses, is as good as can be bought, a trowel, labels, flower pots of various sizes, square propagating pans, some squares of glass, one of Brown's or Dreschler's patent fumigators, some insecticides, flowers of sulphur, and a few camel hair pencils, besides a few other articles that are more for show than use. Of course a strong potting board, a pail, step ladder, and two or three brushes and brooms, and the necessary tools for the stokehole, are absolutely necessary. We may as well mention here that plain serviceable and strong tools and utensils are far better than showily got up cheap goods, although the former may cost a lot of money if judged by appearance only; in all cases it is far better to have good tools (although they are expensive) than cheap ones that will do no service, as it is certain that cheap tools are dearer in the end. Another thing to be borne in mind is, never buy a lot of useless articles, never mind how much they are puffed up, as success does not lay in the tools, but in the cultural skill displayed.

The form of house is not of much consequence, so long as it is well built and ventilated, but we shall make a separate chapter of this subject, to deal fairly with it.

The general routinal treatment we shall leave till the last, as also some remarks on propagation and raising plants from seed.

II.—GREENHOUSES AND FRAMES.

MANY and various are the houses or glass structures that are made expressly for amateur gardeners, and, as they range in prize from £5 to £50, it is as well to point out the best forms of house, bearing in mind cost and general suitability to the purpose in hand. Of course, with existing structures, very little can be done, as it is, as a rule, expensive to meddle with old buildings, the wood very often being half decayed, and the nails rusted in; consequently, in separating or removing portions of woodwork, they are very much damaged, and, in many cases, are rendered quite useless. It also frequently happens that another obstacle presents

FIG. 1. LEAN-TO HOUSE.

itself, viz., the house will not fit another place, and we know from sad experience, that it costs as much to alter such a house as to build a new one. We may as well mention here that we always deal with Mr. Lascelles, Bunhill-row, London, and find his prices moderate, and the articles he supplies are, as a rule, first class. Wood, workmanship, and shape are as near as can be perfect, and, considering the price the articles are made at, it is indeed a remarkable fact that so few persons possess really serviceable glass houses.

Lean-to House.—The most general house is the lean-to, which is shown at Fig. 1. The cost of erecting one of these varies according to the manner in which it is built, as some persons have heavy sashes and timber, and, in some cases, ornamental guttering, fancy designs in painting, &c., all of which cost money, and have the disadvantage of making the house considerably darker, which causes the plants "to draw" and makes it more difficult to keep them in good order than it would be in a light place devoid of superfluous woodwork. A house, 12ft. square, built in this style, would cost at least £50, and in some cases it will be found that £75 will not cover all expenses. If, however, it is desirable to study economy, a house of the same size as that mentioned can be put up for about £35 in the style of Fig. 2. As will be seen in the figure, no top sashes are used, but simply ventilators, which answer quite as well; front sashes are, of course, necessary, but need not necessarily be so heavy as those generally

FIG. 2. LEAN-TO HOUSE.

used. In the example before us there are three front sashes, and five glazed ventilators at the top, and a door at one end. The cost of erecting the house three years ago was £28 17s. 6d., without heating apparatus, which subsequently cost £12 10s., thus making a total of £41 7s. 6d. for a good house 12ft. by 8ft., staging, heating, building, and all complete. Now, had heavy sashes and timber been used, about £20 more would have been charged and, besides the additional price, a great deal less light would have been admitted. In this instance 3in. timber was used, consequently great weight was avoided, the staging was made to accommodate plants of a large size as well as small pots, each shelf being a foot wide. The uprights and stays were made of sound yellow deals, and the glass used was 21oz. Belgian, which is, by the bye, a very useful and serviceable article. Fig. 3 is a sectional view of the house.

We will here give the plans for a lean-to greenhouse, as no doubt some of our readers are amateur carpenters, and with a little care such persons can be their own greenhouse builders. We propose to take in hand a house 10ft. by 12ft., 5ft. 9in. high in front, and 9ft. high at back, a very handy size for general work. Indeed, we have seen very fine plants, and grapes too, grown in such a house, and it was entirely built by the gentleman

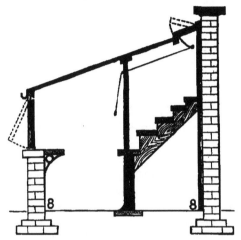

FIG. 3. SECTIONAL VIEW OF LEAN-TO.

himself. Fig. 4 is a ground plan of the house, showing the walls, back

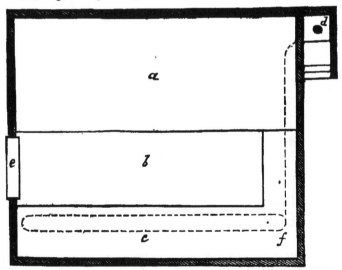

FIG. 4. GROUND PLAN OF LEAN-TO.

stage (a), path (b), front stage (c), boiler and stokehole (d), and stone door sill (e); the pipes are shown by the dotted lines, a single flow to the corner (f), and then a double flow along the front of the house, as shown, with a single return back to the boiler. All must be 4in. pipes, or sufficient heat will not be obtained. Fig. 5 is the front elevation of the

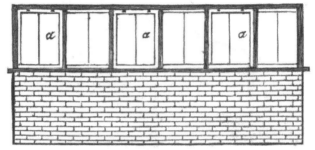

FIG. 5. FRONT ELEVATION OF LEAN-TO.

house. In the first place there is a 3ft. brick wall around the house, and this must be of 9in. work if carried up in mortar, or 4½in. if put up with Portland cement; but in any case if the district surveyor sees the place,

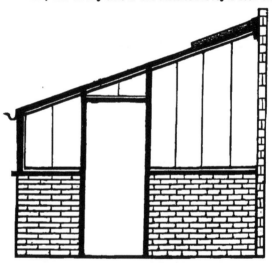

FIG. 6. SIDE ELEVATION OF LEAN-TO.

he will insist on 9in. work. A two course footing will be found necessary for the security of the building. On the top of the wall a 2in. wooden plate must be laid, and well bedded in either mortar or cement, as the case may be. This plate should overlap the wall on either side, and on the outside a groove should be cut out with the plough to allow the water

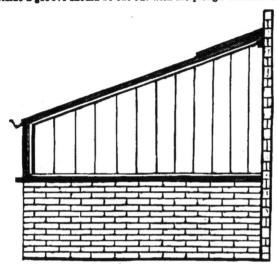

FIG. 7. SIDE ELEVATION OF LEAN-TO.

FIG. 8. ROOF OF LEAN-TO.

to drip off instead of running down the wall; this is very necessary, or the wall soon becomes green and unsightly, besides causing the plate to rot where it is laid on the wall. Upright quartering 3in. by 3in. is used for the corners, and divisions between the sashes, and along the top of these, a plate 4in. by 3in., is laid to form the front of the roof.   There are three fixed, and three swing lights (a), which are sufficient for all practical purposes. Fig. 6 shows the end view where the door is, and Fig. 7 the other end. It will be seen that the sash bars reach from top to bottom of the house at the ends, and the glass is held in its place by iron brads, besides the putty. By this plan there is no fear of the glass falling out by the jar consequent on the slamming of the doors, &c. The roof is shown in Fig. 8 and it will be at once seen by what means the ventilation is

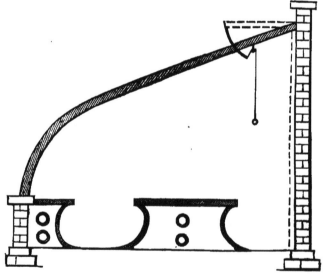

Fig. 9. CURVED ROOF HOUSE.

obtained. Four sashes 3ft. square, rising on hinges, occupy the upper portion of the roof, and the lower portion is formed of sash bars, a plan that greatly increases the light admitted, besides materially decreasing the cost of building ; a 3in. by 4in. beam goes across the roof, where the top lights close down, and one upright support takes its bearing in the centre of this beam. It will be found quite an easy matter to build such a house as we have described, as all the parts can be purchased in a prepared state, and ready for use. A saving of at least 25 per cent. will also be effected by building houses in this manner, therefore there is a double advantage in building your own greenhouses. If the amateur desires to make every part himself he will find very minute directions in " Carpentering and Joining for Amateurs " (Bazaar Office).

Curved Roof House.—Where the object is to obtain the lightest house possible, the curvilinear form offers the best design for the fulfilment of the object in view; but, at the same time, the price is much more than a plain lean-to, or span, as in many cases bent glass has to be used, and this is rather expensive. It is not often that amateurs go in for this style of house, but still, where it is desired to grow plants for exhibition, it is sometimes of use to have such a house. Iron is the best material to use for the sash bars, and in some places the whole of the building may be of iron, doors and staging of course excepted. In Fig. 9 we give a sectional view of a house that was built by a good firm, and which looked very well. It was built of wood and iron, and for

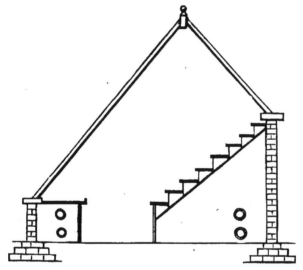

Fig. 10. HALF-SPAN HOUSE.

stability it was unequalled. This style of house is good for conservatories, or greenhouses, as the plants are not liable to " draw " so much as in ordinary lean-to houses, and, as before mentioned, light is a great point in the culture of some plants.

Half-span House.—Houses with short back roofs, or, as some persons call them, half-span roof (Fig. 10) are very useful, and as they may occupy the same positions as the lean-to houses, they afford greater facilities for the culture of plants in general. They are easily built, and may be put up by anyone who has any skill at carpentering, although span-roofed structures are more troublesome to erect than lean-to's. The great advantage in using them is that a portion of the back light being utilised, especially where houses face north or north-west, the additional light and heat

gained are being of great service. This style of house is particularly
useful against low walls, and in similar situations.

Span Roof House.—The span roofed house is, however, the best for
plant culture, where it can be erected, and, unless vines are grown, should
take the place of all others. The cost is not excessive, and although more
trouble to put up than a lean-to, anyone handy at carpentering could
easily put one up. A handy size is 12ft. wide, and of course as long as
desirable. Less width will generally be found to cramp the paths, &c.,
although 10ft. wide gives a very good centre path and side stages; but if
a centre stage is required, then the house must be of greater width.
There are several styles of span-roofed houses, but the two examples
given will be found useful for all general purposes. Fig. 11 shows a

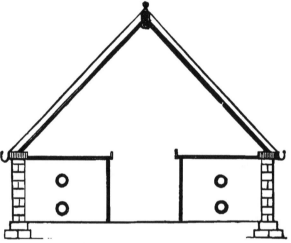

Fig. 11. SPAN ROOF HOUSE.

very cheap form of this style of house, and at the same time one that is in
much favour with growers for the London markets, especially for soft-
wooded stuff. As will be seen from the cut, there are no side lights; the
ventilation is provided for by means of sliding sashes, or ventilators that
open on hinges as described before. As a rule a central path is made
about 2ft. 9in. or 3ft. in width, and there are two side stages, or rather
benches, the farthest edge of which is about 9in. from the glass. In
the second example (Fig. 12) there are side lights, and of course, the place
is much higher and more expensive. This kind of house is useful for all
the ordinary kinds of plants, both hard and soft wooded. It is also one of
the best forms of house for growing specimen plants. Where it is possible,
the best plan is to have a centre stage, and side stages, with paths
around; this allows of the proper distribution of the plants, and more

suitable positions to some of them than can be obtained in a lean-to.
For this reason we prefer a span-roofed house for all ordinary collections
of plants.

Frames.—As these are necessary adjuncts to a greenhouse, a word or
two on them may not come amiss here. The uses to which they may be
put are many, and their use is of such a varied character that to omit
a notice of them would be to omit one of the most important parts of our
book. In the first place there is the common melon or cucumber frame,
that answers all ordinary purposes. It should, be stood on a concrete
bottom with a channel in front to allow the water to run clear away, or

Fig. 12. SPAN ROOF HOUSE.

damp will do much damage. We find that the common frames answer all
practical purposes, on account of their portability, and from the ease with
which a dung bed can be made under them. The best size is that technically
termed "two-light frames," with 6ft. by 4ft. lights, as more lights cause
a difficulty when making up a hotbed. We do not think it necessary to
give an illustration of these as they are so generally known. The only
point is to have them made of the best yellow deal as free from knots and
shakes as possible, and painted three coats with the best lead paint.

In the matter of conservatories and window eases, it is not our inten-
tion to treat of them here, as, although they are sometimes affected by

wealthy amateurs, yet, in the majority of cases, the greenhouses above mentioned, or modifications of them, are the rule amongst persons who make a hobby of gardening themselves, and do not employ gardeners to do the work for them. Window cases or conservatories do not come within the scope of the present work.

III.—HEATING.

THIS is rather a difficult matter to treat, as the wants and requirements of such a large community as the amateur gardeners are so great that one might write a volume without exhausting the subject. In the first place, the sort of greenhouse to be treated is a great consideration, for, as the term is now generally applied, a band box and a winter garden may be termed greenhouses at will, provided there are a few plants in them. We have seen "greenhouses" (?) about 4ft. by 6ft., and about 7ft. high, and to which no apparatus could be affixed to heat the small space thoroughly, unless an extravagant amount of fuel in proportion to the size of the place was used. Of course, it is an easy matter to heat any place when expense and fuel are no object, but with the majority of gardeners the cost is one of the most prominent points of consideration in the subject of heating. In small places the cost of fuel especially is a great drawback to many of the affairs offered for the purpose in hand. Patent fuel being required by many stoves is a great objection, as this fuel cannot always be obtained in country places. Another objection to many stoves is that the fire does not last sufficient time, and the consequence is that the frost gets in and destroys the whole of the plants. In a garden where a large amount of glass has to be kept at a nearly uniform temperature, the gardeners have to visit the fires during the night—a very unthankful office, by the bye. Now, there are few persons who would like to leave their beds on a cold, and, probably, frosty night, for the sake of attending the fire of a small house in which there is perhaps only a pound's worth of plants; and, therefore, the stove should be so constructed as to burn at least eight hours, if not longer; and in the case of simple stoves that give out heat only and do not retain it like hot water, this slow combustion principle should be very nearly perfect, or failure will result. In hot water apparatuses of course it is an advantage to have the fire kept in for as long a period as possible; but at the same time, if there is a sufficiency of water heat will be given out for a long time after the fire is out, and circulation ceases.

Nothing less than 4in. pipes should be used in a house of any size; and if frost is not too severe, and the boiler and furnace have been fixed in a proper manner, a good heat should be given off for twelve hours at least.

B

In fact, we have had boilers fixed under our own superintendence that would give a good circulation of water (hot, not warm) for fifteen hours right off, without any attendance during the time, but as boilers are very often set by country bricklayers, three or four hours' non-attendance is sufficient to let the frost into the house. Heating by means of flues is a very good plan where firing is no object, but when coals are up to 25s. per ton, it will be found to be a case of penny wise and pound foolish to have flues. The lamps or stoves to burn mineral oils do for small places only, and gas is not always to be obtained.

Heating with Mineral Oils.—The stoves for this purpose are of various construction, and also degrees of utility, and most of them are advertised to do more work than they are really capable of doing as a regular thing. It must be borne in mind that a glass house is a far different place to warm than a room, and, taking all points into consideration, requires at least three times as much heat to keep out the frost in proportion to the size of the structure. What would keep a room 12ft. square at a nice heat would not keep the frost out of a greenhouse 6ft. square, unless such house was very much sheltered. Now, for all practical purposes, a sufficient heat must be given to keep out frost, and at the same time no great amount of smoke must be engendered by the (imperfect) combustion of the oil. To this end the wick after it is lighted must be turned down under the dome, so that a sufficient amount of oxygen shall be consumed to ensure the perfect combustion of the oil. It should also be remembered that smoke is simply unconsumed fuel, and the more smoke made the greater the amount of fuel that will be required. This should be remembered by all persons who have the charge of any kind of heating. A good stoker is a truly valuable person in either a dwelling or an engine house, and should be kept when obtained.

But to return to our oil stoves, anyone with care may use one of Hinck's or Dietz's kerosine stoves in a house that has not more than 500 cubic feet of interior capacity; over that, large sized stoves must be used, or more than one of the smaller size, but of this it is only possible to give a decisive opinion on a personal inspection. We would have it understood that we only advise the use of oil stoves for small places, as some other plans are more effective, and not more expensive. In all plans of heating of course price is a consideration, and therefore we advise readers to use oil stoves for small houses.

Both Messrs. Heaps and Wheatley and Dietz and Co. make a good form of stove for using mineral oils. They are somewhat similar in construction to Wright's gas stove, and consist of a boiler, mineral oil lamp, and three hot water pipes, and they do their work well, and from the increased heating surface obtained by using hot water, a greater heat is given off than from a lamp alone. We have seen both in operation, and think them well worth the money charged, and all things considered, they will be of far more use in small conservatories than any simple lamp. A friend of ours who has one of each maker's apparatus in use, says there is no difference in the oil consumed, and the heat given off is about the same, while compared with the simple lamps, or stoves, as they are called, two of this new apparatus give off as much heat as, or rather raise the temperature in the small conservatory he has higher than, what three lamps he has been using will, thus showing a clear saving of nearly a gallon of oil per week. Three lamps cost him £4 10s., and the two apparatus in question cost him altogether about £6.

Heating with Hot-air Stoves.—Under this we class all the various stoves that are heated with coal, coke, or cinders, and which give off dry heat. In the majority of cases these are for more than one reason objectionable. In the first place they give off dry, overheated, and deleterious fumes, especially if they are made of wrought iron, and as a natural consequence the plants do not succeed well. In the next place they are generally dirty and untidy, and lastly they have a nasty habit of going out when most wanted. The last objection is the trouble of attendance, which, if not very great, is not a cleanly job. Of course very much of the pleasure of a greenhouse depends on the nature of the work that has to be done by the owner, for if there is much dirty work to be done the place soon loses favour, and then comes discontent, and eventually failure. In choosing a stove, have one with a cast-iron fire bucket, or one that is lined with fire bricks, by which means direct heat is kept from the wrought iron, and the fumes given off are reduced to a minimum, so increasing the probabilities of growing plants successfully. In addition to this cast-iron or brick fire pail, it is also necessary to have some contrivance to hold water to be evaporated, and so tend to regulate the dryness caused by the stove. Of course the amount of moisture that is necessary will be regulated by the number of plants in the house, and the quantity of water given.

Nearly all the stoves that have chimneys answer well, with care in stoking and by using cinders and coke broken small for fuel; they must be small, or they will cake together. We can, however, only speak of Green's Patent Suspension Stoves from experience, as we have generally had hot-water apparatus under our charge. There are, however, many other stoves with flues that answer well if they are constructed as described above. It is all very well to purchase a stove without a flue for the reason that there is no smoke, but, though no visible smoke exists, there are fumes of a most deadly nature both to plant and animal life that get dispersed over the house in which the stove is inclosed, and eventually ruin or destroy the whole of the plants. There is indeed the one probability that the glazing of the house is so bad that sufficient draughts obtain admission to blow off the vapours that would otherwise accumulate; but in many places the house is comparatively air tight, and so the plants die.

The size of the stove of course regulates the size of the house it will heat, but one of Green's Suspension stoves, that burns about a bushel and a half of fuel daily, will heat from 5000ft. to 10,000ft. of cubical capacity, according to the situation and exposure of the house. To a certain extent the space that can be heated by stoves is unlimited, but of course the larger the space to be heated the greater must be the heat given off by the stove. A drier atmosphere will thus be obtained, and the growth of the plants will be thus seriously affected. It also equally applies in heating schools, &c., with stoves that if there is not sufficient heating surface to give off sufficient heat without overheating the stoves, very undesirable results will follow : severe colds, itching of the eyes, and sometimes sore throats, are caused by this means alone, all of which, we venture to say, would never appear were the stoves sufficiently powerful to heat the place while at a comparatively low heat themselves. With plants the effect is also bad, and it is far better to have two stoves at a moderate than one at a fierce heat.

In fixing these stoves two things are requisite : a draught sufficient to keep the fire alight fairly, and sufficient piping to exhaust the whole of the heat before it reaches the chimney.

The first is easy to attain if the pipes can be led into a chimney belonging to the dwelling house, but some difficulty will often be found in obtaining sufficient length of pipe. We have found it the best plan to take the pipe upright for three or four feet, and then turn it off at right angles, and take it across the house into the chimney ; this, of course, allows of the whole of the heat, that would otherwise be blown out of the roof, being utilised. The joints should be made good with red lead and oil, so that no fumes escape, and the whole is then complete—complete at least so far as the fixing goes; but the more important item of stoking still remains. This is a point that requires much attention, as on it the durability of the fire depends. In the first place light the fire with shavings or paper and short pieces of wood ; when these are well alight put in a little coke broken small, or perhaps a few cinders, but no coal. If coal is used the greatest probability will be that the fire will cake and go out, and consequently the frost will get in and the plants will be lost. As soon as the fuel first put on is well alight, fill up the stove with dry fuel, and partially close the air inlet at the bottom. With a little care the fire may be kept well alight from eight to twelve hours, or as long as can reasonably be expected with the amount of fuel consumed.

Heating with Gas.—This is one of the vexed questions of the day, and will never be definitely settled until we can have gas at a good pressure throughout the night, and at a moderate price ; and even then the risk attendant on this system of heating will debar very many persons from using it. It must in all cases be remembered that the low first cost of an apparatus of any kind does not imply that it will be cheap in the end, in fact it is very often quite the reverse, as cheaply made articles as a rule are not so well made as those for which a fair price is charged.

Joints and rivets are insufficiently fastened, plates are cracked because the holes are not drilled large enough, and, worse than all, the arrangements are such that in the case of an apparatus that depends on hot water for the heating medium, the water in many cases will not circulate. We have had a good experience of gas apparatus, and in no case have we found that the work done, in proportion to the cost, equal that done by good sound fuel in a plain conical boiler. The plates used in the manufacture of gas apparatus are generally very thin, and the action of the gas where it burns against them soon causes them to break into holes, and so allow the fumes of the gas to escape, to the great injury of both plant and animal life. Common burners are also used in many of the contrivances, and the result is that the gas is not thoroughly burnt, and consequently an exorbitant quantity of gas has to be used in proportion to the heat obtained. A good burner that allows the gas to be well oxygenated makes very little smoke, and consequently there is not so great a waste of heat as where large deposits of soot are formed. All parts of the apparatus that comes in contact with the flame should be of copper, and where a boiler is used it should be entirely of copper, so that the greatest amount of durability shall be insured.

There are two plans of heating with gas, with or without hot water. In the latter case, heating by means of the gas alone, George's Patent Gas Calorigen is about the best apparatus there is, as by its use a supply of fresh heated air is supplied to the interior of the place to be heated, whilst the products of combustion are carried out into the outer air, thus obviating all inconvenience that generally arises from the fumes of the gas. The whole apparatus is of neat appearance, and is constructed to burn well, independently of draughts.

Next to the Calorigen, a plain conical tube, with straight chimney, gives the best results, provided down draughts can be guarded against. A plain ring of lights impinge on the sides of the cone near the bottom,

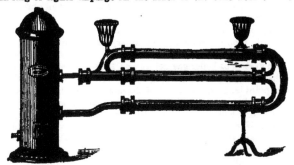

FIG. 13. MESSRS. WRIGHT & CO.'S GAS BOILER.

and of course heat it to the top. No bottom is required to such an apparatus, but the joints and seams must be perfectly sound and tight, and to ensure this all joints, &c., should be luted with red lead and oil, which will make the joints tight. Open gas fires should on no account be used, as the fumes given off will destroy all the plants.

In the more important class of apparatus, i e., that in which water is used as a heating medium, there are various makes of more or less excellence, but all of them require the services of a gasfitter or hot water engineer to fix them to the best advantage. In all hot water arrangements it must be remembered that hot water ascends, and the cold portion contained in the pipes descends, therefore it is of the greatest importance that the point most distant from the boiler should be the highest, and that this part should contain an air pipe to relieve the pipes from any air or vapour which may from time to time accumulate. It is almost useless to attempt to specify any particular one amongst the many kinds of apparatus that are offered to the public, and as we are writing for the benefit of all persons, we only recommend those we have tried and found answer. Of course, we do not for one moment think or wish to imply that those we mention are the only good ones; on the contrary, we know that there are many that are good if properly fitted up.

The gas boiler made by Wright and Co., of Birmingham, of which an illustration is given overleaf, is a good one, and does its work economically and well. The Shrewsbury gas boiler is also very good. Mr. Mussett, of Winstanley-road, Clapham Junction, S.W., also makes some very efficient apparatus at reasonable prices. There are also many other makers who supply good articles at fair prices.

We would give a word or two of advice to all about to use gas for heating conservatories. In the first place employ none but really competent workmen to fix the apparatus when bought; make all joints and crevices secure with red lead putty, have hot water pipes fixed so that they rise to the point farthest from the boiler, and, lastly, buy a good article. It is a good plan to have a written warranty with each apparatus, a warranty that specifies exactly what the boiler will do, and that it is in a proper order to do it. If this rule were always observed fewer mishaps would happen.

Heating with Hot Water.—This is a plan that, if done well, always answers well. Whether we take the ordinary saddle boiler, Week's tubular conical, Cannell's, Lynch White's, Ormson's, or Deard's apparatuses, or the Cowan system of boiler gas retort and lime kiln combined, it will be found that the purpose is thoroughly answered by means of the water. The chief point is, however, which of the many boilers in use is best suited to an amateur's use. In all our experience we ourselves have had no trouble with any boiler when it was fixed properly, but with anyone who has to keep clean, smooth hands it is a different matter. A saddle boiler is very awkward to feed by anyone not used to the work, as it is necessary that a lasting fire should be kept up, or failure will probably result, and we have generally found that one failure means disgust and neglect afterwards. What we have found to answer an amateur's purpose best, are the plain conical and tubular-conical boilers, as when they are properly fixed they will go twelve hours with each stoking, and maintain a good circulation during the time. As they are fed at the top there is little trouble in stoking, the chief thing being the lighting; but when once alight the fire should not go out for months if it is required to be kept in.

In all hot water work it should be remembered that hot water ascends and cold water descends, and in many cases this will be found the key of the whole affair. It is, we are quite well aware, possible for water to be driven along pipes lower than the flow from the boiler, but it is only by the expenditure of a lot of power in driving the water over a high siphon (from 5ft. to 10ft. high) at the point where it comes from the boiler, so that the water is really descending through the heating pipes. And even then we have known cases where the pressure was so great that no circulation could be obtained. In all cases it should be a matter of compulsion that the boiler should be set below the pipes, so that the least quantity of fuel and expense in fixing should be incurred. We are often asked by friends to look at their boilers, &c., and are sometimes much surprised that the apparatus works at all, as in some cases there are so many dips, and other obstructions, that the water circulates under the greatest difficulties, and in many cases we have found that sinking the boiler five or six inches has been the cause of a rapid circulation, and, consequently, rise of temperature in the houses heated. Therefore we recommend that boilers should be set as low as possible, consistent with the proper stoking arrangements, &c., that will be suggested by a man who is conversant with the work. For an amateur's use we would recommend either a plain or tubular conical boiler, properly set, and with close fire doors and dampers, so that the combustion of the fuel may be under perfect control. A boiler of the kind mentioned, properly fixed, and with close doors and dampers, may be with propriety called a slow combustion boiler, as the fire will easily last for twelve or fourteen hours. Fire lumps or fire bricks should be used where the fire impinges on the walls of the furnace, and it is not a bad plan to use fire clay instead of mortar between the bricks. Movable fire bars should be used in preference to cast gratings, as it is easier to replace a fire bar that is burnt through than to get a new bottom for the furnace. If possible to avoid it, the fire should not touch either the flow or return pipe, or some awkward results will sometimes follow.

The pipes used for heating the house should always be 4in. in diameter, and for ordinary work without troughs, or the house will be kept too moist as a rule. Either iron or brick supports should be used for the pipes, and they should be so arranged that they neither sink nor shift about. The joints should be made of Portland cement, or else india-rubber rings should be used, the latter being perhaps the better joint when there is a danger of the pipes sinking from any cause. The connections with the boiler must of course be made with proper cement, and all joints that are screwed together must be made watertight, so that rust may not eat holes in the pipes. An air pipe must be fixed into the flow pipe at its highest point, and this may be of composition gas tubing. The air pipe in all cases must be carried up higher than the top of the supply cistern or the water will be wasted. The cistern should be about a foot above the highest point in the pipes, so that the pipes shall always be full of water. Where one flow and return are insufficient to heat the house, two flows and one return may be used advantageously, provided the boiler will heat them at no greater cost than it would one. Where two houses are heated it is advisable to have valves to regulate the flow of water, and for greater convenience the cooler house should always be that farthest from the boiler.

Besides boilers for fixing in brickwork there are portable conical boilers, that can be placed anywhere, and if the pipes are jointed with Truss's, Read's, or Jones's patent expansion joints, or with rings described as above, and cast iron supports are used between the pipes, so that they are nowhere made fast to a wall, the whole apparatus can be removed at the pleasure of the owner, and in an hour or so. We leave it to the opinions of our readers as to which is cheapest—to give 35s. for a stove such as Hincks's, and use it to exclude frost only at a cost of from 6d. to 9d. per day, or to have a properly fitted up portable arrangement, which costs about £12 to £15, burns at a cost of about 4d. per day (if the house cinders are used), and which will maintain a steady equable heat, and if an extra sharp frost sets in can be made to give out a much greater heat.

The conical and tubular-conical boilers can be had of anyone who does hot water work, while for large places Weeks's patent duplex upright tubular boiler is the best of its class for large houses, especially where the larger sizes of boilers can be used. Deard's patent boilers, both fixed and portable, are good ones, and simple to use. Read's patent portable "Challenge" boilers are good for the use of anyone who desires to do but little stoking, as they burn but slowly, although they do the work well. There are also other boilers in great variety, but the purchaser of any of the above will find that he has a good article for the money.

The points to be observed are—First, a boiler large enough for the work, as it is false economy to have a boiler too small. Secondly, that the boiler shall be properly fixed. Thirdly, that the pipes are large enough, and of a sufficient length to heat the house properly; and lastly, that an experienced hot water smith be employed to do the fixing, &c. If these terms are carried out, success will follow as a necessity.

Heating with Flues.—This old-fashioned method is hardly worth describing at the present time as it is so little used, but for the benefit of those who may like this plan, we give a few hints. In the first place a furnace is required, and this must be constructed so that the flames and heat *rise* into the flue. The construction of the furnace is very simple, as it consists of a long furnace, about a foot high, and a little wider, if convenient, with an ashpit under; it is also desirable to have good fire bars, as the common ones soon burn through. The flue should rise from the top of the furnace in a slanting direction, and should have no dips or sudden falls in it, or in many cases failure will result, as hot air, like hot water, always rises. In building the flue, it will be necessary to raise it the thickness of a brick on edge above the floor of the house, and this is done by placing the brick so that the edges of two tiles (10in. square) lie on each brick; these must be well bedded in mortar, and when the whole of this foundation is laid, three bricks on edge should be built up on each side, on the tiles, and this should be covered in with other tiles, well mortared together, or the smoke will escape. The flue when finished will have an interior size of about a foot high and from five to six inches wide, and as it will get very hot it will be necessary to use good materials. It will be found the best plan to employ a good bricklayer to do the work—if possible—a man who is used to the work, as it is necessary to have good work, but at the same time it is far cheaper in the end to have a properly fitted hot water apparatus. It will be found that unless fuel is cheap, a great loss will result in a very few years—in fact, more than would pay for the first cost and maintenance of a hot water apparatus, which would, moreover, be of far greater practical use. The smoke, too, from most flues is simply a nuisance, oftimes to an intolerable degree, whereas there is but little smoke from properly set boilers, for as a rule these latter consume their own smoke. The stoking is also a subject that few persons will undertake, as the fire wants attention every few hours, and from experience we can confidently say that it is no pleasant job to have to get out of bed at three or four o'clock in the morning to look after the fires, and perhaps find it raining or snowing hard.

In concluding our notice of heating we may add that a few mats thrown over the roof and front of a house to exclude the wind from the laps in the glass, will often save a great deal of firing, while a stout canvas cover, such as a rick cloth, if fastened so as to leave a space between it and the glass, will make a difference of some two or three degrees. The hardier the plants the less heat will be required, therefore it is as well to keep the plants as hardy as possible.

IV.—HARD-WOODED PLANTS.

BUTILONS.—This is a class of plants of which the variegated forms, if well grown, are very beautiful, and most certainly deserve a place in every collection, especially if bottom heat can be obtained. The chief secret in growing fine plants for decorative purposes being quick and at the same time sturdy growth — ends only to be obtained by liberal culture. The majority of the abutilons are semi-hardy, and as a rule, do with indifferent treatment; or when we say do, we mean are obliged to do with the rough treatment they ofttimes receive. They are all interesting for the blossoms, but *A. Thompsoni* and *A. vexillarium* are also very effective for their foliage; *A. Thompsoni* particularly so when well grown. This last does well with the special treatment recommended below, and will repay for the trouble. It is, however, very often the case with these plants that they are placed on one side and so neglected that they are positively worthless; long, straggling things, with two or three leaves on the top of each branch are too often found instead of well furnished plants, as they should be.

In training, the aim should be to obtain good bushy plants of intermediate size, not too large or straggling, or too small. The mode of training is simple; just train them like Cape pelargoniums, without sticks, and they do well. We have also seen them trained over trellises, and they look well, but care is required to keep them in first-rate condition.

Our way with *A. Thompsoni* is to strike cuttings in heat in spring, and as soon as the bedding plants are put out, a bed is prepared for the abutilons. This is done simply by mixing a quantity of well-rotted manure with the ordinary garden soil. In this bed the plants (previously pinched back once or twice, to obtain four or five breaks) are put in about 18in. asunder, and well watered. As soon as the roots begin to run, the trowel is passed round about 3in. from the stem, and this is done several times, until the time for lifting arrives. This plan prevents a too luxuriant growth, and at the same time obtains a good ball of roots round the plants. Before frost comes the plants are taken up and potted in light rich soil, the pots being as small as to only just hold the roots conveniently. Good stocky plants are readily obtained by this plan, and amply repay for any trouble bestowed on them.

Old plants of other abutilons should be cut back hard in spring, and repotted in light rich soil, and, presuming that a light, airy, and comparatively warm place is afforded them, they will be very interesting during the winter. We would advise all amateurs to have a few plants of some of the varieties above-mentioned, as they are very pretty and at the same time not so susceptible to rough treatment as are many of the other and much belauded plants that we so frequently find named in catalogues.

Amongst the sorts we would recommend for an amateur's use the following stand pre-eminent—viz., *A. striatum*, *A. Pattersoni*, *A. Verschaffelti*, *A. vexillarium*, *A. Boule de Neige*, *A. Thompsoni* and *A. vexillarium variegatum*.

Acacias.—These afford some of the most beautiful shades of yellow, and as they are early they combine with the first azaleas, and help to produce an effect that is unattainable without their help. The bright tassels of yellow bloom inserted at the base of the leaf stalks, and the dark foliage, form a beautiful contrast, and is in our opinion more effective in securing admiration than the more gaudy cytisus. Of course the cytisus is an invaluable aid in arranging a large show, and one or two plants are useful but the preference should be rather given to the different acacias, than the last named plant. The acacias we are now referring to are not the common acacias of the garden (*Robinia pseudo-acacia*), but acacias proper, none of which are really hardy. There are several varieties of this family in use in our English gardens at the present time, the commonest of all being, perhaps, *A. armata*, a variety that has small globular tassels of bloom at the axils of the leaves. This variety is frequently seen in markets and on the costermongers' barrows, and ranges in price from 1s. 6d. to 5s. for plants fit for an amateur, while, for large plants, the price varies from 10s. to £5. It may, perhaps, be out of place to mention such plants here, but we once saw a couple about 5ft. high and the same through; they were perfect pyramids, and when in bloom formed very conspicuous objects, although not so showy as azaleas or other plants of that class. It is the rule, however, with the majority of growers, to have the plants very ugly, in fact they are no definite shape, but straggling, scrubby things that are a disgrace to the grower. It is really very little trouble to train acacias into shape, if the training is commenced when the plants are young, but if they are allowed to get old and hard stemmed, then little hope can be held out on the subject of shapely plants, the wood being so very brittle.

In training, the first thing is to determine what form the plant has to assume, and when this is settled satisfactorily, the necessary work of forming the base or frame of the plants must be proceeded with. The framework of these plants must be formed or built up as the plant grows as we before explained, for it is not often that sufficient bottom growth can be obtained after the plant has made a head. The size and height must of course depend on the size of the house, but for general use we find pyramids about 30in. high to be most suitable. Standards are also very useful, and may be somewhat higher than other shapes, but with them it is advisable to have conical heads, as it sets off the bloom to greater advantage. The great point to be aimed at in training acacias is to have a central stem, and to build up the framework of the plant while it is still pliable and young.

Our plan of cultivation with all free growing plants, is to obtain good, sturdy, and at the same time free growth, to obtain the growth as early in the season as is consistent with safety, and to harden off, and ripen the wood perfectly before the wet cold weather sets in. To obtain these results, we consider that as much of the growth as possible shall be made in the frames (in the case of nearly hardy plants like acacias), and, if possible the plants should have a structure to themselves, but of course this is not generally obtainable; and therefore, the lightest and driest part of the house should be set apart for them.

For soil for acacias, we use equal parts of maiden loam and sandy peat, with enough sharp sand to keep the compost open. Manure in no form enters into our compost, as we consider that it tends to make the young wood too soft and sappy, but it is often recommended by some gardeners as a part of the compost.

There are about twenty sorts or varieties of acacia, all of which are useful and of easy culture. We have found the following to be amongst the best: *A. affinis*, *A. armata*, *A. coccinia*, *A. dealbata*, *A. eriocarpa*, *A. lopantha*, *A. pubescens*, and *A. verticillata*, all of which are not yellow.

Acer.—This is a class of a highly decorative order, and may with advantage be represented in nearly all collections of fine foliage plants.

This class of plant is very effective on stems, as standards or half standards, and in these forms gives a more finished appearance to a high structure than it would otherwise have. Of course the larger the tree the larger the house required, and this must be borne in mind when purchasing.

We have grown these plants in rather rich loam and sand, with just a little manure, and they did thoroughly well, the variegated foliage coming very finely in this soil. Pruning must be done in spring, before the growth commences, and the last year's shoots should be reduced to three or four eyes. This causes an abundance of young shoots, that are well furnished. We do not advise too early pruning, as wet will sometimes cause the shoots to die back, as they are not of solid construction.

Amongst those sorts that may be termed the best are *A. albophylla viride reticulata*, *A. atropurpurea*, *A. palmatum*, and *A. polymorphum variegatum*.

Aloysia.—*Aloysia citriodora* is a shrub that should never be omitted from a collection of plants, as its perfume is so fine, and the appearance is so graceful, if the plant is well grown. Large plants are not as a rule desirable, but· if room exists, they may be had on pillars, or trellises against walls. The first point in growing the aloysia, or as it is more generally termed, lemon verbena, is to afford generous treatment, instead of adopting the starvation system, that is so much the practice. The best plan is to obtain well-grown thrifty young plants in spring, and grow them on for the season; as the wood ripens give less water until they are at rest, when the water must be nearly if not quite withheld. About the end of January bring into the light and warmth, and water thoroughly; as soon as the plants break, cut back to three or four eyes, and when the young shoots are about an inch long, re-pot into rich sandy soil, using pots a size or two smaller than they were in before, and as soon as the pots are full of roots re-pot into the pots that are to hold the plants for the season. By this mode of culture good plants are to be maintained for any length of time. It is almost useless to think of keeping this plant in an evergreen state, as it soon goes to the bad if this is attempted.

Mr. J. Groom, of Henham Hall, writing to the *Garden* of Sept.11th, 1875, says: "This little shrub, favourite though it be, is seldom seen in good condition. When confined in a pot it has generally a sickly aspect, but when planted out it becomes a large bush, or forms a handsome pillar plant. In the kitchen garden here, against a south wall, I have two plants of it that are 10ft. in height, and at least 3yds. in width, and the quantity of spray they yield for mixing with cut flowers is surprising. The only care which they require is protection from frost in winter, and to effect this they are generally unnailed in November; the branches are then tied into bundles and enveloped thickly in hay bands; upon these is also put an outer covering of straw, which keeps all dry, their base being covered with coal ashes. When all danger from frost is over in spring the cover is removed, the branches are spread out, and as soon as growth commences all dead wood is removed, the main branches being refastened to the wall; they require no summer training, their young growth being continually cut off for the many purposes of decoration to which they are applied, and to which they are so well adapted."

We can fully indorse Mr. Groom's statement, and besides outdoor work as he describes, the "lemon plant" is very useful in cold houses, where frost is only just excluded, provided they are planted out in the borders. We can with pleasure recall to memory a house where camellias were grown, and where a few plants of aloysia were in the borders, and they throve wonderfully, and were the admiration of all visitors. We may add that they are very easy to grow, and on no account should be omitted from any collection.

Aralia.—This is a family of ornamental foliaged plants, and as such is worthy of a place where good-sized specimens can be used. Small plants of these, as a rule, are not desirable, as they do not show the full beauty of the plant. As a rule it is not desired to have big specimens of these large foliaged plants, and therefore means must be taken to restrict their growth to the proper proportions, not by ill treatment, but by using a moderately poor soil, and very firm potting. This we have found to answer very well for the purpose intended, and by having young plants every three or four years, nice specimens can be kept.

For soil good maiden loam, and enough sand to keep it open, will be found to answer well, provided the plants are potted firmly enough.

For sorts we should prefer, *A. leptophylla, A. Sieboldii, A. Sieboldii argentea variegata,* and *A. Sieboldii aurea variegata.* The last three being perhaps the best for an amateur's use.

Araucaria.—Like the preceding, these are valuable for their habit of growth and graceful appearance, and not for any flowering properties. They are useful where large houses have to be filled, and in such situations are unequalled for effect by any other plants of the same habit; they cannot be shown off to good advantage in a small house. Nearly everyone knows the *A. imbricata*, or Chilian monkey puzzle of gardens, and no doubt has admired it greatly on account of its fine foliage and unique form. When we say foliage, it must be remembered that these plants belong to the pine tribes, and do not bear leaves in the same way as apples or other trees, but, on the contrary, their leaves are more like those of fir, pines, &c.

We have found a mixture of equal parts of maiden and yellow loam, with a little sandy peat, do well for these plants, and keep them healthy; but they must not be overpotted.

A. excelsa and *A. Bidwilli* are very good for our purpose, as are also *A. Cookii* and *A. Cunninghamii.*

Aucubas.—These plants, although not really greenhouse plants, make a great show when well covered with berries, and, as the foliage is pretty, they are worth anyone's notice. In the first place, the plants are perfectly hardy, and at the same time of easy culture; and, another thing, they stand a lot of knocking about, while the price is pretty moderate. Plants fit for our present purpose can be had from ninepence each, while similar plants, if well berried, would cost from half a crown. Of course, a male plant is very necessary to produce pollen, with which to impregnate the blooms of the female plant, which alone produce seeds, or, more properly, berries. The female plants are variously variegated, some of them being more beautiful than others, but all being noticeable for their glossy leaves and fresh and cheerful appearance, which, when the berries are ripe, is further enhanced by the beautiful scarlet of the berries. The bloom is rather inconspicuous, and, in a floricultural point of view, is of no value, the beauty of the plant lying in the foliage and berries. The male plants have generally green leaves, which, if clear, have a bright glossy appearance; they are of course necessary for the production of the fruit on the female plants, but one male plant produces (if it blooms freely) sufficient pollen for the impregnation of hundreds of female blooms.

The process of fertilising is very interesting, and brings out the more delicate skill of the operator. We say delicate, as it is useless to attempt this kind of work in an off-hand manner and with as much care as is generally exercised in cutting a cabbage or other rough job, or the result will most probably be that the greater part of the available pollen will be lost, and the crop of berries will be almost *nil*. The proper mode of operation is to collect the pollen from the anthers of the male plant with a camel's-hair pencil, and then transfer it to the pistil of the female. As we before mentioned, this is an operation that requires great delicacy of touch, especially as only a very few grains of pollen are necessary to each pistil. The time for applying the pollen is when the pistil exudes a slightly gummy substance, and otherwise shows signs of maturity. It, however, often happens that from some unforeseen cause the male blooms are open, and the pollen matured before the female blooms are ready. In this case it is well to collect the pollen on a *dry* pencil, and transfer to perfectly dry sheets of glass, and when all the pollen is obtained, another sheet of glass should be laid on that on which the pollen was laid, and the whole should be placed in a dry, cool place till wanted. Pollen thus saved and stored will retain its vitality for a long time; in fact, we have used it when seven weeks old, and it has given very good results, although not perhaps so good as would have been attained with pollen fresh from the plant.

The cultivation is very simple. Pot the plants firmly in rather sandy yellow loam, allowing plenty of drainage; and during the growing season allow plenty of water; but as soon as the growth is over less water will do. During the summer the plants can be plunged in the borders out of doors, and can be brought in again as soon as required to occupy their situations in the house. One point we have, however, found of great importance, and that is, always keep the plants in rather small pots, so that the roots may not be allowed to ramble too much, and so tend to produce vigorous and unfruitful growth, such growth being most undesirable for our present purpose, however desirable it may be for outdoor work. Short jointed hard wood is of most value for pot work, as it produces the best bloom, while the free growing suckers that spring from the base of the plant as a rule produce leaves only.

For sorts, we prefer the following, as they have given general satisfaction as far as we have had them under our notice. There is, however, a difference in the berries, and as half a dozen would not be too many in a house, one of each would not be too many :—*A. japonica albo variegata, A. japonica arborea vera fœmina, A. japonica aureo maculata, A. japonica aureo marginata, A. japonica lati-maculata, A. japonica longifolia, A. japonica longifolia variegata elegans,* for female variety, and *A. japonica angustifolia maculata, A. japonica arborea vera mascula,* and *A. japonica viridis mascula* for males. *A. japonica viridis fructu-albo* has round white or cream-coloured berries, and green foliage; while *A. japonica luteo-carpa* has oval yellow berries and leaves of a full green, splashed more or less with yellow. The ordinary aucuba of the garden (*A. japonica maculata*) is too well known to render any detailed description of the other rather numerous varieties necessary, as they all are very similar in the habit of growth and form of the foliage, the distinction consisting chiefly in the variation of the leaves.

Azaleas.—These are one of the mainstays of an amateur's house, and should be well represented, so that a continuance of bloom may be kept up. We do not for one instant wish to imply that the stock of hard-wooded plants should be wholly made up of the numerous varieties of azaleas, but still a good proportion should be kept. In colour a very great diversity exists, from white to the brightest scarlet, salmon, purple, red, rose, orange, yellow, and various shades and tints of the different colours; while at the same time variegated flowers are in abundance. Blotched, striped, and in many cases, spotted flowers being produced, rendering a collection of azaleas well worth a visit at any time from Christmas till June, and in some places later. It is a good plan to have a few plants (say two or three) of a sort, and say five or six sorts, according to the

size of the house. Of course, we should not advise more than a proper
proportion of plants, as there are numerous other plants that afford a
fine display of differently habited forms, both of growth and blossom, and
it would be a pity to oust them for the sake of one class of plant—many
of the plants in question affording blue and yellow flowers, an object of
much importance in greenhouse furnishing.

The culture of the azalea is very easy, and in fact anyone can grow them
if a few simple rules are followed. In the first place, potting claims attention—in fact, the way in which the plants are potted has more effect on
the blooming capabilities of the plant than the soil in which it is potted.
We make it a rule to put at least an inch of drainage into 4in. pots, and
2in. into 6in. pots and upwards, as we consider this is the first point in
successful culture. For soil we use three parts sound old peat, one part
best maiden loam, and one part sand. It is, however, a matter of choice
about using the loam, as some persons omit it altogether, while others
use more than we do. But it must be remembered that peat is generally
used for all the heath family of which the azalea is a member, and, therefore, it is necessary to use it in the compost. In repotting, the whole of
the crocks should be removed from the base of the ball of soil and roots,
and the top should also be removed till the fine roots are reached. The
plant should then be put in the new pot, and the soil that is put in should
be rammed firm to prevent the water running through it, and not wetting
the ball of roots inside. In all cases the roots next the stem should be
above the other soil, so that the water may not sink in next the stem, or
death will most certainly ensue. After potting, the plants should be kept
close for a few days, and then may have the full benefit of the air. The
best time for potting is after the growth has been made, as the roots then
elongate, and take hold of the new soil. From October till June the plants
should be in the greenhouse, and the other months in a cold frame, or if
that does not exist, they should be plunged in the borders out of doors.
Water will have to be given abundantly through the blooming and growing
season, and at other times the plants must not become dry, or no bloom
will result. A proper amount of care must of course be exercised, so that
the plants are not swamped one day and dried up the next; but this will
easily be seen by the person who has the charge of the collection.

In regard to sorts, we find the following to be very good and suitable for
the purposes intended, and such a selection as we give is almost sure
to give everyone satisfaction : Admiration, *Amœna grandiflora*, Bijou de
Ledeburg, Brilliant, Cedo Nulli, Comte de Hainault, Concinna, Criterion,
Dieudonné, Duc d'Aremberg, Duc de Nassau, Duke of Edinburgh,
Exquisite, Flag of Truce, Gem, Glory of Sunninghill, Grand Monarch,
Her Majesty, *Indica Alba*, *Insignis*, *Lateritia alba suprema*, Leeana, Lizzie,
Madame Ambroise Verschaffelt, Madame van Houtte, *Magnifica*, Mars,
Ne Plus Ultra, President, Prince of Orange, Princess Alexandra, Princess
Helena, Purity, Queen Victoria, *Sinensis*. All the above can be obtained
of Messrs. Rollison and Sons, Tooting, S.W., to whom we should advise
readers to apply if they have not a nurseryman who supplies them
regularly.

AMBUSA.—This is a class of plants that is ornamental in the extreme, but from its nature it is not well adapted to small houses. There is one variety, however, that has a fine effect anywhere, as it is comparatively dwarf and compact, with finely variegated foliage, and is adapted to pot culture. We allude to *B. Fortunei variegata*, which comes from either China or Japan, and is really good. All the bamboos are semi-aquatic, growing naturally on the banks of rivers and in marshy places. During the season of growth plenty of water must be applied, and if large growth is desired weak liquid manure may be used with advantage. Like all free growing plants, bamboos like a rather porous soil to grow in, and we use two-thirds of fibrous loam, one third thoroughly rotted leaf soil, and plenty of coarse silver sand; we also hold that the plants should not be potted too firmly, or in some cases the young shoots will have some difficulty in pushing through. As a decorative plant, the one mentioned above will (if well grown) be found of great use, either for the greenhouse or for the table, as its foliage is both elegant and shows well under gaslight. For the table, plants about a foot high, in 48-sized pots, surrounded with a plant or two of *Isolepis gracilis* and the spaces filled in with *Selaginella denticulata* will be found to make very effective low centres for tables, and will last for two or three months with ordinary care. We have frequently used a bamboo for the centre, five isolepis (in large 60 pots) around and close to the centre pot, and as many selaginellas in thumb pots as required, which generally amounted to from nine to twelve pots, if the plants were well grown.

Boronia.—In a well-found greenhouse these should always be represented to a certain extent, more or less according to the size of the house. It is, however, a rather tender plant if taken relatively with some of the other kinds, such as acacias, &c., but still, like the chorozemena, it is of much individual beauty.

It is not as a rule necessary, or even desirable, to have too many plants of a sort in a small collection, and if such plants as those mentioned below are represented by one or two good (though not large) specimens, it will be far better than a large quantity of small plants, as the numerous soft-wooded and hardy plants that can be introduced from time to time will generally supply plenty of variety and bloom without the trouble that generally has to be bestowed on the better class of hard-wooded plants. And another, and perhaps one of the more important of all other matters, is that the hardier subjects require less attention than the regular

c

greenhouse subjects. Like many of the other plants that decorate our glass houses in winter, boronias should be placed out of doors from July to September; in pits is the better plan, as then there are greater facilities for protecting from heavy rains and thunder storms. They should not be fully exposed when first put out, but in the course of a week they may have all the sun and air that comes. Potting should be performed once a year, as soon as the top growth ceases, as the roots then extend themselves in preparation for their next year's work. For soil we use peat and maiden loam equal parts, and about one-sixth sharp silver sand, which we find best for general use, although many gardeners use a somewhat different soil. It is a plant that also requires some attention in regard to water, as it must not be allowed to get dry, or disastrous results will follow, especially in summer, as a little drought will soon cause it to lose its foliage.

B. pinnata (purple) and *B. serrulata* (scarlet) are two of the best, while if more varieties are desired, *B. tetranda* (red), *B. Drummondii*, and *B anemonæfolia* (red) can be added.

Bouvardias.—These are, *par excellence*, the flowers for cutting for bouquets, and besides, are of comparatively easy culture. We think that the peculiar beauty of these plants well repays for their cultivation, as no bouquet in winter is complete without them. The almost continual habit of blooming which bouvardias possess when well grown, renders them very valuable to growers of cut bloom, leaving out their intrinsic value. We once had the curiosity to ask some of the salesmen in Covent Garden the value of what they had sold in one morning, and on reckoning up we found that five of them had sold the small lot of £50 worth between them—a sum not to be despised for one class of bloom alone. Of course this was in the season when flowers are expensive, but still it shows the decorative value of the plant. The white varieties are perhaps the most valuable, as their colour is sure to match with almost any other colour, but at the same time the scarlet varieties are good.

The mode of cultivation differs somewhat, according to the season in which it is desired the plants shall bloom, and therefore it is necessary that they shall be prepared accordingly. It must, however, be distinctly remembered that bouvardias are not fond of a cold house during winter, an intermediate house suiting them very much better. In fact, they are better adapted to those who have warm greenhouses than to persons who keep out the frost only, these latter not being able to achieve much success; for although these plants do well in frames during the summer months, they are very susceptible to the cold of our winters. For ordinary work the following practice will probably suit most amateurs, and we know it will suit the plants.

In the first place soil is a consideration, as the plants are rather fastidious in this respect, and they require rich food to do them at all well and keep them in health. We use two parts thoroughly rotted manure and leaf soil and three parts good loam, with enough sand to keep the compost open. Strike the cuttings in a brisk bottom heat in spring, and when rooted pot off into thumbs; still keep in a warm, genial, atmosphere, and as soon as the roots kiss the pot, pot off into large sixties. So soon as these pots are filled with roots, pot into forty-eights, and about the middle of June the plants may be put into airy frames out of doors; give each plant plenty of room to develop itself, and by a careful attention to stopping back during the earlier stages of their growth, let each plant have from six to eight leads. In the end of August pot into thirty-two sized pots, and keep close for a day or two until well established. About the end of September the plants should be housed in an intermediate house, if they are wanted for spring blooming, and just kept moving through the early part of winter; at least 50° should be maintained as the temperature of the house where the late bouvardias are kept. It will be found that the plants kept thus will bloom in the end of February and March, as soon as the sun gets warm. Of course the nearer they can be kept to the glass the better it will be for them, as they will remain sturdy and strong, and be in better condition for a long continuance of the blooming season. In such a house as is required for these plants, coleus, alternantheras, and other plants requiring warmth during winter will do well. Those which are required for blooming in December and early the next year, must have a brisk heat night and day through November and onwards, and they should be kept near the glass. About 70° at night is a very good temperature, but some little allowance must be made according to the weather. Water must be given to meet the requirements of the plants, but it must not be either over or underdone, or bad results will be sure to follow. Bouvardias cannot be grown in the " handsome glass conservatory," such as is fixed to modern villas, unless they are heated, and built up in such a manner as to retain the heat when it is applied. Neither can they be grown in a house from which sunlight is wholly or partially excluded, as they want all the light and sun they can get during winter. Young plants, liberal cultivation, and plenty of warmth in winter, is the only secret of success. Always water with water the same temperature as the house, syringe well occasionally, and fumigate once or twice if green fly appears; we have, however, found that the less the plants are fumigated the better will they bloom, as the smoke appears to affect the foliage, and cause a partial arrest of the due performance of their natural functions.

We have grown all the following and found them good for their respective habits, but perhaps the easiest to do is B. jasminoides. This very much resembles the white jasmine, and by some persons it is mistaken for that flower, although to those who are well up in flowers the difference is so great as to make the two flowers easily distinguishable. The list is as follows: B. candidissima (pure white), Hogarth (scarlet), B. Humboldtii corymbiflora (white), B. jasminæflora (white, very free), B. Laura (fine rose), B. Leiantha (bright scarlet), B. Leiantha compacta (scarlet), B. longiflora flammea (rosy blush tubes, salmon lobes), Rosalinda, (salmon), B. triphylla (orange scarlet, very free), B. Vreelandii (white, tinged with blush). The preceding are all good, and anyone fond of flowers would find a collection of them invaluable for winter use, or, for that matter, summer use as well.

AMELLIAS.—One of the most important plants that are grown for fine blooms is the camellia. Considering the price the cut blooms fetch in market it is surprising that more attention is not paid to the cultivation of this plant by amateurs than is generally the case; but if anyone expresses astonishment at the fact, they are told that "the buds drop off," and the plants cannot be made to do anyhow. To this we would reply that camellias are as easy to grow as any other plant if you only go the right way to work. Dryness of the atmosphere, and want of water at the roots, will generally be found the causes of failure, and the remedy for these evils will of course rest with the cultivator. During the summer camellias can be placed in the borders or other places out of doors, and thus afford a little decorative display, while at the same time they are making growth and bloom buds. We prefer to keep the plants always under cover if they are at all large, as we contrive to get better results from them; in fact, we prefer to have the plants in the borders of a cool conservatory as permanent plants, as they then make the finest growth. Indeed, permanent plants give far better results than any that are in pots or tubs, but as they require a large conservatory to give that room which is so necessary to them when grown in this manner, they are not generally suitable to amateurs. The best mode of cultivation for amateurs is, therefore, in pots or tubs.

Before going into the matter of treatment it may, perhaps, not be amiss to point out a few of the uses to which the blooms of the camellia may be put, and first and foremost amongst these, bouquet making takes a place. White camellias (with other flowers) are much used for bridal bouquets, for the hair, and for buttonholes, and also for table decorations, and the red are used for the same purposes, with the exception of bridal bouquets. A single bloom of Lady Hume's Blush, properly mounted and wired, is one of the nicest flowers imaginable for a lady's hair, as is also a bloom of *Imbricata*; they are also very good for buttonhole bouquets, although for our own part we should prefer a rosebud and a spray or two of bouvardia, backed with a spray of *Adiantum gracillimum*, as we consider a large flower is out of place in the coat. Some of the semi-double varieties come in very usefully in a half expanded state, as they are pretty and not too large. In the decoration of a dinner table, both single and double sorts are very valuable, as they take the place of roses, and besides, they last for many days if they are properly gummed and mounted. Gumming is necessary with all flowers grown indoors, or they soon fall to pieces.

The cultivation of the camellia is very simple, attention to a few easy rules only being necessary for their proper culture. The great faults in growing camellias are too great heat, and very often a dry, arid atmosphere, and too much or too little water. We have very often seen plants kept dust dry, and as a natural consequence all the blooms fell off, as they would had they been kept over wet. Too much dry heat will also fetch off the buds with a run, as will also forcing, or rather trying to force the plants into bloom early. The way to get camellias to bloom well is to keep them just moist enough, and at a temperature of from 45° to 50°, allowing 10° or 12° rise for sun heat; fresh air of the temperature of the house may be admitted, so that mildew is kept down, and little else has to be done. To obtain the blooms early, the plants should be gradually induced to ripen early, so that, according to the natural order of things, they shall bloom early, as the plants will not bear to be forced in the general acceptance of the term. Plenty of light, also early varieties of the plants, are necessary for early work; and in fact, with care, camellias can be had for some months, but they must of course be rather strong in numbers. It should be remembered that camellias are nearly hardy (in some places the single white blooms well out of doors), and in places where frost is excluded they do well if not neglected, but, like all plants, attention is one of the secrets of success. The time to pot camellias is when they cease blooming, using two parts good fibrous loam, one part peat, and enough sand to keep the whole open. Pot firmly and not deeper than before, or it is a great chance that the plants will be killed by the water settling round the collar. Liquid, or other manure is not required, nor is it desirable to apply it, as it sooner or later causes the destruction of the plants.

As a rule insects do not often trouble this class of plants, but scale will sometimes appear, and can easily be removed by hand. Thrip sometimes appears, when a little smoke will settle them. A mildew like that which attacks Cape pelargoniums sometimes shows up; but it is not very often the case, and a soft sponge and some lukewarm soapy water will soon clear it off, but if the place is ventilated, and kept fairly clean, there is very little fear of its appearance.

For a selection of double camellias, we would recommend *Imbricata (red); Alba plena (white); *Lady Hume's Blush (white blushed carmine); Augustina superba (transparent rose, occasionally spotted with white); *Bealii, (crimson); Circe (white; the flowers of this are small, and suited to bouquet making); Comte de Gomer (soft rose); Comte de Paris (salmon pink); *Duke of Lancaster (clear rose); *Eximia (dark crimson, scarlet); Exquisita (rose, flowers small and suitable for bouquets); Fimbriata (white, the edge of each petal is nicely fringed); Frederici, crimson, maroon); Nigra (deep crimson lake, the darkest flower in the family); Wilderii (soft rose). All the preceding are double, of fine form, those marked with an asterisk being old favourites with growers. The following are either single or semi-double, and are very useful for cutting when half expanded. Alba marginata (single red, variegated foliage); Donckelaarii (semi-double, rich crimson, marbled and blotched white); Reticulata (semi-double, bright rosy lake); Sasanqua foliis variegatis, (single red, variegated foliage); *Sasanqua rosea* (single, bright red); *Tricolor* (semi-double, white, deeply flamed with carmine). It will be seen that we have excluded striped and flamed flowers, because, as a rule, they have a somewhat confused appearance, but if anyone wishes for them they are rather plentiful. All the above are suited to pot cultivation, and, if one of each is obtained, make a nice selection.

Cassia.—This is one of those good old-fashioned plants that the rage for novelties has nearly displaced, and consequently it is not seen nearly so often as it should be. Its beautiful golden blossoms, which are borne plentifully from June till the end of the year, are always in demand for cutting, and make a back wall, or pillar, a mass of golden wealth. It is also a fine subject for outdoor decoration, as it blooms till frost cuts it down. Young plants struck in spring, and grown on, make very acceptable plants for autumn decoration, and in fact no house should be without them. Indeed, *Cassia corymbosa* (yellow) is one of those old neglected plants that well repays for cultivation, but from prejudice, or some other reason, seems almost dying out. From the very simple nature of its culture it is essentially a plant for the amateur, and should never be omitted from a collection of hardwooded plants. For indoor use we pot in maiden loam and sand and a little peat, and the plants do well. For outdoors, we plant out in June, and as soon as the frost touches the foliage pot them up (after cutting back nearly to the old wood), and winter in the back part of the greenhouse, or where there is a vinery, in that, just keeping out frost. For beauty of bloom, easiness of culture, and general usefulness, in our opinion, there is no plant to beat this.

Chorozema.—This is a family of plants that is most decidedly ornamental, and although not so easy of culture as some of the other hardwooded plants, will repay for any trouble bestowed on it. The flowers are very handy for bouquets, and the foliage is also very elegant, being of a very fresh green. Trained on a balloon frame the plants when well bloomed form quite " a picture," and for decorating a window are first-rate. Allowed to grow naturally, small plants are very effective, and amongst other blooming plants give a rich, bright appearance that few other plants possess, and many amateurs we have known say they cannot wish for a better return for their care and attention than these plants give. The flowers, which are somewhat pea shaped, are borne well above the foliage, and being on tidy stems are not so awkward to arrange in a bouquet as some others, and for this reason alone are worth cultivation, were the bright colours left out of consideration. The plants can be kept outdoors from the beginning of July till well into September, and are no trouble with the exception of watering. Potting should be performed as soon as the plants cease blooming; the soil we use is two parts peat to one part maiden loam, and plenty of sharp sand. We are aware that some gardeners use a somewhat different compost, but we have always had good success with the above, and of course can recommend it.

For sorts the following will suit the most fastidious, and we know that where we have had them they have given every satisfaction :—*C. cordata* (red), *C. cordata splendens* (red), *C. flava*, *C. ilicifolia* (yellow), *C. Law-*

renciana (orange), *C. macrophylla* (red), *C. ovata* (scarlet), *C. varia* (orange, red), *C. varia nana* (dwarf yellow, red), *C. varia Chandlerii* (orange, red), and *C. varia rotundifolia* (red).

Citrus.—To this family belong the orange, lemon, citron, and two or three other fruits, and it is generally the wish of the proprietor of a greenhouse to grow and fruit one or other of these. Now, however unsuccessful anyone may have been, there is not the least reason why oranges should not be bloomed (if not fruited) in every light conservatory or greenhouse in the land, if our directions are only followed, and in any case it will be found that the bloom alone pays for any trouble bestowed on the plants. The first consideration is, what sort of orange to grow? In this, please yourself, as all the citrus family are pretty, but for our own part *citrus aurantium* (the sweet orange) would be the choice, as it is of no more trouble to grow than the comparatively useless bitter orange, and should fruit be perfected it is useable, whereas that of the bitter orange is of too acrid a flavour to be at all pleasant. The bloom is, moreover, as useful as is that of all the oranges. To grow any of the citrus family well attention must be particularly paid to the soil in which they are grown. This should be sound heavy loam, to which a liberal portion of sand has been added. No manure should be used in the soil, as it tends to promote the growth of fungi, which, in all cases, can be very well done without. During the growing season some liquid manure should be regularly supplied, but as soon as growth begins to slacken, this should be gradually stopped, and clear water substituted. A moist atmosphere should also be kept up while in vigorous growth, and for this reason a vinery is a very good place for the plants at this season; where a dry atmosphere is maintained, the plants are sure to have a starved and stunted appearance, very foreign to what it should be, and, as a rule, the bloom will be poor and scarce. In potting, the soil should be moderately hard in the pot, or the wood will be too soft and sappy, and not ripen properly. It should not, however, be too much compressed, or the plants will not thrive. In a greenhouse the heat must not go below 45° in winter, and in summer of course the heat will depend on circumstances, but in all cases plenty of air is necessary, unless frost is present. We have fruited the Tangerine orange in an ordinary greenhouse heated by a flue, and always found (with some dozens of plants) the preceding treatment answer very well, as we had plenty of fruit and cut bloom. Of course the plants have to be kept clear of insects and dirt, or they soon begin to suffer, as will any evergreen plant.

Properly worked plants must be obtained if flowers are desired, although those raised from seed are interesting from the remembrances they bear. It is, however, many years before they bear fruit.

The sorts we have grown comprise, *C. acida, C. aurantium* (sweet orange), *C. aurantium bigardia* (bitter orange), *C. aurantium sanguinea* (blood orange), *C. limonum* (lime), *C. Medica* (citron), and *C. myrtifolia* (the myrtle-leaved orange).

Coprosma.—*Coprosma Baueriana variegata* is a shrub or plant that is of a highly decorative character, both for the greenhouse and bedding out, although it is rather difficult of cultivation, or rather propagation.

It requires a brisk bottom heat to strike the cuttings, but where convenience exists it well repays for any trouble. In the greenhouse one or two plants look very well, and they may be put out of doors through the summer. The green and white foliage is very conspicuous, and shows up well. Cuttings should be made in March, of young wood, taken off with a heel of the old wood adhering, and put into cutting pots filled two-thirds full of crocks, a thin layer of rich, light material, and on top a layer of sand. Place the pots in a brisk bottom heat in a propagating frame, or into a sweet hotbed, covering the pots in the latter case with bell glasses, and during the time the cuttings are making root only just sprinkle the pots with water, or the cuttings will damp off. When rooted, pot into rich sandy soil, and gradually harden off the same as other bedding plants propagated in a similar manner. Another plan of propagation is to place the plants in a propagating bed, and layer the shoots that overhang the pot. Old plants should be potted in a similar compost to that recommended above, and should be pruned into shape each year if necessary.

Cordyline.—For particulars of *Cordyline indivisa* (blue) see under "Dracæna."

Coronilla.—This is both a pretty and an easy subject to grow, and like the last should be in every collection. We have found the treatment advised for the sorts of cytisus answer admirably in the hands of amateurs, and therefore it is not necessary to enter into a prolonged description.

For sorts either *Coronilla glauca* (yellow) or *C. g. variegata* (yellow).

Correa.—This is a class of plants that commences to bloom in April, and the different varieties keep in bloom till the end of the year. They are really fine plants, and should be in every collection. The blooms, which vary in colour from scarlet to deep crimson in the tube, with a green or light coloured band near the apex, are tube shaped, and are freely produced from the matured wood of the past season. As a decorative plant it is not easy to surpass it. The plant is of erect growth, and therefore does not require to be tied out like many others. In our opinion it is far better to pinch back the points so as to induce bushy growth rather than to tie the branches out with a multiplicity of sticks, judicious pruning being in all cases preferable to sticks, if the plants are naturally shrubby. Of course with young specimens it is necessary to keep the bottoms well furnished, both by pruning and tying out; but, training is not a necessary operation after the plants are furnished, and the growth is set. We find that these do very well with much the same treatment as oranges, so far as temperature and moisture goes, and we have grown both correas and oranges successfully side by side. The plants should be potted in April in good sound peat, to which is added a good allowance of sharp sand, to ensure porosity for a length of years, as it is not advisable to reduce the ball of roots. When the plants reach 12in. pots, potting should cease, and the plants kept in blooming order by being watered with weak liquid manure once a week, by which means they will keep in blooming condition for two or three years; meanwhile young plants can be got on to take their place.

For sorts we should choose *C. bicolor*, *C.* Brilliant, *C. cardinalis*, *C.*

Cavendishii, *C. delicata*, C. Jardin d'Hiver, *C. magnifica*, *C. Ne plus ultra*, and *C. picta superba*. All of these are good and well worth growing.

Cytisus.—This is a plant that is much grown for the London markets, and is well worth growing. Its bright yellow flowers and elegant foliage makes it a favourite with everyone, and a plant or two in a greenhouse gives a bright appearance to what would, perhaps, be only a mass of green foliage. The culture is very easy, and the adaptability of the plants to an amateur's treatment is very great, more so than scores of other hard-wooded plants; and in the first place the cost is very moderate, indeed nice plants in full bloom are to be had from a shilling each in the season. It is one of the most popular spring plants there is grown near London for sale, one large firm of our acquaintance growing from 9000 to 12,000 plants annually. It is well adapted for house decoration, as it lasts in bloom for a long period, and unless large plants only are grown, forms one of the most useful house plants with which we are acquainted. Plants about a foot high look very well for table decoration, only as the flowers are golden yellow, they look white by gas light. Cytisus and Genista are the names the plant is known by in different places, and it is immaterial which is asked for, although cytisus is now the generally accepted name.

The plants should be potted as soon as the bloom is over, using rich sandy loam, and sand enough to keep the soil well open. In the end of June the plants should be put out of doors, and should remain out until September, when they should be brought indoors, and placed in a light position, so that they may start soon after Christmas. They bear forcing very well, and where conveniences exist may form part of the early batches of plants.

For sorts we prefer *C. racemosus* (yellow), *C. racemosus superba* (yellow), *C. Atleeana* (yellow), and *C. filipes* (white), and they are good, although where one or two plants only are grown, the two first will be found to give satisfaction.

APHNE.—This is a class of plants well worthy of general pot culture, both for its foliage and its finely scented bloom. As it is nearly hardy, a cool house suits it very well, and, as the cultivation is easy, it is a very desirable plant for the use of amateurs. It does very well trained on the walls in a partly shaded cool house, and in several large gardens it is trained on the back walls of the camellia house, where it affords the perfume that the camellia lacks, and the foliage works in very well with that of the camellias. As an ornamental perfumed plant, the *Daphne Indica* (red) is second to none, and as it requires no forcing house to bring it into bloom during the short days when fragrant flowers are scarce, of course it is within the means of most persons who have a greenhouse. The two daphnes we prefer for house work are *D. Indica rubra* and *D. cneorum* (pink) ; and *D. cneorum*, though it is perfectly hardy, yet pays for potting-up and housing. The treatment of *D. Indica* is very simple. In the first place, instead of coddling the plants up in a high temperature, 55° is quite high enough for them during the growing season, and if the bloom is wanted moderately early, the same temperature will gradually bring them on. They are of slow growth, although robust looking, and care must be taken to get the wood well ripened. During summer the plants may be placed in a sheltered position out of doors, and brought in at the same time as camellias and other similar plants. A moist atmosphere suits them admirably during the time they are making growth, but when ripening the wood a drier situation is necessary. After blooming pruning may be resorted to ; keep the plants in shape, or they get straggling in a few years, whereas they should be kept as bushy as possible, if good appearance is desired. As a rule, the plants are worked on one of the hardy kinds ; but we advise amateurs to get them on their own roots, as we have found them grow best when propagated in that manner. It will not stand overpotting, blooming best if rather pot-bound. Pot in the middle or end of February ; pot firmly, but at the same time insure sufficient drainage. For soil use two-thirds rich turfy loam, and one-third turfy peat, with plenty of very coarse sand, and it is no disadvantage if some charcoal or crocks are mixed with the soil.

For pot culture it will be found that *D. Indica rubra* is the best, as *D. Indica alba* (white) is somewhat liable to canker ; but still cuttings struck in a cold frame under a bell glass will do very well for a year or two. The first blooms from October to April if the plants are brought on in succession, while the white blooms during summer ; this latter is best planted out in the conservatory borders where there is room. The hardy varieties of daphne will be treated further on.

Dracæna.—This is a class of ornamental foliaged plants that commands attention for general culture by amateurs, as it is so useful for decorative purposes indoors. Small plants a foot to 18in. high, make very useful centres for tables, for windows, and to stand in halls. The foliage is leathery and stands gas well, and if dirty is easily cleaned with a sponge and lukewarm water. *Cordyline indivisa* is, in appearance, much like the dracæna, and as the treatment is much the same, we treat it as a dracæna here. With these, as with all other fine foliage plants, care must be taken to damage the leaves as little as possible, or the plants soon become very unsightly. Leaving out the varieties that require stove and intermediate house treatment, there yet remains a good variety for the greenhouse, which are all comparatively easy of cultivation. Scale is about the only insect pest to be feared, and with ordinary care can be kept down easily, hand picking being the means employed. We have, however, found that thrips will occasionally appear, but in a clean, well kept house their visits will be few and far between.

Dracænas are not very particular as to soil, any ordinary potting soil answering pretty fairly; but, of course, to obtain the best results it is necessary to use the best soil. This we find to consist of equal parts of peat and loam, with enough sharp sand added to keep the soil open enough for the water to pass through freely. The soil should be rather coarse, and not compressed too firmly, as the plants require plenty of water throughout the season of growth, and much compressed soil causes the water to stagnate round the roots of the plants, so causing disease and finally death. For the same reason plenty of drainage must be afforded, and when large pots are used, they should be chosen with holes round the sides, as well as at the bottoms. A rather humid atmosphere, plenty of water and warmth, and a light position are requisite during the growing season; and if the plants are to be removed indoors, they will require to be hardened off, or the leaves will suffer. For a start choose thrifty well-grown plants at a nursery, and grow them on carefully. The modes of propagation will be described at the conclusion of our remarks on plants.

The following will all be found very good: *Cordyline indivisa*, *Dracæna atrosanguinea*, *D. Australis*, *D. Banksii*, *D. Draco*, and *D. Veitchii*. We do not give the colour of the bloom as it is but rarely borne in the ordinary greenhouse.

EPACRIS.—These, too, are worthy of more extensive cultivation, as they are little trouble and very pretty when rightly managed. One of the chief causes of failure with the epacris is neglect when it is out of bloom; and to this neglect very many of the failures are attributable, as the plant is perfecting itself for the production of new blooms, while it is seemingly at rest; indeed, this is the case with the majority of plants, as they undergo many changes while not in active growth. The blossoms are, as most persons know, produced on the young wood, and therefore it is necessary that this should be properly grown and ripened to ensure the setting of the bloom buds.

During the growing season it is a good plan to syringe overhead occasionally, but not often enough to produce mildew. After blooming the plants should be cut down, and as soon as they start into growth should be repotted into pots a size larger, using good sound peat and sand for this purpose. Pot very firmly, and afford plenty of drainage, so that the soil shall not get sour, or the plants will suffer. Once in two or three years is often enough to pot, unless it is desired to have large plants. The plants should be in frames through the summer, as, unlike heaths, they do best under cover as a rule. In some varieties the growth is rather straggling;

but this is of small consequence, each shoot becoming a mass of bloom in its season.

For a selection choose from the following, all of which are first-class: *Epacris alba odoratissima* (white), *E. carminata* (carmine), *E. Albertus* (pink), *E. delicata* (blush, white), *E. densiflora* (blush), *E. elegans, B. grandiflora* (scarlet), *E. hyacinthiflora*, Fireball (scarlet), Lucifer (red), Model (blush), *E. multiflora, E. picturata* (blush white), *E. sanguinea* (red), *E. splendida*, Vesuvius (red), and *E. vesta* (blush).

Epiphyllum.—These are in reality cacti, or, rather they belong to the cactus tribe; but, as they are so often included in collections of plants, of which the majority are hardwooded, we treat of them here instead of further on. As a decorative plant the epiphyllum ranks in the first class whether we use it exclusively in the greenhouse, or also for table decoration and cut bloom (which ranges in colour from pink to deep scarlet), as, in each case, it is very useful. The treatment is very simple, as it is not supposed that an amateur will go to the expense of grafting, &c., which so often proves a source of trouble and annoyance, rather than pleasure. As a general rule, we consider that it is an ill-advised proceeding for an amateur to attempt the propagation of any plant that requires special treatment and a special place to do them in, as, however interesting the process may be, failure is almost sure to cause disgust with the plant and all connected with it, and, therefore, should be avoided. In places where a proper heat and atmosphere are kept up, especially where a range of houses is under the charge of a competent gardener, epiphyllums are very easy to graft, and in most houses under the charge of amateurs cuttings root freely, and form good plants for hanging baskets. *Epiphyllum truncatum var.* is the only variety we shall treat now, as it affords plenty of variety for a beginner. We advise the purchase of young pyramid or umbrella-headed plants as a start, and then if basket plants are required they can be struck from cuttings.

As a rule, the plants bloom best if rather potbound; therefore, for general purposes, it is not well to give too much root room to blooming plants; but, at the same time, young growing specimens should have plenty of room to grow into large plants, as they are the most effective. The soil they do best in is good fibrous loam, lime rubbish, and cowdung rotted to mould. Drainage should be well provided for, or the soil will get sour, and the blooms will not last, a point that is of much importance. Pot in the end of February, and keep close for a few days, after which gradually expose to the full sun to harden the growth, and so promote a large crop of bloom. While in bloom, and during the growing season, plenty of water is necessary; but while the plants are at rest only a few waterings are required. The epiphyllum should be in every greenhouse where a temperature of from 47° to 50° Fahrenheit is maintained during winter.

For sorts make a selection from the following: *Epiphyllum truncatum albescens, E. t. amabile, E. t. bicolor, E. t. cruentum, E. t. magnificum, E. t. purpureum, E. t. majus, E. t. salmoneum, E. t. splendens, E. t.*

tricolor, E. t. violaceum, E. t. violaceum superbum. It may as well be mentioned here that the best plan is to select from a large collection, and have a varied collection of colour, or the plants will appear very similar to inexperienced eyes.

Erica.—As these, as a rule, require more attention than an amateur can give, we omit them from this book, as we are desirous of meeting general, and not special, requirements here.

Eurya.—*Eurya japonica variegata* is a plant that requires a rather warm house to do well, but as it is so handsomely variegated, it is worth a little extra trouble. During the summer syringe once a day, and keep the roots well supplied with water, but after the middle of October this should not be persisted in, and the plants may be kept in a cool house during winter. Although it is nearly hardy, it makes finer growth in a warm greenhouse than in a cold one, and consequently the better plan is to give it the former. We make it a rule to pot twice a year, in February and June, until the plants have attained their full size, and then pot only once a year. The soil used is equal parts of fibrous loam and peat, and a little sharp sand, and we find these do well. After it has attained its allotted size ordinary greenhouse treatment should be given, and the plants will do very well. Insects of all kinds must be kept down, or they disfigure the leaves, and so spoil the beauty of the plants. Training out must be seen to if nice shapely plants are wanted, and any trouble will be amply rewarded.

FICUS ELASTICA.—This plant, which is known as the Indiarubber plant, is very much grown for indoor decoration, as its large glossy foliage stands gas and impure air far better than the majority of the plants generally used for the purpose, and so long as actual frost is kept from it will do fairly well. The culture is very simple in a greenhouse, as, unlike many other plants which we have mentioned, it does no harm to allow it to become pot-bound so long as a sufficient supply of root moisture is afforded. The general plan is to grow the plants as upright rods, well furnished with leaves, although it can also be made to assume bushy form by stopping the points out from time to time, but bushy plants do not, as a rule, look best. Plants should be obtained about a foot high to start with, and these should be grown on to the size desired; but after a certain period the lower leaves will drop off, and the plant will become bare at the bottom. When this occurs the plants may either be placed in a position where the stem is hidden, or they may be exchanged for young ones, or, what is perhaps better, they may be sent to a nurseryman to be cut down, and young plants made of the tops of the shoots. Propagation is a point in the life of this plant which an amateur should not attempt unless he has a propagating pit, and very few amateurs have this accommodation. The soil used by us is sandy loam three parts, rotten leaf soil one part, and from one-eighth to one-sixth part of silver sand. Sometimes we substitute peat for the leaf soil, and we have grown the plants entirely in peat, but the foliage is more lasting in the first-mentioned compost. Scale and mealy bug sometimes attack the stems, but they are easily removed and kept down, and it is only in dirty houses where they occur. The foliage should be sponged occasionally to remove dust.

ENISTA.—This is a very favourite plant for greenhouses and indoor decorations, as its bright yellow blossoms and light elegant foliage have a charming effect amongst other flowers. It is a plant that is very easily grown, and perhaps for this reason it is so popular; but, apart from this, its intrinsic merits fully entitle it to the high position it has attained. The genista is more properly known as the cytisus, and, under that name, full instructions for its cultivation and a list of the best varieties to grow will be found.

Grevillea. — This is a plant of an ornamental character, and is worthy of a place in all fair sized collections. The foliage is ornamental, and of very elegant appearance, while the flowers are of rather a peculiar form, particularly so in *rosmarinifolia*, and for this alone the plants would be interesting. As a comparatively cold house, or an ordinary greenhouse only is required, these plants come within the reach of most amateurs. We would, however, advise our readers to see the plants before purchasing them. For soil we generally use good fibrous loam, and enough sand to keep the compost sufficiently open for the passage of water, as most loams go into a bad state as soon as the fibre decays, unless sand is used. The plants should be repotted when they cease blooming, and they require much the same treatment as cytisus.

For sorts we should prefer *G. alpestris* (red, yellow), *G. Drummondii* (white, yellow), *G. Hillii*, *G. lavendulacea rosea*, *G. punicea splendens* (scarlet), *G. robusta* (orange), and last, but not least, *G. rosmarinifolia* (red).

ABROTHAMNUS.—This is a plant that does well in a house that is heated to about 40° or 45° during winter, and although it is generally used as a climber it makes no despicable pot plant. It requires plenty of pot room, and we always find it do best in a free and moderately rich soil. For pot cultivation, cuttings should be struck in August, and when rooted should be potted as frequently as the roots reach the sides of the pots. They should be pinched back early to cause them to become bushy, and if pinched back early in January they often bloom well according to their size; but the next season they do better, as a rule, if potted, and grown on in the frames or outdoors. It is desirable to use large pots, as the plants require plenty of root room, and at all times they must be carefully looked after, in regard to watering, &c. Where it is desired that they shall form wall plants, they should have large boxes, or, what is better, should be planted out in the borders, and receive liberal treatment, and bloom will then be plentiful.

H. elegans (carmine), *H. fasciculatus* (crimson), and *H. elegans fol. argenteus* are three of the best.

Hovea.—This is a class of plants that is well worthy of cultivation, and from its adaptability for use as a roof or bush plant, it is worthy of extended cultivation. It has pea-shaped flowers, and very distinct foliage, the blooms being produced freely from the axils of the leaves of the last year's growth. The best plan is to raise the plants from seeds, as cuttings are rather difficult to strike. The plant is rather slow growing, and from this it is particularly suited to small or medium-sized houses.

We generally sow on a gentle bottom heat in March, and pot off as soon as the rough leaf appears, using good turf, peat, or loam, with about one-sixth silver sand, to keep it open. Grow on till the plants are about three or four inches high, and then pinch out the points, to cause the young plant to be bushy. As soon as the plant requires a shift, it should have a small one. As the plants grow it is very likely that some of the shoots will take the lead over the others, and when such is the case they should be stopped, and, in fact, it is not a bad plan to stop all the shoots again when they reach about six inches in height. This second stopping causes the plants to become pretty well furnished, and as it were lays the foundation of the future plants. Seedlings require the heat of an intermediate house rather than that of the greenhouse, for the first season, but after the first rest they can be transferred to the greenhouse. It is for this reason that the amateur will find it by far the best plan to purchase plants that are of a very good size from a nursery, as then all the preliminary trouble is avoided, and no other than a greenhouse is necessary. If, however, plants are required for roofs, they had better be raised from seeds, and not stopped until the required height is obtained, when, if they are pinched back, and carefully trained, they will make good plants, and be very ornamental.

The following treatment is more suitable for an amateur, and is that necessary for plants that have been purchased in 6in. pots in autumn. These should be wintered in a light house, as near the glass as possible, and at a temperature from 40° to 45°. It is a good plan to pick off the flowers the first season, if it is desired to have nice specimens; but at the same time it is not absolutely necessary to do so, if the bloom is particularly desired. As soon as they have started an inch or so they should have a shift into pots an inch or two larger, pot firmly, and allow sufficient drainage. Shut up the lights early in the afternoon to retain as much sun heat as possible, so as to ensure an early growth. About the end of April the plants should be just sprinkled in the afternoon with the syringe to ensure a good growth, and should any of the shoots be inclined to run away, tie them down, so that the flow of sap may be equalised. Shade is not required, but a proper amount of water is necessary to ensure success, although over watering is to be avoided. About the end of August air should be freely admitted to harden the plants off. Winter as before, and in the following spring the plants will be very fine in a decorative point of view. After blooming they should have a shift if the soil is full of roots, but if not it can be left for another year. The only insect that is likely to do much damage is the scale, but this is easily destroyed by using a strong solution of "Gishurst Compound," or "Fowler's Insecticide," either of which will destroy it.

The varieties that we have found suitable are *H. Celsii* (blue), *H. purpurea* (purple), and *H. pungens major* (blue).

Hydrangea.—This, although a hardy shrub, is so often grown in greenhouses, and when properly grown produces such a fine effect, that we consider it worth a place amongst the more generally accepted greenhouse plants. *H. hortensis* (pink) is the only one of the family to which we shall refer, as it is the commonest, and most met with. The question to be determined is, whether one large corymb of flowers (as grown for the London markets), or several smaller ones are desirable. for, although the treatment is similar, it is necessary to select the plants for the different plans. Strike cuttings in gentle bottom heat in the end of August, and when well rooted, they should be potted off into 4in. pots, in a free rich soil, containing a small allowance of peat, or if this is not obtainable, leaf mould and silver sand; choose only the lateral or side shoots, and keep them growing in a warm greenhouse, near the glass, throughout the winter. Liberal supplies of water are necessary to ensure large flowers, and, consequently, there must also be good drainage. During the time the plants are in full growth occasional supplies of weak liquid manure can be applied with advantage. If more than one shoot is required, old cut-back plants can be used, but we think the single corymb makes the greatest display, as being larger it is much more conspicuous. The same plants can, by attention to soil and culture, be made to bear blue flowers, and this opens to amateurs a wide field for interesting experiments. It is said that a ferruginous soil will produce the blue coloured, and we have certainly seen masses of hydrangeas in Devonshire, where the soil is strongly impregnated with iron, covered with azure blossoms.

LLICIUM.—*I. Floridanum* is a plant that is by some persons much esteemed, on account of its flowers being perfumed, the scent being very much like that from anisé. The plant is very nearly hardy, and may therefore be treated as described for other plants of a similar nature, putting the plants out of doors during the summer, &c. For soil use good sound turfy loam, to which a little leaf soil has been added, with enough sharp sand to keep the whole open. Pot moderately firm, and do not over water, and the plants will bloom abundantly.

Indiarubber Plant.—See "Ficus Elastica."

ASMINE.—For a cool house plant there is scarcely any one to beat *Jasminum revolutum*. Its flowers are highly fragrant, of a bright yellow colour, and the foliage is of a very rich green. Treated as a shrub it does far better than as a climber, or wall plant, and as it blooms better and earlier in the greenhouse than out of doors, it fully repays for any trouble bestowed on it. For soil we use turfy loam one half, good peat, as used for azaleas, one part, and leaf soil, or rotten cow manure, and sharp sand in equal proportions, one part, potting rather firmly, and not allowing too much room at the roots. We rather prefer to have the plants slightly pot bound, and to assist them with liquid manure, than to have them otherwise.

ENNEDYA.—This is a family of plants that are climbers in the true sense of the word, but we have seen them done well on balloon trellises, and in this form they look very well indeed. All that is necessary is to have the trellises about 15in. high, and to keep them well furnished. The plants should be cut down every third year, so as to maintain plenty of young wood. For soil use loam only, with plenty of sand, and pot firmly. For sorts, &c., see "Climbers."

ASIANDRA.—These plants are well worth cultivation in places where it is desired to have a nice selection of plants, and although they are, like all other good plants, rather more troublesome to grow than flowers such as geraniums, they fully repay for the trouble bestowed on them. They bloom in autumn and winter, and are consequently of much value, as at that season blooming plants are naturally scarce, and as a rule are the more valuable for this reason. In autumn select plants in 4in. or 6in. pots, and after wintering them repot into 8in. pots in February. In selecting the plants choose such as have been stopped at the third or fourth eye above the collar, and have four or five shoots, as unless such are chosen there will be some difficulty in furnishing the bottoms of the plants. For soil, use either loam or peat, the former preferably; use a sufficiency of sharp sand to keep the soil open, as this plant requires a lot of water whilst in a growing state; and good drainage must also be provided to prevent sourness of the soil. Keep in a light position with a temperature of 45° to 48° at night, and a little higher during the day. As the sun gains power, air must be given in the forepart of the day, and throughout the spring plenty of light must be given. As the sun gets very powerful a little shade must be given, and about the end of June the plants should be shifted into pots a couple of inches larger. Before the plants are repotted, say six weeks previously, it is a good plan to stop the shoots, so as to maintain as bushy a habit as possible, or it is probable that some of the strong shoots will have to be cut back, which means a loss of size in the plants. During the whole of the growing season syringe the foliage in the afternoon, and maintain a comparatively moist atmosphere, so that the growth shall be good; and it is also necessary to tie out the shoots to maintain an equal balance to the plants. If everything goes on well, about the end of July nip out the points of the strongest shoots, and in September gradually remove the shading, at the same time keeping a drier atmosphere, to ripen off the wood. Cease syringing, and give plenty of air, and by the end of the year they will commence blooming, at which season they should have a temperature of from 48° to 50°. About the end of the succeeding February cut back moderately, and give a shift into twelve inch pots, and apply a similar treatment to that recommended above, with the exception of the second potting. Red spider sometimes attack lasiandras, but these can be kept in check by plentiful applications of clean water with the syringe during the summer. Brown and white scale also attack them; for the former of which use "Fowler's Insecticide," about 5oz. to the gallon; and for the latter, Abyssinian Mixture, 7oz. to the gallon, well brushed into the bark two or three times while the plants are dormant.

L. macrantha is, in our opinion, only suited for trellises or walls, and for this purpose they should be planted out into the borders, or in large tubs or boxes, giving much the same treatment as that recommended for the preceding. The plants should be grown on the first year in pots, and then turned out. *L. macrantha* is not so suitable for pot culture as *L. macrantha floribunda*, which produces its blooms for some weeks with proper care.

Luculia Gratissima.—This is one of the old-fashioned sweet scented plants that is now much out of cultivation, not because it is inferior to the new plants, or because it is not worth growing, but simply because it is somewhat out of fashion, a reason that in our estimation is not sufficient to warrant its being excluded from more general cultivation. As it is rather difficult of propagation, the best plan is to purchase plants that are of fair size, in autumn or early spring, and grow them on. We prefer to have the plants in 6in. or 8in. pots to start with, unless there is a regular gardener to attend to them, when, of course, the case is different. We have found that a somewhat similar treatment to that described for the hovea answers well, using a compost of fibrous loam, peat, and silver sand. Good drainage must be afforded, as stagnant water is sure to stop growth. Shading from bright sun in summer and maintaining a moderately warm temperature during winter will cause the production of the bloom, in its season. The best place for luculias is planted out in the beds or borders of a conservatory where they have plenty of room to grow. With care they will make magnificent plants in the course of years. Insects are rather partial to the foliage, therefore it is necessary to keep a good look out for them, and destroy them as soon as seen, but let the drawbacks of this sort be what they may, the plant is well worth cultivating.

YRTLES.—In nearly all cases these are to be found in the greenhouses of amateurs, whether large or small, and it is too often the case that while the plants produce foliage they are quite devoid of bloom. This is much to be regretted, as a well bloomed myrtle is a very pretty object, leaving out the usefulness of the blooms when cut. The scent of the foliage and blooms is very grateful to most persons, and for this reason is much sought after. In the south and south-west of England myrtles are practically hardy, and bloom pretty well out of doors, but in less favoured positions the plants have to be protected during winter, or they are very liable to be destroyed by frost. The plants do well in a compost of loam, sand, and leaf soil, potting moderately firm, but not so hard as is the case with azaleas, or fibrous rooted plants of that description; and by keeping the plants in a cool house, and attending to their wants as regards watering, aëration, &c., they will bloom well. The plants may stand out of doors throughout the summer, carefully preventing them from becoming dry at the roots, or they will not bloom. During the growing season plenty of water will be found necessary, and just a trifling shade during the hottest part of the day will be an advantage, although if the pots are plunged in the border it is not really necessary.

For sorts, we prefer *Myrtus bullata*, *M. communis*, *M. c. angustifolia*, *M. c. flore pleno*, and *M. c. latifolia*, all of which are good.

ERIUM *(Oleander)*. — This is a class of old-fashioned plants that is of much beauty, and which affords very useful blooms for cutting for bouquets or table decoration, besides being very useful on the plant itself, as they are produced in terminal clusters on the ends of the branches of the previous year. There is no reason why these should not be grown more extensively than they are, either as large or small plants. In the latter case, however, a pretty brisk heat is required to do them well, and therefore that treatment is out of place here, but at the same time good serviceable plants can be grown by ordinary treatment. We will begin with cuttings. These, as a rule, cannot be struck in the same way as geraniums and similar plants, but require a rather peculiar treatment. The method is as follows : As soon as the young growth is matured, take cuttings about 6in. or 7in. in length, and insert them singly in bottles of water, in each of which a teaspoonful of powdered wood charcoal has been added, then place the bottles in a house where the temperature is about 60° to 70°, and let them remain until pretty well rooted; then carefully pot them off into small pots in a compost of loam and river sand in equal parts, putting plenty of drainage into the pots. Keep in a warm place and they will soon get established. The following April the plants should have a size larger pot, and should be grown on in a warm house, and they will bloom towards the end of the year. But it is not this style of work that the amateur can, as a rule, do, and, therefore, the better way is to grow the plants in large tubs, or planted out in the house, but this latter plan can seldom be carried out. In growing the oleander in pots, the pots should be gradually increased in size as the plants grow, and the soil should be good sound loam and sand. During the growing season plenty of water should be given, both at the roots and the tops, but at the same time care must be taken to avoid the water at the roots becoming stagnant, or disease and death will be the result. No shade is at any time required, and, in fact, the warmest and sunniest spot in the house should be chosen for it. As a rule, it is a very good plan to stand the plants out of doors from the middle or end of May until the end of September, but it is not absolutely necessary to do so.

The best sorts are *Nerium splendens*, *N. s. album plenum*, *N. s. luteum plenum*, and *N. s. variegatum*. The latter is, however, more conspicuous for its leaves than its flowers. There are also some with single flowers, but these we do not give, as they are not so good as those named.

ORANGE.—Oranges come in very usefully both for flowers and fruit, and, if only for the former, they are worth cultivation. Few persons who have not tasted a ripe orange from the tree have the least conception of the delicate and refreshing flavour of this popular fruit, of which, if imported from abroad, it is almost devoid. A ripe sweet orange, gathered in the cool of the morning, is simply delicious; while it surpasses everything for quenching thirst, and also for cooling the system. Full directions for their culture are given under the head of " Citrus."

Oleander.—See " Nerium."

PHORMIUM.—This is an ornamental plant of some beauty, and is suitable for houses where there is plenty of room and where there is plenty of height for the full development of the leaves. Its stately habit of growth renders it particularly useful for large conservatories and similar places, and, while in a comparatively small state, it is useful for room decoration to a certain extent, but, of course, other and more graceful plants should be associated with it if the full effect of its peculiar beauty is to be obtained. This plant, which is also known as New Zealand flax, has broad green, or variegated leaves, according to the variety, and will with little trouble attain a height of five feet or more. In Lord Meath's garden, at Killruddery, co. Wicklow, Ireland, the leaves of a fine specimen (*out of doors*) attain a length of from 10ft. to 14ft., the whole forming a magnificent clump of foliage. But of these out-door plants we have nothing to say here, pot plants being at present our speciality.

For soil we use sound fibrous maiden loam and leaf soil, in equal portions, and about a sixth part of coarse, sharp sand. Plenty of drainage is necessary, and plenty of pot room is important. Repot each spring, giving a liberal shift, and potting rather firmly, keeping close for a few days, until the roots may be supposed to have recovered from the check consequent on repotting. Plenty of water is necessary during the season of growth, and during the hot months the plants may stand out of doors.

For sorts, *P. Colensoi variegatum, P. Cookii, P. tenax,* and *P. tenax variegatum* will all be found of use, the variegated sorts, of course, being most effective for house decoration.

Pimelea.—These are plants that are of rather difficult culture, and unless the amateur means to go in for gardening in its entirety, are of no value to him; but where anyone means to grow his plants well, they amply repay for all trouble bestowed on them. They are a class of plants that are especially liable to the attacks of red spider unless properly grown, and then there is little fear of trouble from any kind of insect. Pimeleas are not suited for houses where the minimum temperature is less than 45°, in winter, as they are never actually at rest, the same as most other hard-wooded plants.

About the end of March or early in April young healthy plants in 6in. pots should be repotted into some 2in. or 3in. larger, using a good fibrous loam chopped into lumps about the size of walnuts, and not sifted; to this should be added about one-sixth of sharp sand; pot the plants firmly, and stand in a position where they will receive no side air, for a fortnight or so. The stage on which the pots stand should be kept moist, and the plants should be gently syringed over every morning. Shade must be afforded from hot sun throughout the growing season, a point that is too frequently neglected in the cultivation of these plants. As the blooms that season will be of little worth, it is as well to remove them as soon as they begin to open, cutting the branches midway between the bloom and where they were out the previous year. This will prevent the branches becoming too long in proportion to the size of the plants. Cause the plants to make as good growth during the summer as possible, both by careful shading and by judicious watering, syringing thoroughly every day, and in such a manner that the *under*, as well as the upper side is wetted, so that the red spider shall be kept down, as no amount of care causes the plants to recover from their ravages. About the end of August more air and less shade may be given, and the syringing may be discontinued, so as to harden the plants off a little, and they must be wintered in a light position, where the minimum temperature is not less than 45°. They will require water throughout the winter, but not so much as during the summer. In spring repot as before, giving from 2in to 4in. larger pots according to the state of the roots, and treat as before, with the exception of removing the blooms, unless the plants are required for exhibition. After the bloom is over cut back as before described, and great care must be taken that the water from the syringe touches every part of the foliage, or the spider will get in and the plants will be spoiled. Very little training will be required, only a few sticks just to hold the branches down, so that the plants shall be well furnished, and perhaps a few sticks to hold the branches in their place when they get large, but these latter are not always required.

For sorts select from *P. spectabilis*, *P. s. rosea*, *P. Hendersonii*, *P. elegans*, *P. decussata*, *P. hispida*, *P. mirabilis*, and *P. Neippergiana*, all of which are good. *P. hispida* and *P. Neippergiana* do best in good sandy, fibrous peat, but the general treatment is the same as with the others.

Pittosporum.—This is a class of plants which is well worthy of cultivation, although not very largely grown now. It stands well and is seldom sickly, while it bears its pretty fragrant flowers freely.

In the cultivation of these plants a fair amount of pot room must be afforded, and drainage must be well provided for. Any good soil answers, and we have found the following compost answer well: turfy loam three parts, thoroughly decomposed cow manure one part, and leaf soil and sand one part, pot rather firm, and grow on in a cool house. The same remarks apply to these as to other plants in regard to training, watering, &c. The plants can stand out of doors from July to September, and a light situation indoors should be given them for the rest of the year. Repotting should be done in March, and keep close for a few days after. Some of the pittosporums have proved hardy in Ireland, but it is doubtful if they would stand in many parts of England without protection.

It may not perhaps be amiss to mention that *P. Tobira* is grown in tubs in some parts of the Continent, and in winter are stored away in cellars or sheds, and there is no reason why this plan should not be carried out in warm places in England. This plant should form a companion to the myrtle where the latter is grown in tubs or large pots.

For sorts we prefer *P. Tobira, P. Tobira argenteo variegatum, P. undulatum, P. eugenoides, P. Mayii,* and *P. crassifolium,* which are all good.

Pleroma.—This is a plant that somewhat resembles the Hovea in form, but as it has a better habit than that plant, and as the bloom is brighter, it is of more value for pot culture. We have found the blossoms very useful for bouquets that are used during daylight, but by artificial light the blooms lose their brilliancy, and are not very effective. As a conservatory plant while it is in bloom it stands pre-eminent, when well done, and, although not suitable for a cold greenhouse, it well repays for any trouble bestowed on it; it will not do in a house where the temperature is less than 40° in winter, so it is useless for an unheated structure. The best mode of procedure is to purchase plants in 6in. pots, in autumn, and to place in a greenhouse until about March, when the roots will probably be sufficiently active to warrant the repotting of the plants, using 9in. pots for the purpose, and for compost use good fibrous loam and about one-sixth of clean sharp sand; allow plenty of drainage. Pot firmly, and stand in a close place for a few days. Care must be taken all through their growth to protect them from hot sun, by shading, and it is well to protect as early as March. Care must also be taken to keep the strongest shoots trained to the outsides, and the weaker ones to the middle, so as to equalise the growth. As the weather gets warm the plants should be syringed in the afternoon, and plenty of water must be given to the roots. About August discontinue syringing, and give more air and light to harden them off for their season's rest. The next season repot as before, giving another 3in. shift, and treat as before until August, when they should be removed to the open air under a tall hedge or trees, where the sun has no power on them. Bring them in about the middle of September, and place near the light, winter as before, and be careful the sun does not injure the foliage, and the plants will probably bloom in spring. By careful stopping and training, and by keeping relays in readiness, there is no difficulty in keeping up a sufficient stock for all ordinary work; and without them a collection of plants would be incomplete.

Plumbago.—These plants are more suited for climbers or wall plants than for culture as bushes, but as they are so very ornamental when well flowered, and as by the following mode of treatment they can be made to do well, we treat them here rather than under the head of climbers. It is a plant that has a long, straggling habit of growth, and is more suited for walls or pillars for this reason; but at the same time, where there is plenty of room, the plumbago does well trained over a balloon trellis. The plumbago does best in a moderately warm house, and it is not a good plan to have it in any other house than one that can be kept comparatively warm. In the first place, plants should be obtained in autumn that have been stopped back to about 2in. from the collar, and which have five or six shoots or branches. A balloon trellis should be fixed in the pot and the branches trained over it, and by careful stopping about twice in the season, and training the shoots out carefully, the frame will be covered the first season. A moderate pruning must be given the next year and the plants must be re-potted into larger pots, using a free open soil for the purpose. We use good fibrous loam and sand, and a little peat, and in some cases a little thoroughly decomposed manure is admissible if the other soils are poor. Planted out in the borders of a warm conservatory, or in a warm greenhouse, these form some of the best plants out for walls and pillars, and should be more extensively grown than at present.

P. *Capensis,* P. *rosea,* and P. *Zeylanica* are all good, although, perhaps, the preference should be given to the two former.

RHODODENDRONS.—The greenhouse varieties of these are very beautiful, and, by using a little care in their selection, a fine and varied display can be had with no very great amount of labour. Of course, with all plants used in indoor work there is a certain amount of trouble; but with some plants it is less than with others; and with rhododendrons the trouble is but small compared with the results obtained. In the first place, it is necessary that plenty of root room be afforded, as rhododendrons, although not rooting so vigorously as many other plants, do not succeed well if too much cramped for space. The best plan is, however, where space exists, to plant them out in the borders of a conservatory, and then their full beauty is obtained. Good sound fibrous peat will be found the best soil, to which should be added enough sharp silver sand to keep the soil well open, as the soil cannot be removed from amongst the roots, the close fibrous nature of which causes them to form solid balls, the whole or partial destruction of which would cause the death of the plant or loss of the greater part of the foliage—a great point with expensive varieties. As rhododendrons only require the exclusion of frost, a cold house is all that is necessary, although many of the sorts force well—a large conservatory that it is desired to keep well furnished with as little fire heat as possible being as good a place as any for the reception of these plants. As a rule they should be repotted every year, as soon as they have ceased blooming, not giving more than a 2in. shift; press, or rather ram, the soil down hard by the side of the old soil, or the water will escape by the sides of the pots, and as a consequence, the plants will become dry, and if the evil is not rectified in time, they will soon die, or become injured irreparably. By using a little care in training, it is quite easy to maintain the plants in good form, without much pruning or cutting back, which, unless the plants are very straggling, should not often be resorted to, other than to reduce the size should it become too large. At no time must the plants get dry, although the supply of water should be diminished in winter, but during the growing season almost unlimited supplies should be given. For this reason plenty of drainage should be given, or in many cases the soil becomes sour and stagnant, and the plants necessarily suffer. The hardy varieties we will treat further on, as they are only useful for temporary work.

For sorts, the following will be found a good selection, and will, doubtless, please anyone choosing from it: Princess Royal, rich rose; *argenteum*, white, black spots; *Falconerii*, creamy white; Countess of Haddington, blush white; *campylocarpum*, primrose yellow; *ciliatum*, blush and white; Dalhousie, blush-white; *Dennisonii*, white, lemon throat; *Edgworthii*, white; *fragrantissimum*, white shaded blush; *fulgens*, crimson scarlet; *Gibsonii*, blush white; *jasminiflorum*, white; *Javanicum angustifolium*, orange yellow; *McNabii*, blush; *Nuttallii*, white; Prince of Wales, reddish orange; Princess Alice, blush white; Princess Helena, soft pink; Princess Mary, white; *tubiflorum*, dark reddish purple; *retusum*, reddish orange; *Veitchianum*, white, yellow base; *virgatum*, white. This last is most remarkable from its being the only one having axillary flowers, but all the others are desirable either for their blooms or scent, which latter in some kinds is very fine.

Roella ciliata.—This, from its peculiar appearance both of foliage and blooms, is worthy a place in all collections of hardwooded plants, and, as it is quite distinct from the generality of greenhouse hardwooded stock, it contrasts favourably with all of them. It is not a plant that is inclined to make over large specimens, or to outgrow the space allotted to it. For decorative purposes it is very effective, as its very distinct, purple-tipped white blooms, almost covering the surface of the plant, and quite hiding the rusty appearance of the foliage, which is the chief drawback to the general beauty of the roella when out of bloom. In no case must this plant be subjected to *cold* treatment, as that simply means an earlier or later death from mildew. A minimum temperature of 45° or 50° must be maintained in winter without sun heat, and the plants must be kept near the glass, as they are essentially light-loving subjects, and must not be shaded at any time, either by shading the glass or by placing tall plants over them, or their great enemy, mildew, will soon put in an appearance and cause destruction. Plenty of drainage must be afforded, and for soil, use good fibrous peat, with about one-sixth part of sand added, potting moderately firm, as it is a rather free-rooting subject, much more so than would be generally supposed from its apparently weak habit. The best time to commence the culture of the roella is about the beginning of March. Obtain healthy plants in 6in. pots, give a shift into pots 2in. larger, and, as before mentioned, give plenty of drainage, and pot moderately firm. As this is a plant that requires training, a sufficiency of sticks should be put round the edge of the pot in the new soil to avoid damaging the roots, and to these sticks the shoots should be trained as much as possible. Care must be taken to remove the blooms as soon as they appear, and this is about all the pruning the plants will require, as they are very regular growers. Admit no side air for two or three weeks, and damp the stage on which the plants stand, but on no account must there be syringing over head. Attention must also be paid to watering, giving water only when they require it, and then giving sufficient to pass through the pots, for, like most of the plants from the Cape, these do not like an indiscriminate supply of water, too much moisture at the roots causing bad health. Keep the plants in an airy, light, house, near the glass, and during the spring and early summer months close early in the afternoon to retain the sun heat as much as possible. During the summer give plenty of air during the daytime, and wet the stages and pots, but not the foliage, as the latter would tend to make the plants more readily susceptible to the attacks of mildew. About the middle of August leave air on all night, and keep them quite cool through October, after which close the house at night or the plants will be chilled. Remove all bloom buds as soon as formed, as it is not well to let the plants exhaust themselves in blooming the first season. Keep through the winter near the glass, in a house where the temperature is not less than 45° at night, and keep the plants neatly trained out and tied. This is necessary, as the plant, being naturally of a procumbent habit, soon forms an unsightly straggling mass if left to grow as it pleases. About March repot and treat as before if exhibition plants are required, but if they are required for decoration only, let them bloom, which they will do freely if permitted; after blooming treat as before described, and each year treat in the same manner. The roella does not require to be placed out of doors during the summer, but rather the reverse, as cold or cutting winds cause a more rusty appearance, and does the plant no good. Mildew is the chief foe to be combated, and for its better prevention all dead flowers must be removed; and for a cure flowers of sulphur must be freely applied on its first appearance. The only insect that will live on the roella is brown scale, and that can be easily kept under by the aid of a small brush, as it does not increase very fast.

ERICOGRAPHIS GHIESBREGHIANA.— This is a plant that is suited to a warm conservatory or greenhouse only, but as it can be done very well with some of the plants we have already mentioned, and as it is very useful from a decorative point of view, we give the cultural directions for it. Its fine feathery scarlet flowers are set off to great advantage by the bright green shining leaves, and from its comparatively easy culture it will be found very useful where a little convenience exists to meet its requirements. In the first place it is necessary to get the plants on early, so that good useful plants shall be made during the summer, and so that they may have time to mature their growth ere winter sets in. As a general rule late-struck plants do badly; and as they do not get thoroughly matured, they, as a matter of course, do not bloom at all, or, if they do bloom, it is very poorly.

As soon as the plants have ceased blooming they should be placed in a brisk and moist bottom heat for a week or two to get them into free growth, when the tips of the shoots will strike freely if properly treated. Cutting pots should be prepared by half filling them with crocks, on which a little coarse fibrous peat should be laid, and then the pots should be nearly filled with sharp propagating sand. The cuttings should be inserted about an inch or so apart, round the sides of the pots, which should have been thoroughly watered and drained previously to inserting the cuttings. These pots must be placed in a close moist heat, where they will strike freely, after which they should be potted off singly into small pots, and nursed gently on in a moderate moist heat. We have done this part of the process in an ordinary cucumber frame, where the bed had become sweet, and the plants throve very well; but, at the same time, if a propagating frame exists in the greenhouse, it is best to strike all cuttings therein. When well rooted the points should be pinched out to induce a bushy growth, and, when this has been attained, or rather, when the young plants have broken freely, they should be placed on a light, airy shelf, until the middle or end of May, when they should be repotted into 4in. pots, and gradually hardened off preparatory to placing outdoors in a cold frame. The time for putting them out would depend on the state of the weather; but well on into June will do if the weather is hot, but if cold the plants may remain for another week or so in the house. When placed in the frames, the pots should be plunged in half-spent leaves, and the plants should be syringed once or twice daily, according to the weather. If treated thus, and the frame is closed early, the plants can be finally shifted into 6in. pots about the end of July.

During September the syringing should be gradually discontinued, and the frames should be drawn off every fine day to harden off the plants, and induce a good supply of bloom. About the last week in September the plants should be removed to a warm greenhouse, and they will soon commence to bloom well. During winter a temperature of 50° to 55° should be kept up. For soil use peat and loam in equal parts, with enough sand to keep it open.

Sparmannia Africana.—This is a really good cool house shrub, that is nearly always in bloom. It, however, attains a pretty good size, and therefore requires a pretty high house to grow in. The blooms are produced in rich masses, and are white in colour, therefore it is the more valuable a plant for use in large places; but, at the same time, comparatively small plants give very good results. The best plan is to strike cuttings under bell glasses in a moist bottom heat in February or March, and as soon as rooted pot off into small pots, keeping in a warm light position until well rooted, when the plants should be put into 4in. pots. When the plants are about 3in. high the points should be taken out so as to induce the plants to become bushy. About June the plants should be put into six or eight inch pots, and when rooted into the new soil should be placed in frames out of doors, gradually hardening them off. Bring in early in September and place in a light position, and with care they will bloom well. Repot again in March, using a mixture of peat and loam for the purpose, adding just enough sand to keep the soil well open. Pruning must be resorted to to obtain bushy plants. These shrubs also look well as standards, and well repay any trouble that may be afforded them. The usual means must be taken to keep down insects, which, however, are not very troublesome if the plants are well managed. After the third or fourth potting the plants should be allowed to get slightly potbound, and liquid manure should be applied during the season of growth—a practice that tends to encourage the formation of blooming wood. As a continuous blooming, cool house, or conservatory plant, this cannot easily be surpassed.

Statice.—These plants are pre-eminently suited for greenhouse culture or for exhibition, as they combine a good habit with a comparative ease of cultivation, although, like several other plants, 45° is quite as low a temperature as they should be subjected to in winter, or no great success will be attained. On no account must the plants be rested in the ordinary acceptance of the word, but must be kept growing all the winter, or the results will be far from desirable. Statices bear large heads of papery texture, which may nearly be classed with the everlastings, but, strictly speaking, cannot be considered as such. The calyx varies from lilac to blue in different plants, and the corolla (which soon drops off) is white, and the leaves, which are leathery in some of the varieties, are 4in. or 5in. wide and from 8in. to 12in. long. The season of blooming varies, but with the following sorts, if treated as we direct, the principal flowering stems will be thrown up in spring, and a succession of side blooms will be continued until autumn. At no time is it advisable to place the plants out of doors, or to give full exposure to the sun; they also like a rather closer atmosphere than the generality of hard wooded plants; but at the same time they must not be kept too close or too far from the light, or success will not be attained. *S. profusa* is about the best of its class, and the treatment for this one applies to the whole family. Plants should be selected in autumn which have been stopped at 3in. or 4in. from the soil, and should be such as have not been cramped up in small pots, as such plants never do well as a rule. The reason of this is that the plants being free rooters get stunted if kept in small pots for too long a time, and when this occurs they never afterwards grow satisfactorily. During winter they should be on a shelf near the light, and kept at a night temperature of about 45°, by which means the roots will be kept active throughout the winter, a matter of much importance. They must not, of course, be grown on at the same rate as they are in summer; but still growth must not stop entirely if good results are desired. Early in March the plants should be put into 9-inch pots, using good turfy yellow loam, with enough sharp sand to keep it open. The soil must not be broken too fine, and the plants must be potted firmly. Plenty of water must be given, and, consequently, good drainage must be afforded, or the pots will get waterlogged, and the plants will suffer in consequence. For a week or two after potting, keep the plants rather close, and do not over water; and afterwards place in the light, near the glass, but away from cold currents of air. Shade must be given to protect the plants from hot sun, but · it should not be kept on longer than needful. Throughout the summer syringe in the afternoon, being careful to syringe underneath the leaves, to keep down red spider, which soon does irreparable mischief. During the first season it is advisable to pick off the flower stems, which will be thrown up all through the summer; but the second season the first crop of bloom may remain. In the hot sunny weather a bed of coal ashes is preferable to a dry stage, for, if they are treated in this manner, the large leaves afford so great space for evaporation that the plants would frequently suffer from dryness. As autumn approaches, discontinue the use of the syringe, and give more air. Winter as before, and remove all bloom that may appear before spring. In March, give another shift as before, and let them be similarly treated, but allow the blooms to open; while in bloom, syringing should be discontinued, or the flowers will damp off. The plants should not be out of the growing house long, neither should the successional blooms be allowed to open that year, but should be removed as they appear. The side shoots should be carefully tied down, so as to form a nice base to the plant, and care must be used not to split the shoots out, as they are very brittle. Treat in the same manner each year until the plants get into 24in. pots, when they may be kept in good order for years by the use of liquid manure. After the second season, unless the plants are intended for exhibition, they may be allowed to bloom for their full season; but if for exhibition they should not bloom fully until in 18in. pots. These plants are subject to red spider, thrip, and aphides. For the first the cold water cure should be applied, while for the two latter fumigation is the only remedy.

For sorts, select from the following, always having the first two in a collection: *Statice profusa, S. imbricata, S. brassicæfolia, S. Holfordii, S. macrophylla, S. macroptera, S. propinqua, S. Rattrayana,* and *S. sinuata.* All are good and useful, but the first two are the best for general work.

───◦◦◦───

THEA.—Thea, or tea, is a plant that from its economical value is of much interest, besides having a good appearance and pretty blooms. It is also of comparatively easy culture, and does not require excessive heat; a house where the temperature does not fall below 40° in winter suiting it very well. It is quite a different plant from the " tea tree " (so-called) of the out-door garden, which is in reality *Lycium barbatum.* Whether the thea will produce leaves in England of any value economically is a doubtful question, but still, in a collection of plants, it is very interesting. The plants should be repotted every spring in a compost of three parts yellow loam, thoroughly decomposed manure or leaf soil one part, and enough sand to keep the compost open. Plenty of drainage must be afforded, or the soil will become sour. During the summer liquid manure should be occasionally supplied, and the plants must at no time get thoroughly dry. The plants should be placed in frames during the summer, and treated much the same as camellias or oranges, getting the wood well ripened before bringing into the house, where they should have a light airy position afforded them, and be treated the same as oranges.

The sorts are *Thea Assamensis, T. Bohea, T. viridis,* and *T. v. variegata.* The first is the hardiest, though the second, in our opinion, is one of the best.

───◦◦◦───

VERONICA.—The shrubby veronicas, though not in reality greenhouse plants, are yet very ornamental, and in the north of England and on cold wet soils well repay for house room. And, again, some of the varieties are not hardy even so far north as London; so they, consequently, require house room, as they only stand out during the summer. We have usually grown these in a compost of two-thirds loam and one part leaf soil, with enough sharp sand to maintain the necessary porosity of the soil. The flowers are produced in axillary spikes varying from one to four inches in length, and as the colours vary from white through pink to blue they are very ornamental. Cuttings should be struck in January, and planted out in the open in May, pinching them back once or twice to make the plants bushy, and in October taking the plants up with a good ball of earth attached, and potting them carefully. The old plants can be cut back and planted out of doors, afterwards treating them the same as young plants.

For sorts select from *V. Andersonii*, blue; *V. A. fol. var.*, intense blue, attractive foliage; *V. atropurpurea*, rosy purple; *V. angustifolia alba*, pure white; *V. decussata*, dwarf blue; *V. d. alba*, dwarf white; V. Gloire de Lyon, bright red; *V. imperialis*, amaranth red; V. *lobeliodes*, fine blue; *V. multiflorum*, rosy carmine; *V. speciosa*, blue, cream coloured variegation; V. Mlle. Claudine Villermoz, indigo blue; V. Crème et violet, flesh pink, stamens violet; V. Blue Gem, light blue, very dwarf and free; V. Marie Antoinette, pink; and *V. rosea alba*, rose.

WITSENIA CORYMBOSA.—This is a plant which, if well grown, repays for the trouble; but we do not advise its culture, as all the specimens we have seen have had some objectionable feature. We have not had it ourselves, but have seen it in the collections of numerous amateurs, but never well grown. In nurseries we have seen it well done, as also in places where regular gardeners are employed. A particular friend of ours, who had the best specimen we ever saw, had grown it in the same manner as *Cassia corymbosa*. Where it is desired to have a plant it is the best plan to purchase in a 6in. pot, and treat in the same manner as cassia.

ANTHOCERAS SORBIFOLIA is a plant of recent introduction, and will probably prove what it is stated to be—hardy; but at the same time we doubt if it will be hardy throughout the whole of England and Scotland. The flowers are white, with a flesh tint, and are produced at the same time that the leaves unfold; they are disposed in racemes, which attain a height of from seven to eight inches. The flowers are well figured in a plate issued with the *Garden* for Dec. 18th, 1875. Messrs. Veitch have since exhibited plants which were forced. For soil use fibrous loam and sand, and treat the same as nearly hardy subjects—veronicas, for instance. The plants are at present both scarce and expensive, but will probably soon reach a moderate price.

V.—SOFT WOODED PLANTS.

GAPANTHUS.—This is a very old-fashioned plant, but at the same time its magnificent heads of bloom render it a fit associate for the choicest plants in the land. The flowers are blue (or white in *albiflora*), and are borne on stout footstalks, and vary from fifteen to twenty-five in number, forming a magnificent head of bloom. There is also a variety with striped leaves, but this we do not consider an advantage, except when the plant is out of bloom. It is as well to mention that all offsets must be kept removed during the growth, or the plants soon become weak, and give but few blooms. These offsets should be potted into small pots, and placed in a little bottom heat, when they will root freely, and if treated in the same manner as the old plants will make good blooming specimens. The soil we use is one-half sandy loam and one-half thoroughly rotted manure, with sufficient sand to keep the whole of a proper porosity; the pots should be filled one-third full of crocks to insure proper drainage. Pot the plants about March, and place in a greenhouse or on a gentle bottom heat, and as soon as the pots are filled with roots, repot into a size larger until sixteen or twelve sized pots are reached, in which sized pots they should bloom. During the whole of the growing season abundance of water should be given, but which should be nearly discontinued during the season of rest. As soon as the bloom is over the plant should be placed out of doors until autumn, when it should be removed into dry cold frames or pits for the winter. In spring remove all dead fibres and exhausted soil, and treat as before. With established plants it is an advantage to raise some in a pit as well as in a greenhouse, as the season is prolonged by this means.

For sorts, *A. umbellatus*, blue, *A. u. maxima*, blue, *A. u. variegata*, blue, variegated striped foliage, and *A. u. albiflora*, are the sorts mostly catalogued, and are all good.

Ageratums.—These plants, which are somewhat extensively used for bedding purposes, are also very useful for the conservatory if well grown. Whether the dwarf or tall sorts are chosen, they come in useful, although, in our opinion, the larger sorts are best for the cool conservatory, and the more dwarf kinds for outdoor work. The culture is very easy, and within the reach of everyone who has a hot bed on which to raise the seed, for although ageratums can be raised from cuttings, the same as other bedding plants, they are done easiest from seeds. We sow the seeds in January, in heat, on sandy soil, barely covering the seeds, and as soon as the young plants are large enough, we prick them off into thumb pots, and place in heat till they grow freely, and then they are brought into the warmest part of the greenhouse. Those for bedding we rarely repot, but those for indoors we shift as the present pots are full of roots, and keep on shifting until the end of June, when the pots used are 10in. or 12in. When these pots are full of roots, the plants are watered with liquid manure twice a week, and they soon bloom well, and make fine specimens. During the whole of the hot weather the plants are well syringed with cold water daily, to keep down red spider, and after July the plants are kept in a cold frame until wanted indoors, but those for bedding purposes are put out in the end of June.

For sorts we use the old tall form of *A. Mexicanum* which varies from azure to greyish blue, and the white Imperial Dwarf, and for bedding the latter named variety, Imperial Dwarf (blue), Tom Thumb (blue), both indoors and out, but particularly in warm situations in the country. It is also very useful in a warm light house for cut blooms, from Christmas till April, but it must be kept clear of insects.

Alonsoa.—These are showy plants, useful alike for indoor use, or summer decoration outdoors. The culture is very simple, being in fact the same as that for the ordinary stock of the greenhouse. Some of the varieties will bloom nearly the whole year round. They require a good rich light soil, similar to that which is used for several other plants, and as the plants go out of bloom they should be cut down, and they will bloom again in six weeks or two months. *A. incisifolia*, scarlet, and *A. Warscewiczii*, deep orange, with black centre, are two of the best for the purpose in hand.

Amaryllis.—This is a class of bulbous plants that is well worthy of cultivation in every collection, and, although there may be some little trouble in growing them to perfection, they yet repay for all care bestowed on them. Like many other plants, they have had their rise and fall, and although rather more in fashion than they were a short time back, they are not so much cultivated as they should be. Some of the varieties are evergreen, and some deciduous, and although the former require to be kept in a drier state during the season of rest, they must not be kept so dry as the deciduous kinds. The soil used should be good sound fibrous loam, to which enough sand has been added to preserve the

natural porosity of the soil, and so prevent the pots becoming water-
logged from the liberal application of water that is so necessary during
their season of growth. Give plenty of drainage, and not too much root
space, although it is not advisable to contract the roots too much, and
good spikes of bloom will be produced. A temperature of not less than
50 degs. is necessary in winter, and about 75 degs. in the growing season.
The deciduous kinds should be dried off in winter, while the evergreen
kinds should have a diminished supply of water only.

For sorts select from the following, which are all good : *A. Ackermanii*,
A. aulica, *A. a. superba*, A. Amazon, A. Brilliant, *A. calyptrata*, A. Cleo-
patra, *A. conspicua*, *A. crocea grandiflora*, *A. delicata*, A. Diadem, *A. Eclipse*,
A. Edith. A. Excellent, *A. falcata*, *A. Johnsonii*, *A. J. psittacina*, *A. longifolia*, *A. pardina*, A. Prince of Orange, *A. regina*, *A. vittata*, A. Vivid, and A.
William Pitt. It must, however, be borne in mind that amaryllis require
a warm greenhouse to do them at all well, and it is quite useless to attempt
their culture in a cold greenhouse where the frost is only just kept out,
as in such a house the bulbs rot away.

Anagallis Brewerii.—This is an old-fashioned plant, bearing blue
flowers in great profusion, and is alike suitable for indoor or outdoor
work. The culture is of the easiest, as it will do in almost any good well-
drained soil. The treatment is the same as the ordinary stock of soft-
wooded plants, and need not be further described. The red *A. Parksii* is
also good.

Asparagus Decumbens.—This is a plant that is very useful, on
account of its fine feathery spray, which works in well for bouquets and
other floral decorations. In the house it can be trained against arches,
&c., and has a very light appearance. The culture is very simple : a
large pot filled with one-third crocks, and then filled to within an inch
of the top with rich, moderately light soil, being all that is required if
liberal waterings and plenty of air is given. The bright pea-shaped
berries, or the insignificent blooms, are of far less use than the spray,
which is very fine and chaste. As a useful plant for cut spray this stands
pre-eminent.

Astilbe.—See " Spiræa."

EGONIAS.—These plants, which are of comparatively easy culture, contain both blooming and fine foliage specimens, and the greater part of them can be done in a greenhouse, that is, kept at about 40 deg. There are also some hardy kinds, but of these we do not intend to treat here. The fine foliage kinds are very useful for any kind of wall decorations, the larger foliaged kinds being particularly useful for the purpose, as they grow so that the leaves quite hide the pots when the latter are suspended against a wall. The colours of the leaves are very rich, from silver to rich bronze, of a very metallic appearance. A single plant in a small vase also looks well on a table, and as the plants stand the gas pretty fairly, they do well for table decorations, or for sideboards, mantel shelves, &c. Of the ornamental foliaged kinds, those of the *Rex* section are very useful, as they will stand a good amount of cold if it is not accompanied by a damp atmosphere. At one time they were classed as stove plants, but experience shows that they can be used for decorative purposes in almost any greenhouse where the temperature is kept at from 38 deg. to 40 deg. through the winter.

The culture is very easy, and the various hybrids of the various kinds, caused by crossing *B. rex* with other varieties, are really beautiful. The aim in winter in a cool house should be the preservation of the foliage that is already formed, rather than the production of new, and this can only be done in a place where the atmosphere is not surcharged with moisture. Where the temperature exceeds 50 deg. the plants can be kept growing, and so maintain plenty of foliage. Repot once or twice a year, using equal parts of peat and loam and plenty of sharp sand, or perhaps, where the loam is heavy, one third should be used to two-thirds peat; pot moderately firm, and while giving sufficient water do not overdo the matter, so that the plants become waterlogged. For this reason plenty of drainage must be given, or the same undesirable results will follow. With the tuberous rooted kinds, a somewhat different style of treatment must be pursued, as the plants rest through the winter. Our plan is to pot in the end of March, in somewhat rich sandy loam, affording plenty of drainage, and to place the plants in the light. Here they soon break, and in due course produce their flowers. Most of the varieties require sticks to keep them in form, and as the plants can stand in the greenhouse throughout the season they require some assistance, as they sometimes get a little drawn. Plenty of water is necessary during the growing season, and an occasional watering with liquid manure will be found of great advantage. When the plants have bloomed out, the supply of water should be lessened, and as the foliage dies off watering should be practically discontinued, but the soil must not become dust dry. During the winter the roots should be kept in a place where the temperature is about 40 deg., as in a much cooler place they would rot. Although begonias are generally termed stove plants they can, as a rule, be treated as greenhouse plants, the only necessity being that the temperature shall not fall below 40 deg. Of course, for winter blooming, a stove is necessary, as the heat given to the begonias would prove very injurious to the other plants in the greenhouse; but for summer and autumn decoration the plants are excellent. Of course the fine foliaged kinds are useful all through the year, but the latter kinds are not.

For ornamental foliaged plants select from the following, which are all good : B. rex, B. Marshallii, B. Duchesse de Brabant, B. Queen Victoria, B. Comte de Lemminghe, B. Chas. Lievens, B. Diadem, B. nebulosa, B. Sambo, and B. Snowflake. For blooming kinds select from B. Breigeii, white flowers and buds ; B. spatulata, white ; B. nitida, rose ; B. Saundersonii, deep rose ; B. manicata, flesh ; B. Trœbelli, crimson-scarlet ; and several of the intermediate hybrids. In fact, where there exists the means of raising the plants from seeds, a 5s. packet of seed will produce a good collection. M. Victor Lemoine, of Nancy, has also raised some double-blossomed varieties, which are excellent, but expensive at present. They are B. Gloire de Nancy, bright vermillion ; B. salmonea plena, rosy salmon ; B. Mons. Lemoine, orange vermillion; B. President Burelle, red, shaded scarlet; and B. W. E. Gumbleton, rosy salmon with orange centre. He has also some semi-double varieties of much excellence.

Brugmansia.—These plants are well worth cultivation on account of their beauty, and also on account of their easy cultivation, and, as they are nearly hardy, they are very suitable for cool houses—in fact, more so than many of the more fashionable plants. A pretty large pot should be used, according to the size of the plant, and plenty of drainage must be afforded. For soil use either peat and loam, about one-third of the former to two-thirds of the latter, or use good sandy loam alone. A goodly amount of sharp sand should be allowed to keep the whole open, as a water-logged soil is not conducive to the welfare of the plants. Ordinary greenhouse treatment should be given, and the plants will not fail to produce their fine blossoms in due season.

For sorts B. lutea (yellow), and B. sanguinea (red), are the best and most effective.

CALCEOLARIA (shrubby). — Nearly every one is acquainted with this class of calceolaria, which is so much used for bedding purposes, but only a comparatively small number know what fine decorative plants they are when well grown. This is much to be regretted as a well grown shrubby calceolaria in a 6in. or 8in. pot, is really a very handsome and showy subject, useful alike in conservatory or dwelling house. It will be found more convenient to grow these in a pit or frame, as they are not so much attacked by fly in such a place, and also make sturdier plants. They are, however, a little later in blooming, but this is fully compensated by the better habit obtained and smaller trouble incurred. So long as frost is excluded, and the plants are kept moist, and receive plenty of air on favourable opportunities they will succeed very well in a frame, but should excessive moisture be applied or should the plants be frozen, then good pot plants will not be obtained. In the case of the amateur cultivator, it is a question as to which is the best time to strike cuttings of these plants, as unlike those set aside for bedding purposes which are best struck at the end of September, the plants for pots are required of a pretty good size if large plants are wanted, but if it is only desired to have medium sized plants they can be treated as the bedding plants are until spring. If large plants are required they should be struck in August, putting the cuttings in a cold frame facing the north, and as soon as rooted potted off into sixty-sized pots; and as soon as the roots kiss the sides of the pots, re-potted into large sixties, or 3in. pots, in which they will remain until the end of February. The points of the plants should then be pinched out, and as soon as they break they should be potted on into forty-eight sized pots. If there are from four to six breaks to each plant it will be sufficient, but should such not be the case the plants should be stopped again, when the requisite number of breaks will probably be obtained. As soon as the roots kiss the pots the plants should be transferred to their blooming pots (either 6in. or 8in.) and the shoots should be tied out so as to develope fully, a point of much importance. Every effort should be exerted to maintain the foliage green to the base of the plants, and to attain this end the plants should be fumigated at the first appearance of green fly. From the end of September the plants should occupy a light airy pit, or frame facing the south, and as the warm weather arrives the pots should be plunged in coal ashes, as it is very essential that the roots should be kept cool, as in the native habitat of the plants. Very little manure should be used in the soil, but as the flower spikes are thrown up, weak liquid manure should be given two or three times a week. We follow the above plan successfully, and find that the plants are less liable to be attacked by insects than in an ordinary greenhouse, and from May till August the plants are all that can be desired. We place no reliance in old plants, but still, as is seldom the case, if a house is devoted to calceolarias, they pay for attention. For soil use one-half good fibrous loam, one-eighth thoroughly rotted manure, and the remainder leaf soil, and enough sharp sand to keep the whole open. Bedding varieties should not be potted, but should be inserted about 3in. apart over a bed in a cold frame, and after breaking (the tops should be taken off early in March or about the middle of April) should be planted out where they are to remain. By this means the "disease" will be obviated. Should frosty weather ensue, the plants should be protected with inverted flower pots, a piece of slate or crock being placed on the hole — we have thus often protected more tender plants than calceolarias, the chief object being to protect from the drying winds that at times accompany frosts.

We mention a few good shrubby calceolarias; but, with the general grower, we would advise the use of seed in preference: Aurea floribunda, yellow; Excelsior, orange-brown, gold cap; Firefly, orange-crimson; Pluto, dark crimson; Aurora, crimson face, scarlet back; Clio, deep dark crimson; Sparkler, crimson, gold cap; Beauty of Montreal, bright crimson; Crimson Queen, scarlet tinted, bronzy crimson; Prince of Orange, red; Mrs. W. Paul, dark crimson; and Starlight, bright red.

Calceolaria (herbaceous).—These, like the preceding, are very useful for both house and conservatory decoration. Unless a stock of named plants exists it is scarcely worth while to purchase named sorts, as a packet of seed from a first class firm will produce a good percentage of flowers nearly, if not quite, equal to many of the named varieties. The chief reason for using plants from seed is, however, the cheapness of the process, for one or two good named sorts would cost half-a-crown, while a hundred or so can be obtained from a packet of seed costing that amount. The seed should be sown about the middle of July on pans of light soil, which should have been previously soaked with water. Care must be taken to make the surface of the soil level, and also to sow the seed as evenly as possible, a matter of some little difficulty with fine seeds like calceolaria, musk, lobelia, &c., as the seeds fall in bunches from inexperienced fingers. The seeds should be just covered (no more) with fine soil, a sheet of glass should be laid over the pan, and the pan should be placed in a shady part of the greenhouse until the young plants show the first leaf. The glass can then be gradually removed. As soon as they can be handled, the plants should be pricked out into pots or boxes, keeping them about two inches asunder, and, as soon as they begin to crowd each other, each alternate one should be transplanted into other pots or boxes, so that the plants are about four inches apart. By the end of September or early in November they will be nice and strong, and fit for wintering, and the best place for them is in a dry pit, where frost is excluded, or on the shelf of a greenhouse. Give only enough water to prevent the plants flagging, and keep all dead leaves removed. At the first appearance of green fly, fumigate with tobacco, as this blight does a vast amount of harm. About the end of January the plants should be removed into their blooming pots, using those from 7in. to 9in. in diameter, giving plenty of drainage, and a compost consisting of one-half good fibrous loam, one-fourth thoroughly decayed manure (cow manure preferably), and one-fourth leaf soil. To this should be added sufficient coarse sand and powdered charcoal to keep the whole open. Take the plants up with good balls of earth and roots, and pot them moderately firmly. A good watering should be given through a fine rosed watering pot, and the plants should be put on an airy shelf in a cold pit or greenhouse, where frost can be just excluded. For the next week constant attention is necessary, watering, aëration, fumigating, &c., all being of paramount importance to the future wellbeing of the plants. Care must be taken to give plenty of room, and to support the flower stems with small neat sticks. About May the plants will commence blooming, and continue to do so for a couple of months. As soon as the bloom is over, if the plants are cut down and placed in a somewhat shady border of light rich soil, they will afford plenty of stock for the next year; but, at the same time, we advise the use of seedling sorts. Clear liquid manure, not too strong, is very useful for the herbaceous calceolarias, if employed in moderation; but it should not be used too often after the flowers show colour, as it tends to mar the clearness. The chief points in the culture of herbaceous calceolarias are plenty of air and light, attention to watering, &c., and the destruction of fly as soon as it appears. Shrubby calceolarias can be raised from seeds as well as the herbaceous kinds, and results as good can be obtained.

Calla.—Calla, or *Richardia Æthiopica,* or the white arum lily, is one of the most useful plants of its class. It can be had in bloom at any season, and can be grown as a window plant anywhere where frost is excluded, while its fine white spathe and yellow spadix render it peculiarly interesting. It can also be treated as an aquatic, sub-aquatic, or terrestrial subject, and in all cases it repays for cultivation. Like most of the aroids, it likes a moderately open compost, well enriched, and during the season of growth it is very greedy of water, in fact, if the plants have good drainage and a proper soil, it is scarcely possible to give them too much. Of course there is a medium in all things, and a careful cultivator is sure not to exceed this. There are two or three different modes of culture, two of which we have followed very successfully. The best plan in our hands is the following :—As soon as the plants have ceased blooming, weak liquid manure is applied until the end of June, and meanwhile a trench has been prepared, like that for celery, well-rotted manure being used, and in this the plants are turned out, and kept well supplied with water during the growing season. A partially-shaded situation is chosen, and a mulching with cocoa fibre refuse, or other fibrous material is given, as it tends to keep up a moist soil with fewer waterings. While planted out all the flowers are removed, so that the strength of the plants is concentrated in the strong crowns. The plants are taken up about the end of September, and potted carefully in rich and rather open compost, well watered, and placed in a close pit for a week or so, and thence they are removed to the greenhouse, where by forcing some and retarding others a continuation of bloom is maintained for a long time. The other plan, which is not so good as the preceding, is, however, more suited to small gardens where there does not exist in any form a kitchen garden. As soon as the plants cease blooming in spring the plants receive a liberal shift, disturbing the roots as little as possible, using a good open rich soil. They are then placed in a moist pit for a few weeks until they commence growth, when plenty of air and water is freely given. From the middle of June the water is given more sparingly, and the plants are gradually exposed to the air. The plants are plunged in coal ashes out of doors until the middle of August, giving only enough water to keep them from shrivelling. In August they are replaced in the pit and well watered, and they soon commence growth, when by forcing some and retarding others a succession of blooms is maintained. In all cases plenty of drainage must be given, and close sticky soil must be avoided.

The two sorts we find good are *C. œthiopica* and *C. albo-maculata.*

Campanula.—Campanulas, or bell flowers, are amongst the most beautiful plants grown, both for form and colour of the bloom and the form and fresh green appearance of the foliage. The dwarf varieties are really very fine for pot culture, and form masses of light green foliage covered with a greater or smaller quantity of bright flowers, that render the plants very acceptable either for rooms or the cool greenhouse.

A comparatively rich sandy loam suits the plants, if plenty of drainage is afforded. We keep them in cold frames during the winter, and introduce them as required, unless, indeed, it has been found necessary to keep them in the greenhouse altogether. The chimney campanula is quite out of place in a small house, and, besides, it is not of any great decorative merit, the dwarf kinds only being really admissible to the greenhouse. As a rule, campanulas should be repotted in autumn, potting firmly, and the crown of the plant being kept just a trifle raised above the soil, or at times they will fog off through the water lodging around the necks. The plants should be repotted each autumn, when they may be divided into as many plants as there are rooted crowns, if numbers is the chief object; but if moderate sized plants are desired, then the old plants should not be too much divided.

Of sorts there is a pretty wide selection, especially as the greater part of the whole family can be cultivated in pots. *C. Garganica,* pale blue, 6in.; *C. G. alba,* white, 6in.; *C. Carpatica,* blue, 9in.; *C. C. pallida,* pale blue; *C. C. alba,* white; *C. turbinata,* purple blue, 9in.; *C. t. floribunda,* blue; *C. t. alba,* white; *C. Barrelieri,* 6in., blue; *C. nitida,* blue, 6in.; *C. n. flore pleno,* blue; *C. pulla,* 6in., blue; and *C. rubra,* red, 6in., we have found to answer well for the purpose named, and at times we have used the Canterbury bell (*C. media* and *C. media fl. pl.*) very successfully, the plants being grown out doors until just before the flowers opened, and then carefully potted up and watered, keeping in the shade for a few days, when the blooms open and form very handsome plants. The new variety, *C. media calycanthema*, in which the calyx is of the same colour as the corolla, is also very handsome done this way.

Canna.—These are used very much for subtropical gardening, but at the same time, a few plants transferred into the house late in the year have a bright appearance for a month or so. It is, however, for the flower garden that the canna is chiefly grown, and for this reason it is advisable to treat them for this purpose alone, and, if it is desired to introduce a few plants into the greenhouse late in the season, they can be grown in the borders or kitchen garden.

As cannas can be raised from seeds as well as division of the roots, we give the treatment from the first. Seeds should be sown in light soil in January or February, in a brisk bottom heat, and, when large enough, should be potted off singly into small pots, using rich moderately light soil. As soon as the roots kiss the sides of the pot, re-pot into 4in. pots, and get the plants hardened off by the end of May, so that they can be put out early in June. A deep, rich, loamy soil is the best for the plants while out of doors, and good drainage is a necessity. Plants to be put into the greenhouse should be taken up and potted into large pots about the end of August, well watered, and kept close for a week, when they may be stood out of doors until the time arrives for frost, and then they can be housed. So soon as the frost cuts down the foliage the old plants should be taken up, placed in boxes, and kept moderately dry until March, when they can be divided and started in the greenhouse preparatory to bedding-out in June. Besides the ordinary green foliage some of the plants have leaves finely marked, which thus forms an additional attraction, while the flower (which somewhat resembles that of the gladiolus) is very hand-some.

Here is a selection of really good sorts, and well worth cultivation. *C. Annei*, large glaucous foliage; *C. A. discolor*, purple stems, orange flowers; *C. A. fulgida*, zebra-marked foliage; *C. A. rosea*, tall, orange flowers; *C. Auguste Ferrière*, very large oval green leaves, orange-red flowers, eight feet high; *C. aurantiaca zebrina*, brown barred foliage; *C. coccinea vera*, scarlet flowers; *C. Daniel Hooinbrench*, bright yellow flowers; *C. Deputé Heron*, leaves glaucous, flowers sulphur and orange; *C. excelsa zebrina*, dark veined long leaves; *C. expansa rubra*, dark leaves, blood-red flowers; *C. insignis*, large foliage rayed with chocolate; *C. limbata major*, undulated foliage, red flowers; *C. metallica*, magnificent reddish bronze leaves; *C. Rendatleri*, long narrow violet leaves, orange flower; *C. Schubertii*, ruby flowers; *C. tricolor*, very fine foliage, streaked and mottled with creamy white, and margined with red, red stems; and *C. Warszewiczii major*, scarlet flowers, green musæ-like foliage, dark margins. Of course all these will not be grown, but on no account should *C. tricolor* be omitted, as it is so very beautiful.

Carnation (Tree or Perpetual).—These are without doubt some of the most useful plants grown for cut bloom, and as the culture is of the easiest t is a matter of much surprise to us that they are not more grown by amateurs than is at present the case.

We strike the plants from June till the end of September in the ordinary manner, and when well rooted pot them off into 3in. pots, and when well rooted in these, about the end of August, we give a shift into 4in. pots, in which the plants are wintered the first season. As the plants are nearly, if not quite hardy, all the light and air possible are given, and undue moisture avoided. The second season the plants are grown on and not allowed to bloom, two or three shifts being given until the plants are in 12in. pots. Meanwhile the shoots are trained out into their places, and the general contour of the plant arranged. When the pots are filled with roots liquid manure is supplied, and about the middle of September the plants are taken indoors, giving plenty of air for some days. By maintaining a temperature of 45 deg., and applying sulphate of ammonia as liquid manure, plenty of bloom is obtained in the proper season.

For soil we use good fibrous yellow loam, and sand enough to keep the whole sufficiently porous to admit of the free passage of water. By this system late bloom is obtained.

Where heat can be afforded without detriment to other subjects in the house, the following is as good a plan as any. From November to the end of February cuttings should be taken, and struck in bottom heat; as soon as rooted they should be potted off and gradually hardened, so that they will bear removal to the greenhouse, where they should remain till April. They should then be planted out on heavily manured ground, and watered in, if necessary. In June go over the plants and take off the tops, and about once a fortnight take off the tops of any of the side shoots which may appear likely to bloom. About the end of September the plants should be carefully potted up, and shaded for a week or ten days, being careful to keep the plants in a healthy state of moisture, and give an unlimited supply of air until frost sets in. Commence fire heat in the early part of November, gradually working up to and maintaining a night temperature of 60 deg., admitting a free circulation of warmed air during the day. Fumigation must be resorted to if fly should put in an appearance, and for mildew flowers of sulphur should be thoroughly dusted over the plants, washing it off after three days, being very careful to remove all dirt from the plants.

The following are very good sorts for general purposes : Garibaldi, rosy scarlet; Souvenir de Malmaison, blush white; Bride, pure white; Covent Garden Scarlet, scarlet, very fine ; Dragon, scarlet ; Boule de Feu, scarlet ; Prince of Orange, yellow, edged crimson ; La Belle, pure white ; Jean Bart, bright scarlet ; Oscar, yellow ; Henshaw's Scarlet, good scarlet ; Lee's Scarlet, a very good serrulated scarlet ; Valiant, rosy scarlet ; Rembrandt, large crimson ; Maiden's Blush, blush white. Rather more trouble will be found with the yellows than with the other varieties, but at the same time the yellow sorts are often the most esteemed.

Centaurea—These are white-foliaged plants of much use for bedding purposes, and also for the decoration of the greenhouse during the cooler months of the year; and as they have a somewhat snowy appearance, they blend well with richer forms of coloured foliage. The culture is simple.

Sow seeds in August on sandy soil, and prick off into small pots, and as

soon as the roots fill these repot into large sixties. Winter the plants
in these, and in March repot into 4in. pots, and in these the plants can
stand until June, when, if large plants are required, they can be repotted
into 6in. pots. During the summer the plants can be stood out in the
frames, or where grown as bedding plants they can be put out, and the
contrast afforded will be very good. A moderately rich and sandy soil
is necessary, and freedom from excessive moisture is essential. The
plants can also be raised from cuttings taken off with a heel attached, and
struck during summer in a frame facing the north, or in a slight bottom
heat in spring.

For sorts choose from *C. argentea plumosa*; *C. gymnocarpa*; *C. Ragu-
sina*, and *C. R. compacta*.

Chrysanthemums.—These, though hardy, if grown for indoor decoration, require such special treatment as to render them worthy of a place
amongst greenhouse plants. Whether the pompones, ordinary sorts, or
Japanese varieties are grown, the show of colour and varied form will be
very great, and supposing that a fair collection exists, a very good display
of colour will result. Indeed, the varied colours render the greenhouse
very gay for some of the dullest months in the year. In all cases it is,
however, very necessary that proper attention and liberal culture be
given, or the plants will not be so brilliant either in foliage or bloom;
and as good foliage is as much an essential as fine blooms, plants that are
deficient in that respect are certainly not good specimens of culture. With
all flowering plants bare stems, as a rule, indicate some error in the cultivation, and to exhibit such plants on the stage of a greenhouse generally
shows up their defects. The methods of cultivation are legion, and nearly
everyone who grows for market or home use has some particular part
or parts of his treatment different to his neighbour's. But whatever plan
is pursued, the object is the same, *i.e.*, the production of well furnished,
free flowering plants, of not too great a size. For the use of an amateur,
large plants are frequently in the way, as are also those which attain a
great height, unless, indeed, the bloom is required for cutting for exhi-
bitions, when the best plan is to allow the plants to attain their maximum
growth, as finer flowers are then produced, but as only one or two blooms
are allowed to each, plants grown for cut blooms are certainly not very
ornamental.

In the end of March or the two first weeks in April, strong cuttings, 3in.
or 4in. long, should be inserted three in a 3in. pot, and the pots should
be plunged into a gentle hotbed. When well rooted the plants should be
hardened off somewhat and potted singly into 3in. pots. Keep close for a
few days and then give air more or less freely, according to the weather.
As soon as the young plants have grown about 2in. the points should be
pinched out, so that the plants may be induced to break freely, a point of
much moment. As soon as the pots are full of roots (not pot bound) give
a shift into 4in. or 6in. pots, paying particular attention to watering
and stopping back where necessary. About the end of May the plants
can be removed to their blooming pots, 8in. or 10in., and the pots should
be at once plunged in a bed of coal ashes. The soil used for potting

should be composed of three parts good loam, one part rotten manure, and one part good rotten leaf soil, with, perhaps, a small quantity of the raspings of a farrier's shop. To these a sufficient quantity of sharp sand should be added to render the whole sufficiently porous to admit of the free passage of water. Drainage should be particularly cared for on account of the large quantity of water the plants require during their season of growth. The plants should not be stopped after the middle of June, but the branches should be kept well tied out, both to admit a free circulation of air and to maintain a comely, well-balanced shape. As the pots become filled with roots liquid manure should be supplied, and continued until the blooms begin to open, when it should be discontinued. Another plan is to turn the plants out into good soil in April and carefully grow them on outdoors, potting them up in the end of September. Small plants are easily obtained by layering branches, and when rooted, gradually severing the branch, and then potting the young plants without injuring the roots more than can be avoided. Chrysanthemums bloom well in a temperature of 38 deg. to 45 deg., provided plenty of air is admitted to keep down mildew. Fly must be got rid of by fumigation, and mildew by dusting the parts over with flowers of sulphur.

The following are some good plants for pot culture, though old :— *Anemone flowered :* Antonius, yellow ; Empress, lilac ; Prince of Anemones, lilac blush ; Lady Margaret, white ; King of Anemones, crimson purple ; Firefly, bright scarlet. *Pompones :* Aigle d'Or, yellow ; Heléne, rosy violet ; Madge Wildfire, bright red, gold tips ; Mrs. Dix, blush ; Rose Trevenna, rosy blush ; the Little Gem, delicate peach. *Japanese :* Bronze Dragon, rich bronze ; Prince Satsuma, golden yellow ; Tasselled Yellow, good yellow. *Chinese, or ordinary :* Aurea multiflora, pure yellow ; Beverley, ivory white ; General Slade, Indian red, orange tips ; Gloria Mundi, golden yellow ; Golden Beverley, rich gold ; Golden Queen, canary yellow ; Josiah Wedgwood, rosy carmine ; Lady Slade, lilac, pink centre ; Mount Etna, rich red ; Miss Mary Morgan, delicate pink ; Mrs. G. Rundle, white ; Prince Alfred, rosy crimson ; Queen of England, ivory white ; Queen of Whites, large white ; Rifleman, dark ruby ; *Rosa mutabilis*, delicate peach ; Sam Slick, ruby, bronze tips ; Yellow Perfection, golden yellow. The above plants, if obtained true, will be found to answe all requirements, and all the plants are good both in foliage and flower.

Cineraria.—These are amongst the most ornamental, and, at the same time, most easily grown plants there are, and as a half-crown packet of good seed will produce a vast assortment of colours, they should be grown by everyone possessing a house where frost is excluded during winter. The colours range from pure white to purple and crimson in selfs, and all the various colours banded with others, as white banded with crimson, white banded with blue, blue banded with white, &c., all of which contrasts are very effective, and look excellently as individual blooms. Some of the named varieties are fine, but, at the same time, many of the " strains " of seedlings of the last few years are (except in the view of professional florists) as near perfection as possible. In all cases it is advisable

to grow cinerarias in pits or frames, with just enough heat to keep out
frost, but, as the generality of amateurs cannot afford heated pits, the
plants should be grown in frames until frost sets in, and then removed to
a light airy position in the greenhouse to bloom. Seed should be sown
under glass in July and August, and as soon as large enough, should be
potted off into small pots, and kept close for a few days. As soon as
the roots kiss the sides of the pots, give a shift into others an inch larger,
and continue to do so until 8in. pots are reached, when liquid manure
should be applied, and as soon as the plants get pot bound, they will
commence to bloom. With the edged varieties, as soon as they commence
to show colour the liquid manure should be discontinued, and clear water
substituted, or the flowers will become muddy and not look well. With
old plants the culture is much the same, dividing the plants early in
August, and repotting into small pots, potting on as before directed. For
soil use the following compost : Two parts of fibrous loam, one part leaf
soil, and one cow manure, with enough sand to keep the whole open,
for if once the plants get water-logged they are spoiled. It is therefore necessary to provide plenty of drainage to each pot, and to stand the
plants where the water will run away easily, instead of placing them in
saucers where, as is too often the case, the stagnant water is not removed.
Pegging out the foliage, and tying out the blooms, will of course be necessary to make the plant appear at its best. After blooming, such plants as
it may be desirable to keep should be cut down to within 6in. of the
pots, so that they shall afford plenty of suckers to provide plants for the
next season. Green fly must be kept down by frequent fumigation, and
should mildew appear, flowers of sulphur should be dusted over the
infected plants.

As possibly some of our readers may desire a few named sorts, we give
a selection of some really good kinds—*Selfs* : Adam Bede, bright rose; Blue
Beard, deep blue; Brilliant, bright crimson; Capt. Schriber, light blue;
Duke of Cambridge, crimson; Eclipse, rosy carmine; Eclat, shaded purple;
Reynolds Hole, scarlet crimson; Snowflake, pure white; Uncle Toby, deep
purple. *Edged and banded* : Agrippa, white, rosy crimson edge; Amazon,
light ground, crimson edge; Auricula, white, heavily tipped blue; Brides-
maid, white, purple margin; Chancellor, deep purplish crimson, white
circle and disc; Chas. Dickens, white, rosy crimson edge; Evyln, light
ground, tipped crimson; Flora, pure white, crimson edge; Ino, white
ground, heavily tipped crimson; Juno, crimson, white ring; Meteor,
crimson, white ring; Miranda, white, blue edge; Orb of Day, rich glossy
crimson, white ring; Zoë, rich crimson, light ring. As it is impossible to
suit anyone's taste by a mere description, we would advise those who
require a collection of really nice sorts, all distinct, to visit a good collection in the blooming season, and select the varieties that they prefer,
as tastes vary greatly.

Clivia.—See "Imantophyllum."

Coleus.—These are foliage plants, unsurpassed for beauty of colour or
richness of foliage, and whether grown as large or small plants, they are
extremely useful for decorative purposes. Their culture is very simple;

no expensive manures or medicaments are required, but unless a minimum temperature of at least 55 deg. is maintained, the plants cannot be wintered successfully. In such a case it is far better to purchase plants in April, and grow them on carefully for the season, and then throw them away, than to encumber the house with what will prove to be so much useless rubbish before the winter is out. The following is the plan we follow most successfully, as it saves us the trouble of wintering old plants.

In April we purchase a quantity of plants in thumb pots, cost about 2s. 6d. per dozen. We then transfer them into 3in. pots, and place in a warm part of the house, keeping moderately moist. As soon as the plants are about two inches high the points are pinched out, and this causes the plant to break freely, and as each break gets to be about two inches long we repeat the process, until a good framework is obtained on which the future plant can be constructed. As soon as the roots touch the sides of the pots a two inch shift should be given, and this should be repeated until 10in. pots are reached, when, with care in training, watering, &c., magnificent plants will have been made, as the structure prepared at first would carry a very fine head of foliage. For compost we use one-half rotten turf from an old pasture, one-fourth thoroughly rotted cow manure, and the other fourth composed of sharp sand and leaf soil in equal proportions. Pot moderately firm, and water freely when growth has commenced, giving occasional doses of liquid manure (not sulphate of ammonia), especially during the hot weather, as the plants grow very rapidly then. Plenty of air and light must at all times be afforded, so that the plants are short-jointed and the wood firm, long spindling shoots not holding the leaves firmly, consequently soon becoming bare. Great care must be taken that the plants do not suffer for the want of water, or the lower leaves will fall and render the plants unsightly. A well-grown plant should be of a globular or pyramidal form, and the lower leaves should cover the edge of the pot, so that neither bare stems nor soil are visible. The chief points to be observed in the culture of coleus are, free rich soil, plenty of water, and a warm temperature, and careful attendance. The bloom is insignificant and of no decorative value, so when there is the least appearance of a flower spike the point of the shoot should be at once pinched out.

The following are all good and effective sorts, and are well worth cultivation: Golden Gem, scarlet, edged gold, fringed edge; Brilliant, bronzy red, yellow edge; Hermit, dark purple, fringed brown; Sunrise, deep bronze red, edge beaded gold. Her Majesty, the same as preceding; Cloth of Gold, fine yellow self; Beauty of Widmore, dark marone, belted with rose and green, and edged with silver, very fine; Refulgens, deep velvety purple, beaded bright green; Warrior, intense black velvet, belted pale yellow; Princess of Wales, reddish carmine; Verschaffelti, rich crimson; Diadem, rosy crimson, gold edge; Mr. J. H. Claringbull, dark scarlet, wide golden edge; Mrs. Galbraith, bright scarlet, tinged purple, edged white. If a couple of each of the above are obtained in spring and carefully grown on, they will form a splendid collection.

Crassula.—See "Kalosanthes."

Cuphea.—*C. platycentra* is very old-fashioned, very pretty, and withal very easy to cultivate. It is useful either as a pot or a bedding plant, and, besides being simply pretty, the whole plant is both strong and interesting.

The old-fashioned plan was to raise the plants from cuttings which strike freely in March or April if placed on a brisk bottom heat, but by far the better method is to sow seeds in January or February, and then grow the plants on in rich sandy loam. Grow to nearly the size required, repotting from time to time, and, when large enough, let the plants fill the pots with roots, and then give ample doses of liquid manure occasionally. For vases, pots, window boxes, and various uses outdoors, cupheas come in very useful, and for the conservatory they are fine subjects. In fact, we often wonder why they are so little grown now.

Cyclamen.—These are plants that should be represented in every greenhouse and conservatory, as their decorative power is so great for a bulbous plant. *C. Persicum* is, perhaps, the best of the family for pot culture, but *C. Coum, C. Europæum, C. Atkinsii, C. repandum,* and *C. Ibericum* are all useful according to their different forms. The culture is comparatively simple, and with ordinary care success is certain, but while the plants are in active growth they must neither be neglected nor coddled up.

We have found the following methods answer well in practice, although quite opposed to the old-fashioned practice of drying off the bulbs in summer, a practice that only tends to destroy the bulbs and render them the reverse of floriferous. The plan (to begin at the beginning) that we now practise is as follows: In October we sow the seed in broad pans, using a compost of leaf soil, sand, and fibrous loam, and then stand the pans in a warm hotbed until the plants are pricked off, in about six weeks from sowing. The pans will be all the more suited for the purpose if they are covered with flat sheets of glass, as it greatly hastens the vegetation of the seeds, and, at the same time, a hotbed is not necessary, as a warm greenhouse or stove will do as well. When large enough we pot off into small pots and place on a shelf in a warm greenhouse until February, when they are potted off into 4in. pots, using good friable loam five parts and thoroughly rotted cow manure three parts, with a good quantity of sharp sand. We then grow them on briskly until the first week in May, and then transfer them to a pit or frame, and gradually harden off ready for planting out the last week in the month. Meanwhile we prepare a bed for their reception, either on a north or a shady border. This bed is deeply dug and pulverised, and a liberal dressing of thoroughly rotted manure and coarse sand is added to make the bed both rich and friable. We plant the bulbs out about a foot asunder, being careful to retain a good ball of earth to each, and not cover more than one-third of the bulb with soil. A good watering once a week and a sprinkling with a syringe every day is all that is required during the summer. About the second or third week in August the plants are taken up, with good balls of earth adhering, and potted into six or eight inch pots, placing them in a close frame for about ten days after they are potted, and then admitting air as necessary, at the same time paying due attention to watering, &c. About the end of September the pots are found full of roots, and the plants are then removed to a shelf near the glass in a warm light greenhouse. Here, with attention, they bloom for a long period, and about May they undergo the same treatment as before. Care must be taken to afford plenty of drainage at all times, and insects must be scrupulously destroyed. So much for *C. Persicum.* For the hardy kinds a somewhat different treatment is necessary, but as they are quite hardy, they do not require to be placed in a greenhouse at all. They should be potted into four or six inch pots, using soil as before recommended; and, after potting, should be plunged in a pit or frame facing the north. About October the position should be changed, and the plants face the south during the winter. Air ought to be given at all times, except in actual frost, and during fine weather the lights should be thrown right off. In the place of partly burying the bulbs, as in the Persicum section, the crowns of the bulbs of *C. Coum, C. Europœum,* &c., should be about half an inch below the surface of the soil, as in many cases the roots start just below the crown of the bulb, instead of the base.

During the summer we treat the hardy cyclamen much the same as the tender section—that is those for pot culture—but, of course, permanent plants do best in sheltered borders in a rockery. In all cases it is absolutely necessary to give hardy cyclamen a deep, rich, and well-drained border, where they are permanently planted; and it is also requisite that the plants should be protected from violent hail storms and very heavy rains, as the leaves being persistent during winter, are very liable to be damaged if not protected.

For sorts of *C. Persicum,* the following are distinct, but a packet of good seed will produce a great variety of colours and markings : *C. Persicum album, C. P. delicatum, C. P. punctatum, C. P. purpureum, C. P. roseum, C. P. rubrum,* and some others to be obtained at nurseries. For hardy sorts, *C. Atkinsii, C. A. carneum, C. A. roseum, C. Coum, C. C. carneum, C. C. vernum (marmoratum), C. Europœum, C. Ibericum, C. I. album,* and *C. repandum.* For making a selection for pot culture alone, we should use the Persicum section only, unless, indeed, quiet instead of showy plants are required.

DACTYLIS.—This, like the foregoing, is nearly hardy, and is much used out of doors as an edging plant in fixed designs, as its neatness renders it particularly useful in this respect. The plants can be wintered in a cold frame, or in the greenhouse, where they are of value on account of their foliage and general appearance.

They are easily propagated by division, using a sharp sandy loam for compost, and keeping the plants close for a day or two afterwards.

For sorts, *D. glomerata variegata*, and *D. g. elegantissima* are the best.

Darlingtonia.—*D. Californica* is one of the so-called carnivorous plants, and is of American origin. As a curiosity of plant life it is both curious and interesting, and the structure of the plant is alike wonderful and beautiful, albeit it is destitute of the gaudy characteristics of many of our more ephemeral beauties that "bloom and soon decay." It requires a warm house to grow it well, a house where the minimum temperature is at least 50 degs., and a north-west aspect suits it well. A moist but not saturated atmosphere is required, and plenty of root moisture is necessary. The best medium in which to grow this plant is chiefly chopped sphagnum mixed with about a fourth part of heath soil and charcoal, the whole surfaced with chopped sphagnum. Plenty of drainage must be afforded, and large pans are far preferable to pots, the plant being on a mound, raised a little above the surface of the pan. Dr. Moore, of Glasnevin, has one of the finest specimens in Europe, and we believe his treatment is much the same as the preceding. To an enthusiast in horticulture this will be found one of the gems of the greenhouse, but it requires skill and attention to do it well.

Dionæa.—*D. muscipula* is another carnivorous plant, and does well with the foregoing treatment, and it is far easier of cultivation. It should be in pots one-third filled with crocks, and the compost should be one-third fibrous peat, and two-thirds sphagnum, and some very sharp sand, and perhaps a small quantity of charcoal. It requires a moist atmosphere, and where this cannot be obtained in the house the plants should be grown under bell glasses. The dionæas are very interesting subjects, the one named being about the best for the use of an amateur. Some of the Droseras, also, thrive well with the above treatment.

CHEVERIA.—These are what are termed succulents, and some of them are very fine when in bloom, while others are more conspicuous for their foliage. The culture is very simple, that of the secunda glauca varieties, particularly so, as the chief point is to keep them through the winter, or until bedding time, as they will remain in the house throughout the summer and autumn. They are very good plants for decoration, receive no injury from drought, blooming profusely in the season, and bearing hardships that would utterly destroy less succulent plants. For all the secunda type, a good, fairly rich, sandy loam is necessary, using comparatively small pots, and plenty of drainage, but if they are required for house decoration it is advisable to use 4in. pots, and a somewhat richer soil. *E. metallica* forms a fine specimen in a 10in. or 12in. pot, especially when it is in bloom, and everyone knows its value as a bedding plant. Echeverias are easily propagated from seed sown in August, from cuttings of the flower stems used at the same time if possible, these stems producing offsets, and from offsets which are produced more or less freely from the base of the stems. These should be placed singly on small pots of sandy soil, kept just moist, and they soon strike root. A frame is the best place for the purpose, keeping it nearly close. The young plants should have a shift in March, and if not used for bedding purposes should be placed in the frames in June, giving them a shift into 4in. pots in which they may bloom; or they may be shifted into 6in. pots, when the foliage will be finer. Plants taken up from the ground should be potted firmly into small pots and kept nearly dry through the winter, as damp is the greatest enemy to be feared. All the echeverias are useful for the foliage, and the bloom of all of them is interesting, especially in a mixed collection of plants. The plants can be kept indoors or out during the summer, and if not watered by accident occasionally, will not flag, unless drawn up weakly from want of light and air. They are also very easy to propagate, and anyone who has only a sitting room window can grow a very nice collection. They are, however, not quite hardy.

E. pulverulenta and *E. formosa* have both mealy, silvery leaves; *E. rotundifolia* is a cross between *E. metallica* and *E. secunda glauca*, and the leaves are nicely tinted on the edges; *E. fulgens* is good both for foliage and flower, but for the latter particularly, it bears orange red flowers, with sometimes a yellow tinge; it blooms with ordinary greenhouse treatment in March, earlier if forced into bloom by a higher temperature. *E. secunda glauca* is good from its form and glaucous leaves; *E. secunda globosa* is one of the best of the series; *E. metallica* has large fleshy, massive foliage, of a rich metallic hue, and is very handsome; *E. agavoides* is very fine, with scarlet flowers, plant very much like an agave; and *E. atropurpurea* is good for its bloom, the same as the preceding, the colour being purplish red.

Epiphyllum.—See "Hard Wooded Plants."

Erythrina.—These are plants that are very ornamental when in fruit, and should be represented in every greenhouse. The plant is nearly hardy, and of an herbaceous nature, having particularly ugly root stocks, from which the roots spring. It is very easy to grow, and although it does best in a large pot, still moderate-sized specimens can be obtained with care. The height varies from 2ft. to 4ft., and the foliage is not bad looking, but the chief thing is the bloom and seeds, both of which are bright scarlet.

The soil that suits it best is a sandy loam, or peat, giving water during the growing season, and treating much the same as cannas. The seed pods, when they open, contain many orange red or scarlet seeds, which have the appearance of coral. The blooms are somewhat pea-shaped, and vary in length according to cultivation and sorts.

The only two we have grown are *E. crista-galli* and *E. profusa*; but from what we have seen of *E. conspicua*, *E. marginata*, *E. ornata*, *E. Belangerii*, and *E. Marie Belanger*, we should say that they are well worth cultivation. Cool treatment and proper rest are the chief points in the culture of Erythrinas.

UCHSIAS.—This is one of the most important of all the soft wooded plants, and requires a very small amount of attention to produce ordinary small plants for summer use. Not that it is the least bit necessary to grow them in the house through the summer, but only during the earlier stages of growth. In very few cases do amateurs go in for show plants—rather the reverse—small well grown plants in 4in. or 6in. pots being all that is desired, and where such sorts as Conspicua, Mrs. Ballantyne, Vainqueur de Puebla, Talma, &c., are nicely grown, but little more is desired.

Now it depends on which part of the year these plants are desired, whether early or late. If early the cuttings should be got in before Christmas, but if not

required until autumn they may be struck from January to early April.
As soon as rooted they should be potted off into thumb pots, and kept
gently moving until March, when they should be placed in 4in. pots in a
light position, growing on freely, and the first batch will be ready in
May and June under glass. Those intended for autumn should be pinched
back in May, and as soon as they break placed in frames and closed for
a few days. Then they should have plenty of air and light, and about
June should have a shift into pots a size larger, and, with due attention
to watering, nice plants for decorative purposes will be had in August.
Cuttings struck in April and grown on into 6in. pots will bloom well from
the end of August until near Christmas if taken indoors as soon as the
wet season commences, and kept at a minimum temperature of 55°.
Liquid manure must, however, be given in this state of cultivation, using
sulphate of ammonia in preference to other more gross manures. For
general use the preceding is good if due attention to stopping, watering,
&c., is paid, the principles of which are described farther on.

We do not advise any amateur to attempt winter or early spring
fuchsias, as they do not pay for the trouble involved in growing them.
As, however, some of our readers may possibly desire to grow exhibition
plants, we will describe the process of culture. In September, cuttings
should be taken of the desired sort, from robust tops free from bloom.
If the cuttings have leaves produced in whorls of three, so much the
better; but this is not absolutely necessary—only an advantage. These
should be inserted in 4in. pots, one-third of which should be filled with
crocks, and then the pots filled with a compost of leaf soil, loam, and
sharp sand, in equal proportions. Put from six to eight cuttings in each
pot, and water in, giving a good watering to settle the soil. The cuttings
should then be placed on a light shelf in the greenhouse for the winter.
Early in March the plants should be potted off into 3in. pots, using the
same compost, with, perhaps, a little less sand. The strongest shoot, or
break as it is technically termed, should alone be permitted to remain,
pinching the others off. As they attain 8in. or 10in. in height small
sticks should be placed to them to prevent them bending or knuckling
over; also the points of the shoots should be taken out, so that side
shoots may be induced to break. If the plants can have the benefit of
a little warmth until the end of April so much the better, always provided
that proper care is taken to maintain as equable a temperature as
possible. As soon as the roots kiss the sides of the pots, it is better to
give a moderate shift, instead of waiting until the roots become entangled,
and then giving a large shift. This repotting should be kept up until 6in.
pots are reached, which should be about the second week in May, gradually
hardening off meanwhile. Careful attention must be paid to stopping and
training, so that a good framework should be obtained, bearing in mind
that the plants will be from 2½ft. to 5ft. high, when finished. By the
end of May, if the plants have progressed in a proper manner, they will
be ready for transferring to the blooming pots, which may be 10in., 12in.,
or 14in., according to the size and habit of the plant.

For soil use one half chopped fibrous loam, the other half leaf soil, and thoroughly decayed manure, with enough coarse sand to keep the whole sufficiently porous. Pass through a ¾in. sieve, not finer. Potting should be performed carefully, pressing the soil firmly around the ball of earth and roots, but yet not making it as hard as a gravel path, place a neat stake from 3ft. to 5ft. long in the centre of the pot, tying the plant loosely to it. Now select a light, yet warm and sheltered, spot out of doors, and stand the pots on pieces of slate to prevent the ingress of worms. Carefully attend to watering and training, as before, and allow the plants to remain until the second week in June. Then plunge the pots into ashes, tan, or other material, turning them round once or twice a week to prevent them becoming lopsided or drawn. Liberal supplies of water must be given, and liquid manure should be given twice a week. Pinching should be discontinued about five weeks before the show, when the plants should be a perfect pyramid of foliage and bloom. Slight shade should also be given about a fortnight before the show. The composts given above should be used for all classes of fuchsias, either for show or ordinary pot work.

The following, although not, perhaps, the newest, are good sorts for both form and colour. Dark single: Lord Elcho, Gipsy Girl, Senator, La Favorita, Prince Imperial, Souvenir de Cornelissen. Double: Rifleman, Percy, Universal, Amy Hoste. Single whites: Schiller, Rose of Denmark, Lady Heytesbury, Rose of Castille, Hugh Miller, Guiding Star, Maid of Kent, Fairest of the Fair. Red, with white corolla, single: Conspicua, Maria Cornelissen, Marchioness of Bath. Double: Vainqueur de Puebla, Mrs. Ballantyne, Emperor of the Fuchsias. To these may be added Arabella Improved, Mrs. Marshall, Improvement, Nabob, Water Nymph, Avalanche, Blue Boy, G. Grant, Purple Prince, Sultan, and White Lady. In our opinion the first twenty-four are the best for all purposes. Variegated foliage we object to, as it detracts from its bloom, which is the strong point in all fuchsias.

Funkia.—The variegated form of this plant is very effective in spring, and forms a very desirable foliage plant either for the greenhouse or drawing room. The culture is very simple, all that is necessary being plenty of drainage and very good loamy soil, with plenty of sand to keep it open. As the plant is herbaceous, and dies off each season, it is necessary to treat it in the same manner as other plants of a like nature, withholding water during the season of rest, still not allowing the soil to become dust dry. Funkias are hardy, so that about the end of May the plants should be removed to the frames, and thence should be plunged out of doors until they die down, when they should be repotted and placed in the frames, from which they can be brought into a warm house as occasion may require, and a temperature of from 48° to 55° will soon bring the foliage out to perfection.

For sorts choose from *F. Fortunei foliis variegatis*, *F. ovata variegata*, *F. O. foliis aureis maculatis*, and *F. undulata medio variegata*, but preferably the second and third one named.

AZANIA.—These are showy, nearly hardy bedding plants, and, from their habit and bloom, should be in every collection. In many places they are quite hardy, while in others they require to be housed; but in all cases it is better to keep a few store pots in readiness to fill up blanks or to guard against loss, while in places where the bedding system is pursued it is a good plan to have the stock in small pots at planting time, as in this state they are most manageable, and work into the designs more readily. We take cuttings in August and insert them eight in a pot in sandy soil, half filling the pots with crocks. These pots we place in a frame or on a bed of ashes until about the middle or end of October, when they are placed in a cool house until March. We then pot them off into comparatively small pots (2½in. to 3in.), and in April place in a frame till required for bedding or for the furnishing of baskets, vases, &c. Too much heat or water should be avoided, and all insects should be kept down carefully. A good sandy loam suits the plants best.

For sorts select from *G. pavonia*, yellow; *G. rigens*, orange; *G. splendens*, orange; and *G. splendens fol. var.*, orange.

Geranium.—See "Pelargonium."

Guernsey Lily.—See "Nerine."

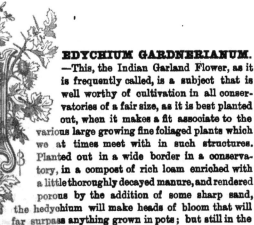

EDYCHIUM GARDNERIANUM.
—This, the Indian Garland Flower, as it is frequently called, is a subject that is well worthy of cultivation in all conservatories of a fair size, as it is best planted out, when it makes a fit associate to the various large growing fine foliaged plants which we at times meet with in such structures. Planted out in a wide border in a conservatory, in a compost of rich loam enriched with a little thoroughly decayed manure, and rendered porous by the addition of some sharp sand, the hedychium will make heads of bloom that will far surpass anything grown in pots; but still in the latter they are not bad if they are properly grown. Occasional supplies of liquid manure are also very beneficial in producing increased strength and vigour, and we can assure our readers that the 5s. the plant costs is not thrown away.

For pot culture the following answers well : Purchase the plant in winter, and as soon as it shows signs of growth repot into a pot or tub at least 15in. or 18in. in diameter, giving about 3in. of drainage. Water thoroughly until growth pushes freely, and then apply pure water in an almost unlimited amount, occasionally giving a dose of liquid manure. By forwarding some and retarding others, a continuance of bloom can be maintained for some months. As soon as the bloom is over the flower spikes should be cut down, and the strongest of the others left through the winter, when some of them will produce early spikes of bloom. If the flowers are fertilised artificially they will produce seeds of a bright orange scarlet colour, very showy and interesting, but of course the production of seeds weakens the plants a little. In spring, when the plants are repotted, the rhizomes can be divided, and many plants will be made; but in our opinion one or two good specimens are preferable to a number of smaller ones, the size of the plant rendering a large number out of place in any but large conservatories. The second season the spent earth can be partly removed, and the plants repotted into pots or boxes only an inch or two larger, or if this is not convenient, into the same sized pots or boxes, which are large enough to carry (with the aid of liquid manure) from eight to fifteen flower spikes, which makes a handsome specimen.

There are red, orange, yellow, and white hedychiums, which any good nurseryman can supply, although we believe they are mostly unnamed.

Hæmanthus.—This is a very showy class of bulbous plant well worth cultivation, and we have found it do well treated in the same manner as the Guernsey lily. In fact, we have had finer blooms when treated thus than in any other way.

The best we have seen (not stove varieties) are *H. coccineus*, red; *H. albiflos*, white flushed pink, sometimes pure white; and *H. puniceus*.

Heliotropium.—Heliotrope is one of the constituents of most bouquets in the season when it is in bloom out doors, and in winter it is very much esteemed, as it is one of the best-scented flowers to be had. Heliotrope is not difficult to grow if certain simple rules are followed, but if they are neglected, small success will follow. There is little labour required to produce bedding plants; simply strike the cuttings in the autumn and winter them in store pots, or keep old plants until early spring, and then strike cuttings and grow them on briskly, whichever is most convenient. In either case we find that it is the most convenient plan to strike the cuttings in a moderate bottom heat, and to strike in sand only. The advantage in keeping old plants is that sometimes plenty of bloom is had without any trouble, especially if a warm and moderately dry atmosphere is kept up; in fact, such a house as that in which tricolour pelargoniums are wintered will suit them nicely, providing bloom is not the chief point aimed at. Another plan where bloom is required, is to take up the plants used for bedding, and, after potting them up, place in a moderately brisk bottom heat for a fortnight, and then cutting them back, place them in heat until they break freely; gradually hardening them off so that they be brought into a house at a temperature of about 50°. With care in training, &c., repotting about the end of February, nice plants full of bloom may be had during April and May. Planted out, and trained over a trellis in a conservatory, where a minimum temperature of 50° is maintained, heliotropes will bloom for the greater part of the year, and few plants answer better.

For soil, use good fibrous maiden loam two-thirds, and thoroughly decomposed manure one-third, adding sufficient sharp sand to maintain the whole in a porous condition. We strike in sand, and pot off into the above compost, in which the plants both bloom and grow freely.

For conservatory decoration we, however, pursue the following plan. In July or August insert about six cuttings around the edge of a 6in. pot, affording plenty of drainage, and choosing strong terminal shoots for the cuttings, which should be about 1½in. long. Stand the pots in a close frame, and shade from the sun, keeping the pots fairly moist. In about a month the young plants should be potted off singly in 3in. pots, still keeping the plants in the frame, but admitting air freely. As soon as the pots get fairly filled with roots, repot into 48-sized pots, stand in the frame for a week or ten days, and then either remove the lights altogether or stand the plants out. Some of the plants will have a single stem only, and others will be bushy, and the former should be nicely staked and reserved for standards, as plants of this form, about three or four feet high, are extremely useful. So soon as there is the least chance of frost, the plants should be placed on an airy light shelf in the greenhouse, and should receive only just enough water to keep them alive during the winter. As soon as the plants start in spring, they should be turned out of the pots, the balls of earth should be reduced somewhat, and then repotted into pots one size larger. At the same time the branches of the bushy specimens should be shortened somewhat, and the plants should have more heat and moisture, to induce them to break freely. About May give another shift, and also give less fire heat, and increase the supply of fresh air. The plants should then be divided into two batches —one to be placed in the frames in June after being repotted into 8in. pots, the others to be kept in the conservatory, where the plants will bloom for a long time—many months, in fact. Those placed in the frames should be brought into the conservatory in September, and, by maintaining a temperature of 50° to 55°, an abundance of bloom will be obtained until the late plants are ready. The first batch should be wintered and treated as before described.

Standards should be run up to the height desired and then stopped, afterwards stopping the shoots and training them into a nicely-balanced head. The same general treatment applies as above. The old *H. Peruvianum* makes a good plant to cover trellises in the conservatory, giving an abundance of bloom for many months in the year. The soil used must be the same as mentioned above.

The best sorts for pot culture or bedding are Surpasse Guascoi, lilac to French white; M. Semeul, reddish purple; Mrs. Lewington, dark purple; Miss Nightingale, darkish purple; Hurst Metternich, French white; Madame Fillion, violet, white centre; Jersey Beauty, lavender; Mme. J. Amy, light blue; Mme. Bourcharlat, dark blue; Mons. Cassanave, dark purple; and Souvenir de Leopold I., light lavender lilac, very free and dwarf.

Humea.—*H. elegans* and *H. purpurea* are two very useful half-hardy perennials ; but they succeed best if treated as biennials, and as the seed is very moderate in price, we recommend that course. We sow the seeds thinly in rather sandy soil in April, and transplant into small pots (thumbs) as soon as the first leaf appears. After the young plants root into the fresh soil, gradually harden the plants off, and place in cold frames about the end of May, being careful that the temperature does not fall below 45°. As soon as the pots are full of roots (but not pot-bound), repot into one size larger, paying particular attention to watering, and keeping free from insects. Continue repotting as necessary, but giving only one size larger each time, keep the plants as close to the glass as possible, when it is necessary to keep the lights on, and syringe the plants every evening during hot weather. Early in September remove the plants to a light position, near the glass in a greenhouse, where a temperature of 45° to 50° is kept up, admitting as much air as can consistently be allowed, and repotting from time to time as requisite, as the chief secret in growing these plants is to keep them steadily growing. About the end of May they can be again transferred to the frames, treating as before. From 12in. to 15in. pots will be found necessary to bloom the plants well, and during the whole of their growth no check must be given. They will bloom from about July till the end of October, or even later, and as the plants are very imposing in appearance, and the flowers are nicely perfumed, they are very welcome additions to the stock. In growing them a slightly moist atmosphere rather than a dry one should be kept up.

The best soil to use is a good rich light fibrous loam, with enough sand added to secure the necessary porosity, as when growing vigorously they require plenty of water, they also necessarily require plenty of drainage.

The two varieties we name are fairly distinct, and are certainly good, viz.: H. *elegans*, reddish brown ; and H. *purpurea*, brownish crimson.

MANTOPHYLLUM.—These plants are also called by the name of Clivea, at least so far as two or three of the varieties are concerned. The culture is very simple, and provided proper attention is paid them at some seasons, at others they can remain under the stage of the greenhouse. The chief point is to grow them well and freely during the summer, and to give them rest during the winter. We have grown them successfully in the same manner as amaryllis, and also in the following manner : In March the plants are repotted in a compost of loam and leaf soil, with the addition of some sharp sand, potting the plants in from 9in. to 11in. pots, and watering in accordance with the growth. Give the same heat as the other stock receives, and as the weather becomes warm give air freely, so that the plants shall be fairly hardy. The blooms should be supported by neat stakes, and as probably there will be several heads, they should be trained apart so that a fine head of bloom is shown on each plant. After the bloom is over it is well to keep the plants growing vigorously until the leaves begin to ripen, and then gradually leave off watering until the plants are in a dormant state, when they can be placed under the stage.

The sorts we have grown are I. *Aitoni*, I. *miniatum*, and I. *cyrtanthiflorum*. The colours are shades of orange red, and the flowers are produced in large numbers.

Indian Garland Flower.—See "Hedychium."

Iresine.—This is a class of plant much used for bedding, and from the metallic bronzy colour of the foliage, whether dark red or bronze coloured reddish green, it contrasts favourably with other foliage plants of a brighter hue. The iresines are, however, plants that require a brisk heat to grow them on at certain times, that is, to obtain presentable plants for bedding out; but at all other times a minimum of 45° will keep them in fair health. The way we manage them is as follows : We take up the old plants in September, or strike cuttings in the end of July, and grow them on in pots, housing them in September, giving a light place near the glass, at the same time not over-watering for the winter. In the beginning of March cuttings are taken off and struck in nearly all sand, placing the pots in a brisk bottom heat. The old plants from which the cuttings were taken should also be placed in heat, and will supply an abundance of cuttings. When the cuttings are rooted they should be potted off into a compost of loam and leaf soil, to which a large amount of sharp sand has been added; return to heat again, and when the young plants are about 3in. high pinch out the tops, and as soon as the plants break freely gradually harden off, and bed out in June. Some of the plants may, however, be grown on in pots, and by shifting frequently until 8in. pots are reached, stopping from time to time, and paying due attention to watering, fine decorative plants will be made.

The following three varieties are good, viz., *I. Lindeni*, dark-blood red leaves, tall; *I. acuminata*, taller than the next, but variegated like the latter, having brighter colours, fine for pot work; and *I. Herbstii*, dark crimson, ribs and stems of a carmine colour, but on some soils the plants have a reddish bronze colour instead of coming true.

Isolepis gracilis.—This plant, which is in reality a rush, is most useful for various decorative purposes, both in rooms, in the greenhouse and conservatory, and for table decorations, consequently it should be grown in every greenhouse in the land; but, while it will do anywhere if frost is excluded, still it is far preferable to grow it in a house where at least a minimum of 45° is maintained. In fact, a higher temperature would produce better results, but as in many cases this cannot be had without injuring the other stock, the former temperature must suffice. Where sufficient heat is at hand the plants can be kept growing briskly throughout the winter, while in cool houses the plants should be in a large state before winter sets in, so that the chief point shall be to preserve and prolong the beauty of the plant rather than to cause a fresh growth to be made. Of course, allowance must be made to meet any special features in the case, but the following treatment will be found to produce excellent results : Pot the plants (after dividing the old stools) in a compost of sandy loam, leaf soil, and thoroughly rotted cow manure in equal parts, adding enough sand to keep the whole open. Keep the plants close for a week or ten days, and then air can be admitted more or less according to the season. Repotting can be done at almost any season where heat is readily obtainable, but in cold houses this operation is best done in April and August, having two batches of plants for the purpose. Few insects attack the isolepis, but slugs and snails must be guarded against. In no case must the plants become dry at the roots, or the foliage will become brown and unsightly, and the beauty of the plant is thus lost. It is the best plan to propagate by division, for although seeds are to be obtained, they cannot be relied on, as they should be sown as soon as ripe.

ALOSANTHES.—These plants, which are so much esteemed for decorative purposes during the season, are of easy culture if ordinary care is used; but it is a sign of careless cultivation to see them 3ft. or 4ft. high, and the clusters of blossoms consisting only of four or five, instead of several dozens. The scarlet variety is most effective for decorative purposes; but if the blooms are cut and wired for table work the flesh coloured or pink variety is also very useful. As plants for the decoration of rooms they are at times useful, but as their habit is erect they are better suited for conservatory work, as they can be there worked in to greater advantage. The flowers are also sweet-scented, which is an additional advantage. The best way to grow the plants is as follows :—In August, or early in September, take cuttings about 3in. long, choosing shoots which have not bloomed; strip off a few of the bottom leaves and insert each cutting singly in a 3in. pot, using a compost of loam, leaf soil, and pounded brick or crocks in about equal proportions. Place these pots on a shelf in the greenhouse or in a warm pit, keeping them as near the glass as possible, and giving only enough water to prevent flagging. When well rooted, remove to a cool dry greenhouse for the winter, giving but little water, so that the plants shall be kept at rest till the spring. Early in March the plants should be repotted into 8in. or 10in. pots, using a somewhat heavier soil and also plenty of drainage. After potting, the plants should be carefully introduced into a growing temperature, and induced to grow freely, but at the same time care must be taken that the plants are kept near the glass, or they will become long and spindly, and of small value. As growth commences some of the plants will have several shoots, while others will have one. In the former case remove all but seven or eight; and in the latter pinch off the top to induce the formation of young shoots, as it is these shoots that will bear bloom. About the end of May the plants should be plunged in a bed of ashes outdoors, or they may be stood on a hard surface, as the plunging is not absolutely necessary; but at the same time it is necessary to give them a hot and open (though sheltered) spot from the time of repotting until the fall, when they should be taken into a cool house before the weather becomes too cold. Here they can remain until they open, maintaining a temperature of 45° to 50°. Some may be got on earlier by giving more heat, while some may be retarded by keeping them a little cooler, so that a succession can be kept up. If due attention is paid to watering, staking, &c., during the summer, fine plants, covered with large trusses of flower buds, will be produced by autumn, and then the only question is to get the buds open at the time desired, and this is done by the routine already described.

The sorts we prefer are *K. coccinea superba* and *K. coccinea*, crimson; *K. versicolor*, flesh or pink. *K. splendens* is also very good; but the first two are the best of the lot.

ACHENALIA.—This is a class of greenhouse bulbous plants which, though of great individual beauty, is still much neglected. Indeed, at the time when the plants most require attention, as a rule, they have the least of it, probably owing to the fact that their blooming period is then over. The bulbs are comparatively cheap, and are to be had at most nurseries.

About October or November the bulbs should be put into 6in. or 8in. pots, placing from seven to twelve bulbs in the 6in., and from twelve to eighteen in the 8in. pots. It is as well to mention that here a little discretion must be used, as in many cases the bulbs will be strong, and then a less number will be required, and then again weak bulbs will require to be much closer together, so that in reality they must be planted according to size. By far the best plan is to place the larger bulbs in the centre and the smaller ones around, as the pots are then more evenly balanced. In potting, about an inch of drainage should be put, then an inch of thoroughly decayed cow manure, and the pot filled up with a compost of yellow fibrous loam and enough sharp sand to keep up the necessary amount of porosity. As the bulbs are very small, it is preferable to fill the pots and then insert

the bulbs, first putting in a pinch of silver sand for the bulbs to rest on.
No water should be given until the plants are growing well, and then
water must be given freely. To grow the plants well they should be stood
on a bed of ashes in a cool frame, keeping them somewhat near the glass,
but taking especial care to exclude frost. It is also a good plan to exclude
light from the bulbs until they are well into leaf. When well advanced
they may be placed on the front shelf of a greenhouse until their beauty
is over, then they should be taken back to the frame to complete their
growth and ripen off the bulbs, as on this depends their value as decorative
subjects.

The best three varieties are L. pendula, red, tipped with purple and
green; L. quadricolor, and L. tricolor, scarlet, yellow, and green. For all
cool houses this will be found a gem amongst bulbs, but no forcing must
be attempted.

Lantana.—These plants are useful for greenhouse decoration and
bedding-out; and whether grown for one or other of these purposes, or
for both, if grown well they are sure to give satisfaction. For ordinary
culture they are well adapted, as they produce flowers for six or seven
months in the year, with no more trouble than is necessary to grow a
geranium. They strike very freely, are easily raised from seed, and
winter well, doing very well in a house where the temperature does not
fall below 38°. Combined with these good points, the flowers are conspicuous, showy, and borne at the ends of the shoots, where they are in
full view, and, what is more important to the amateur horticulturist,
they are not subject to any insect pest to any appreciable degree. In
many places they are used pegged down in place of verbenas, with this
disadvantage, that crimson, scarlet, pure white, and self purple are absent,
the shades generally having more or less orange in them. Nevertheless,
the whole of the plants are well worth cultivating.

The way we manage them is to strike cuttings in August or early in
September, pot off into small pots, and winter in an ordinary greenhouse, repotting in March into 3in. pots, and when the side shoots are
large enough stopping them back, and striking the points in a gentle
bottom heat, by this means having plenty of plants from a small space.
If it is desired to have large plants for decorative purposes, the plants
that were stopped back should be repotted into 6in. pots, and carefully
grown on, choosing a pyramidal form of growth, in which they will
exhibit their flowers to the greatest perfection. Plenty of water will be
necessary while the plants are growing freely, but no liquid manure
should be applied until the pots are full of roots, but then a solution of
sulphate of ammonia may be applied most advantageously, as this manure
is most suited for the production of flowers. The ordinary stock may be
bedded out in the proper season, and will be very useful both for the
display of bloom obtained, and for cutting, but great care must be taken in
the latter case that no *bruised* foliage is used, as it then emits a very
unpleasant smell.

For soil, we find a compost of one part leaf mould and two parts good
maiden loam, and a fair amount of sand answer well, and we pot mode-

rately firm, but not too hard, or the plants will not grow freely. We find, as a rule, lantanas do best without manure.

The following sorts, which we have grown ourselves, are all good, and should be in all collections : Ne plus ultra, centre of truss straw yellow, and shades off at the edges to rose pink tinted with lavender ; *L. lutea grandiflora*, fine yellow ; La Manula, rose pink centre, yellow outside; Julius Cæsar, bright bronze yellow; Marquis de St. Laporta, bronze self ; Favorita, bronze yellow, changing to dark brownish scarlet, and tinted bright purple ; Dom Calmet, pink, changing to peach and yellow; Mons. Felix Aliburt, purple pink suffused with gold; Distinction, orange scarlet ; Imperatrice Eugenie, pale pink, clear yellow centre ; Victoire, white, lemon eye ; *L. Ninus*, canary yellow ; and Mons. Rougier Chauvière, yellow, bordered bright red, changing to scarlet. There are also other named sorts, of which we have not sufficient knowledge to recommend them, but the preceding we know are good. A packet of seed from good varieties raised in heat in January or February, will bloom some time between July and October, and will afford many different marked flowers, some of which are sure to prove useful.

Leucophyta.—This is a plant which is useful alike for greenhouse decoration and for bedding-out purposes, and from its colour is a very desirable acquisition to the stock of plants grown. The colour is a peculiar silvery white, and the growth is quick and slender, presenting the appearance of some marine plant rather than one belonging to the earth. The stems appear to branch and ramify at will, apparently bearing no foliage ; but if closely examined it will be found to be thickly set with long narrow leaves. It is not very difficult to propagate, cuttings taken in August striking freely. We grow it in the same manner as the Lantana, using the same soil, and we find that it does well with such treatment. The only variety with which we are acquainted is *L. Brownii*.

Lilium.—The only one of the lilies proper that we consider is worth the trouble of culture under glass is *L. auratum*, or the golden-rayed lily of Japan, as it is sometimes called. In a spacious house one or two large clumps look well, and diffuse a fine perfume, but too many must not be used or the scent will be too powerful and cause a feeling of nausea each time the house is entered. The way we cultivate these plants is as follows : As soon as we can procure the roots or bulbs we pot them into pots of sufficient size for the purpose required, generally 12in. or 14in. In these we put about two inches of crocks, and on these about the same quantity of compost. We then place the bulb or bulbs on this soil, allowing at the rate of one blooming crown to each two inches in diameter of the pot, whether the crowns are in one or several roots or bulbs. On the bulbs we lay about two inches of soil, pressed down moderately firm. The pots are then placed in a cold frame with a bottom of coal ashes, and no water is given until the plants begin to throw up the flower spikes, when a good soaking is administered. When the spikes are about six inches high, another two inches of rough soil are applied ; and when the roots appear above this the pots are filled up, as by this method we find that much finer blooms are produced. As the stems increase in height, liquid manure may be added occasionally with advantage, and the stems may also be neatly trained out with stakes just strong enough to bear the weight of the head of bloom. During the whole of the time the plants are growing they must be kept as close to the glass as possible, and given the largest amount of air that can be consistently allowed. In fact, it is far better to grow the plants in the frame until the end of May, and then only cover in case of frost. As soon as the foliage dies off we repot the roots and treat them as before described. And here let us draw attention to the fact that there are no roots to beat those grown at home, although they may be more expensive; for home-grown bulbs always retain the thick, fleshy roots at the base, which are absent in imported samples; and this makes a vast difference in the beauty of the flowers. For compost there is nothing better than pure fibrous maiden loam, to which is added enough sand to maintain porosity to admit of the free passage of water. The soil should be roughly chopped up, so as to pass through a two-inch meshed sieve.

There are two sorts we use, viz., L. auratum, the golden-rayed, and L. rubrum vittatum, the red-rayed lily. There are several different forms in both these, and therefore if one comes across a taking flower it is as well to secure the root, but if imported roots are purchased various forms of flowers will be obtained.

Lobelia.—This class of plants, which is rather large, is generally represented in most gardens by the ordinary blue, L. speciosa, and its varieties, and is chiefly used as an edging plant. Sometimes the hardy L. cardinalis is employed in the herbaceous borders, but this is not so often used now as it ought to be. But of these we are not now treating; it is the sorts which have to be grown under glass for at least some part of the year that now require our attention.

Nearly everyone is acquainted with some of the varieties of L. speciosa, and to these dwarf bedding plants we will first direct attention. There are two ways of propagating these plants which are in general use, and the first of these is raising from seeds.

Before attempting to raise a good stock of reliable plants from seeds, it is necessary to have two things, viz., new seed, and seed saved from a good strain of plants, otherwise disappointment is sure to ensue. Premising the seed is as it should be, the next point is to prepare some pots of rich soil on which to sow it; at least two inches of drainage should be allowed to a 4-inch pot, and the soil should not come to within half an inch of the top of the pot. These pots should now be stood in a tub of water, but the water must not be allowed to overflow into the top of the pots, and when the soil is well soaked they should be placed aside for an hour to drain. A small portion of clean seed should then be taken on the point of a penknife, and, by a dexterous puff with the breath, distributed over the surface of the soil. No soil should be put on the seeds, but each pot should be covered with a sheet of glass, the pots having been first placed in a brisk bottom heat, or in a greenhouse where a temperature of 60° to 65° is maintained. When the plants are sufficiently large to handle they should be transplanted at about an inch apart in other pots, and when large enough they should be repotted into thumbs for use, gradually hardening them off as the season advances. The second plan is to cut down old plants in August, and, when they have broken freely, pot them up and place in a cold frame until the weather becomes too damp, and then take them into the greenhouse for the winter. In February the tops may be taken off and struck in heat, and by giving a gentle temperature to the old plants they will produce a large number of cuttings, which may in their turn be struck, so making a large stock of plants. The cuttings, when struck, should be treated the same as seedlings.

Double lobelias should be struck in gentle heat in January, or in a shaded position in August, and wintered in a cool house. In February they should be repotted into 3in. pots, and as the pots become full of roots (not pot-bound) shifted again into 4in. or 6in. pots, as the size of the plants warrant. By keeping them near the glass in a well-ventilated house until April, and then transferring to a cold frame, all the time paying attention to the wants of the plants as regards watering, &c., giving plenty of air, but avoiding heavy rains, good pots of bloom will be had. It is, however, practically useless to plant these lobelias out, unless for the supply of cuttings, as they only make a good display for a short time, and then they are done for the season. A good soil for the above lobelias is maiden loam three parts, rotten manure one part, and sufficient sharp sand to maintain the proper porosity of the soil.

There is a fine lobelia very suitable for the decoration of the greenhouse, and this is the L. subnuda, a species with foliage much resembling some of the Anæctochili. It is one which, although not of very large size, is still extremely useful as a choice decorative plant, especially if small gems are desired for any special purpose. It is a native of Mexico, and therefore does best in the greenhouse. The plants form tufts about four inches, or a trifle more, in diameter, and the leaves are ovate, about an inch long. They are serrated at the margins, of a brownish purple colour, the midrib and veins being bright green, thus forming a very elegant contrast. The under surface of the leaves is deep purple, while the flowers—which are produced freely on stems about six inches high—are of a very pale blue, and do not add much to the beauty of the plant. It is therefore a good plan to remove them as soon as they appear, unless seed is required, and then a spike may be left, as the plant seeds freely. The way we grow this plant is to sow seeds in April in a broad pan of sandy loam, distributing them thinly and evenly, and, when the plants are large enough, pricking each one into the centre of a 4in. pot. These plants are then carefully brought on in a warm position near the glass, but shaded from sun. With care in watering the plants soon get a good size and commence to bloom. If preferred, the seedlings may be placed in small pots at first, and then repotted, and perhaps they will do better thus than as we do them. For soil we use fibrous, sandy loam, enriched with a little thoroughly decayed manure, to which some sand has been added to ensure the proper amount of porosity. L. subnuda is also sold under the alias of L. picta, but the former is the correct name.

G 2

For sorts of single varieties selection should be made from the following : *L. speciosa* (true), *L. pumila grandiflora*, *L. pumila magnifica*, *L. speciosa compacta*, Brilliant, Henderson's Lustrous, Celestial Blue, Blue Boy, and Carter's Cobalt Blue, all various shades of blue. There are white varieties, but, with the exception of White Perfection and Duchess of Edinburgh for pot work, we do not recommend them. Of doubles we think that *L. pumila, fl. pl.*, is the best, as culture more than variety causes size and doubleness in the blooms.

MESEMBRYANTHEMUM.—These are rather nice succulent plants, which are very useful in many places, both for bedding out and other purposes, and some of them do not look bad in pots. We grow all of them in the same manner, and with great success, there being only one way to do these plants well. The great secret of success we consider to be the exposure of the plants to the full sun at all times, and not potting in too rich a soil, a compost of lime rubbish, yellow loam, and sand and cow manure, in equal proportions, suiting them well. The way we grow them is as follows : In March we either sow seeds in a little bottom heat, or strike cuttings in a position fully exposed to the sun, and when these are of a sufficient size we pot off into small pots, from which they are repotted into 4in. pots when large enough, or transferred to the open ground if intended for bedding purposes. The whole of the time the plants remain in the most exposed part of the house, and not overwatered, and in due time they make fine plants. It is not, of course, intended that the plants shall perish for want of water, but what we would imply is that water is only given when really required, a saturated soil not being desirable for the well-being of the plants. Mesembryanthemums are best struck the same as cacti, *i.e.*, the cuttings being inserted in dry sand and exposed to the sun till rooted, which operation takes place in a few days. When rooted some moisture may be applied, and, when potted off, the general routine may be followed.

The following sorts are very interesting, either for pot culture or for planting out on rockwork during the summer months. *M. conspicuum*, blooms mauve pink; *M. lupinum*, yellow blooms; *M. tigrinum*, curious foliage; *M. echinatum*, curious foliage; *M. cordifolium variegatum*, creamy variegation, rose-coloured blooms. As in these plants form varies so much, and as the chief beauty lies in the grotesque form of the foliage, it is impossible to describe the best, for what one person would admire others would be disgusted with; therefore we consider it is better to advise our readers to see a collection of these plants before investing ' largely, and select only those which suit their fancy. There are over fifty varieties grown by Mr. Ware, of Tottenham, and he does not, we believe, cultivate the whole of those grown.

Mignonette.—This odorous plant, which is as a rule grown as an annual, blooms throughout the winter months if treated as a perennial. There are several modes of growing the plants for this purpose, but we shall give our own system.

In the first place, never attempt to transplant mignonette, or failure is almost sure to result, as it is such an extremely difficult matter to success-fully transplant things of this sort, which, as a rule, make but few fibrous roots. The best plan is to select the blackest seeds from a packet, and to sow two of these (a slight distance apart) in thumb or small 60 sized pots, and when up strongly to remove the weaker plant, and allow the other to remain. The time to sow is March, or early in April, and a little bottom heat should be used to start the plants. As soon as the pots become filled with roots, but not pot bound, shift into 3in. pots, and continue shifting as necessary, until the second week in September, when the final shift should be given. During the hot weather the plants should stand on a bed of coal ashes, in a north-east aspect, and should be kept supplied with water, on no account allowing them to become dry, or the foliage will get rusty, and the wood hard, and all our labour would be lost.

After the last potting has been given in September, the plants should be removed to a light airy greenhouse, and should be placed near the glass, taking care not to neglect watering, or the destruction of green fly. The flower buds must also be pinched out for the last time, and after this all blooms must be allowed to open. A temperature of about 45° to 50° will cause the plants to bloom well and freely. To this end it is also advantageous to give occasional waterings with sulphate of ammonia, as this induces bloom.

For soil use two-thirds turfy loam, one-part leaf soil, and one-part road grit, with just enough sand to maintain the necessary porosity of the soil. Plenty of drainage must be afforded, and the plant must be neatly staked.

Another plan is to sow seeds in July or August, keeping the plants in a cool north aspect, and by having about three or four plants in a 6in. pot, and giving liberal treatment, the plants can be had in bloom from November till after Christmas, or even later, but of course much depends on the season.

Amongst the many sorts, we have found the following good in practice : Crimson Giant, Parson's New White, Parson's Hybrid Giant, New Dwarf Compact, and Pyramidal Bouquet, all of which are distinct, good, and have some speciality in growth or colour, which, although scarcely worth describing at length, is still of enough note to render the plants sufficiently distinct while growing. As a rule we should advise the use of the whole of the sorts enumerated, and then a good show could be maintained.

Mimulus.—These are nearly hardy, very ornamental plants, and are also of very easy culture. The best amongst them are Clapham's and Henderson's strains, which, though unnamed, are of very great excellence, and we always grow them in preference to named varieties, on account of obtaining a finer show from them. We sow twice in the year, in October and April, using a little bottom heat to get the plants up. When up large enough to handle we transplant into 6in. pots, about twelve in a pot, and those sown in October remain thus until February, while those sown in March remain only until of sufficient strength to be transferred to single pots. If desired they can be transferred to thumb pots at once, and remain there until the roots kiss the sides of the pots, when they should be transferred to 6in. pots, and if large plants be required from these they should be again transferred to 8in. pots, where, if proper care has been taken, they will make plants from 18in. to 2ft. high. Like musk, however, it is necessary to give them a position facing the north during the hot weather, and a large amount of water must be given—in fact, like musk, they require very liberal treatment. For soil we use leaf mould one part, cow manure one part, good maiden loam two parts, and sand one part, and we put at least a couple of inches of crocks in the bottom of each pot. As the pots get filled with roots we stand them in saucers of water, and apply liquid manure once or twice a week.

The colours of the strains of Mimulus we mentioned above vary from white, yellow, brown, maroon, &c., to almost black, and the flowers are beautifully spotted with colours very different from the ground colour of the bloom, thus making very striking contrasts.

As, however, some of our readers might fancy a few named sorts, we give the names of half-a-dozen which we have grown ourselves. Attraction, large scarlet, yellow throat, spotted with crimson; Constellation, canary yellow, deep crimson spots and blotches; Goliah, clear yellow, richly spotted with crimson, very fine; Illustration, yellow ground, crimson lobes, very large and fine; Regulator, cream ground and margin, ruby crimson blotches, very fine; Regulus, deep crimson, canary spots and band; and *M. albus-elegantissimus*, creamy white ground, crimson blotched lobes, and plum-coloured margins. The preceding are all most excellent in form and markings, and form an inexhaustible store for the supply of seeds, but a packet of either Henderson's or Clapham's strain would be found to give quite as good results.

Musk.—Musk, or, more properly speaking, *Mimulus moschatus*, is a good old-fashioned plant, welcome alike in both mansion and cottage. Of course, all our readers are acquainted with the plant, therefore it needs no description; but the method of cultivation is quite another matter. To have a fine pot of musk is generally everyone's ambition, and if the simple rules we give are followed, pretty fair success, if not perfection itself, will be met. In the cultivation of musk, that is if fine plants are desired, a somewhat shaded position should be chosen for the plants to occupy, and it is also desirable that no fierce sun rays drop across them at any time, or the foliage will have a rusty faded appearance. It is therefore better to grow the plants in a place having a north aspect during the summer, and as the sun loses power to bring them to the warmer side of the house. The way we manage the plants is as follows: In January we introduce some roots into a warm position in the greenhouse, and as soon as they break freely we pot them off, about five in a 6in. pot, using rich, fairly open compost; plenty of drainage is also afforded, as the plants require an almost unlimited supply of water during the growing season. These young plants are then stood in a warm, somewhat moist position, and at once commence growth. As soon as they are about 2in. high they are stopped back, and this causes them to branch freely. Sticks are inserted round the sides of the pot at an early stage of the plants' growth, and they are thus kept in a good form for a long time. About the first week in March, June, and August we also put in cuttings, and treat as before described, and thus have musk in good order all the year round, which is not possible unless this practice is adhered to.

We are acquainted with only one kind of musk, *M. moschatus*, but there is also a variety called the giant musk, *M. m. gigantea*, but this is, we suspect, only a sort improved from the common variety, and is consequently not different from the original variety, except in size.

ERINE.—This is a section of amaryllis, and is quite hardy on some soils; but, as a rule, the bulbs are grown in pots for conservatory decoration. The botanical name is *Nerine*, and the name of the Guernsey lily is *N. Sarniensis*. There are, however, other nerines that are worth the same care as the Guernsey lily, a list of which we give. The culture is extremely simple; the plants growing in a good light sandy loam, a fair amount of drainage being afforded, as a matter of course. Procure the bulbs early in September, and pot at once, say, three in a 6in. pot; place the pots on a front shelf in the greenhouse, or in a frame, near the glass, where they can receive plenty of light and air. Keep the soil fairly moist, and growth will at once commence. The flower spikes should be neatly staked, and, as soon as the blooms are well advanced, give plenty of water, and place the plants in a dry, cool, and airy position.

As the bulbs are comparatively expensive, it is desirable to keep them for successive years; but as this cannot be done if the bulbs are starved, it is necessary that they should be replanted. The best plan is to have some boxes a foot or thirteen inches deep, and of a size that is convenient to move about—claret cases for instances—and, after providing for sufficient drainage, have ready some sandy loam chopped fine, but not sifted. Then after blooming turn the plants carefully out of the pots, and place each individual bulb about six inches from its neighbour; then water gently, to settle the soil around the roots, and place in a situation where a temperature of 40° can be maintained, and plenty of air can be given on mild days. The same treatment should then be given as that which is generally afforded to greenhouse plants. When the foliage begins to fade, the water should be gradually discontinued, and, when ripe, the bulbs should be stored away until the next planting season.

For sorts, select from the following: *N. corusca*, bright scarlet; *N. flexuosa*, pale rose; *N. Fothergillii*, vermilion scarlet; *N. pudica*, white; *N. rosea*, rosy red; *N. Sarniensis*, rose crimson; *N. undulata*, lilac rose; and *N. venusta*, crimson.

Nierembergias.—The nierembergias, which are very good for cool houses, are of comparatively easy culture, and as they only require the exclusion 'of frost, say a temperature of 36° to 40°, they are handy in many situations, especially where plants which do not require much heat are grown. We have grown them very successfully as follows, but we do not think the practice is in general use: We strike cuttings in August, and when well rooted pot off singly into small 60 sized pots, using sandy loam for the purpose. In the latter end of September we place these pots on a light airy shelf in the greenhouse, and through the winter give only enough water to prevent flagging. Of course, if a mean temperature of about 45° is kept up, we apply enough water to keep the plants growing, but not otherwise. In the second or third month we repot into 48 sized pots, if the plants are to bloom in pots, but if for out-door decoration, then 3in. pots are used, and the plants do well. For soil we use good sandy loam three parts, thoroughly decomposed manure and sharp sand mixed one part, and the plants are potted pretty firm. A good light airy spot in the house is set aside for the plants, and water is given according to their requirements. When the heat becomes too great, the plants are removed to a sunny frame, and the pots are plunged in coal ashes, which keeps the plants in a healthy condition. When the pots are well filled with roots, a solution of sulphate of ammonia is applied, and plants thus treated never fail to bloom well.

For sorts we use *N. frutescens*, lilac and white; *N. gracilis*, blue; *N. gracilis picta*, blue edged white, a cross between the two preceding; *N. rivularis*, cream; and *N. Veitchii*, pale lilac. *N. frutescens* is the tallest growing plant, and, in our opinion, *N. Veitchii* is the most dwarf, but probably difference in cultivation has something to do with the matter.

XALIS.—These are greatly neglected now, and although they are very pretty, we think they should not occupy too much space in the house. They are dwarf growing plants of very easy culture, and can be propagated freely if desired. Plenty of drainage is necessary, and a good sandy loam is the best in which to grow the plants, which, however, never do so well in pots as in large clumps, in a rockery or herbaceous border, at least during the greater part of the year.

For sorts select from *O. rosea*, rose; *O. tropæoloides*, yellow, rich brown foliage; *O. corniculata rubra*, rich velvety dark brown foliage; *O. Smithii*, pink; *O. rosea alba*, white; *O. arenaria*, dark rosy purple; *O. lobata*, yellow; *O. elegans*, rich purple lake, dark centre; *O. floribunda alba*, white; *O. f. rosea*, rose; *O. pentaphylla*, pink; and *O. purpurea*, purple.

PLARGONIUM. — This is a very large family of plants, and includes what are generally called geraniums, that is, the scarlet and bedding varieties, and the Cape or fancy pelargoniums.

The varieties amount to several hundreds, and it is much to be regretted that they are so numerous, as in many cases they are so much alike that it is quite impossible to tell them apart. This is particularly the case with scarlets, which are so numerous in name that the difficulty lies in distinguishing them by name at all, except in the case of a very few sorts, which are really distinct.

In the tricolor, bicolor, and bronze sections the same difficulties also arise, and while we have grown some 150 sorts or varieties to name, we have not had above thirty that are really distinct. There are, of course, some which can be easily told apart, but as we arranged a houseful once, no one out of the trade, and but few in it, could have told us where one variety ended and the other began. Still they were all true to name.

To commence, we will take the scarlet, and zonal sections first. These, as nearly every one is aware, are the sorts which are chiefly used for bedding out purposes, and are therefore always in request. They are also useful for the decoration of the greenhouse during part of the year, and also for use in rooms, &c. In fact, generally speaking, the scarlet and other zonal pelargoniums are the most useful plants we have; anyhow, they are grown most generally. The first consideration is obtaining good plants for bedding-out purposes, and these we manage to obtain as follows : In August or the first week in September, we prepare some 6in. or 8in. pots, by half filling them with crocks, and then filling up with a sandy compost, loam being the principal ingredient. A number of cuttings having been prepared, are inserted about twenty or thirty in each pot, the pots are well watered and stood in the full rays of the sun. In a short time they become rooted, when all dead foliage is removed, and about the end of the month they are removed into the greenhouse, there to remain until the next March. Only just enough water to keep them alive is necessary, and so long as the house is kept fairly dry, and frost is well excluded, the young plants will do very well. About March they are potted off into large 60 sized pots, and, by affording more moisture and warmth, good plants are obtained in the proper season. A compost of maiden loam, enriched with a little thoroughly rotted manure and made sufficiently porous by the addition of some sharp sand, does the bedding varieties well.

For plants to bloom during winter we always put the cuttings in in June, and about August shift them into 6in. pots. They are carefully grown on until the second week in September, when some are removed into the greenhouse and others into frames. During the whole of this time they are not allowed to bloom, neither are they watered more than is necessary, as the aim is to obtain a potful of vigorous roots, and a comparatively dwarf sturdy head. When introduced into the house a temperature of about 50° to 55° is maintained, and a free circulation of air is allowed, the plants receiving more liberal treatment at the same time. Those left in the frames are not housed until October, and, of course, receive a similar treatment to the others. As the season advances, the maximum temperature may be reduced 4° or 5°, so as to maintain a kind of equilibrium with the outer atmosphere. It may also be found useful to give a small quantity of liquid manure from time to time, but if it can be done without so much the better. To grow plants for bloom during the winter months it is necessary to have a light house, and to give the plants liberal treatment, at the same time using every endeavour to keep the growth as stocky as possible, as on this a vast amount depends.

For summer use, in pots, &c., the cuttings should be potted off singly into 3in. pots in August, and kept through the winter as before described, and then, about six weeks after Christmas, they should be shifted into 4in. pots, and by giving them due attention they will do well throughout the season.

We now come to the bronze and golden bicolor section, as being next to the ordinary scarlet and zonal varieties. These are most suitable for pot culture, and we shall therefore treat of them as pot plants, as the greatest amount of beauty can be got from them as such. Of course, there are bronzes and bronzes, and in the majority of cases it requires considerable management to bring out the good points of the plants— particularly those which are of a very robust nature—as they all require a treatment suitable to their constitution. At the same time, a little judgment used in selecting the cuttings, and a little care in selecting soils, will save much time and anxiety in after work. Thus a very robust, free growing bronze, if propagated from soft free grown wood, will grow to an immense size, especially if the soil is rich, while at the same time the colour will not differ much from an ordinary zonal, but if the cuttings are made from poor starved specimens, and the soil is not over rich, the results will generally be all that can be desired. We therefore advise a poor, rather than too rich a soil, and, as a rule, to pot rather firmly.

The soil we use for bronzes and bicolors is sound yellow loam, passed through a 1in. meshed sieve, and to this is added enough leaf soil and sharp sand to keep the whole open. For weak growing plants a little thoroughly decomposed cow manure can also be advantageously added, but it must not be overdone, or strength will be obtained at the expense of colour.

The way we do this class of pelargoniums is as follows: In February or in August, according to circumstances, we strike cuttings of the sorts we intend growing on in pots. This we do by inserting one cutting in a thumb or small 60 sized pot, filled with sandy compost, and doing so until we have about 12 per cent. more cuttings than we require plants, so allowing for losses. These plants are repotted and placed in the frames about the second week in April, and as soon as the pots are full of roots they are shifted into the sized pots they are to permanently occupy. Care must be paid to stopping, &c., and the plants must be kept near the glass. Water must be given as necessary, and during very bright hot sun it is well to apply a slight shade. In this they resemble tricolors. In fact, as a rule, the treatment may be the same as that for tricolors, allowing some slight difference of treatment to suit the habits of the plants.

In the tricolor or variegated foliaged section, we find two divisions —silver and gold—both of which are very useful in their places. The treatment is the same for both, and although we may be disbelieved by many unsuccessful growers, we assert that there is no more real difficulty in growing tricolors than there is in growing the ordinary zonal varieties, the only difficulty being the propagation, and in this there is no difficulty if it is commenced at the proper time. We strike our main crop or stock in August, and plants for pot culture, to come in late, we strike in March, as at other times we find that, although we can strike the cuttings freely, the plants are not of much service, as those struck during the winter are generally too poor in colour, and those struck during the summer are too large, and oft times too sappy to winter well. Besides, it rarely happens that tricolors retain their colour during the winter, and it is therefore necessary that the plants should not be incited to grow much during that time. We have ere now worked up a stock of about 500 plants from a seedling in less than twelve months ; but if we had desired them for our own use, about one-fourth of that number only would have been raised, as excessive propagation reduces the constitution and vigour of these plants to such an extent that they are too weak for any purpose, and the colour is reduced to a minimum. In this as in other matters, it generally happens that the more haste the less speed. We would therefore desire our readers to remember that in no case should propagation be carried too far, and also that cuttings should only be taken from the strongest and best plants, as weak cuttings do not produce highly coloured plants.

For convenience we generally adopt the following plan : In August cuttings are inserted singly in small sixty-sized pots, previously prepared by filling about one-third full of crocks, and the remainder with sandy loam, the sand used being very sharp. The cuttings are then potted firmly, and after twenty-four hours the pots are carefully watered, and then stood in a frame facing the south, the frame being filled up with ashes to a convenient height. Water is not again necessary for about a week or ten days, when the cuttings are just emitting roots, and after this time water is applied with care. The lights are only used to exclude heavy storms, and care is taken that a too vigorous growth is not induced, as the more dwarf and hard the young plants are the more easily are they managed during winter.

In wintering both old and young plants we take great care to place them in a light airy position near the glass, and to keep the house free from an excess of atmospheric moisture, at the same time maintaining a temperature of about 45°. Very little water is given during the winter, in fact only sufficient to keep the plants in a healthy state, but at the same time excessive dryness is avoided, or the plants would be liable to damp off when watered. All dead and decaying foliage is kept scrupulously removed, and in fact everything that would tend to cause "damp" or decay is carefully removed.

In spring, cuttings can be taken from the old plants, and struck in the greenhouse, always provided that they are exposed to the full sun. For convenience we always strike these in single pots, as they are then so much more readily handled, and, what is more, the roots do not get broken, which is a most important point, as tricolors never have too many roots.

The plants struck in August should be repotted in March, and the old plants from which cuttings have been taken should be repotted as soon as they have broken well. Shift the young stuff into 48 sized pots, and the old ones into pots a size smaller than those which they occupy when cut back. Subsequent repotting must depend on the wants and vigour of the plants, as no strict rule can be set in this respect.

About the second or third week in April the plants—with the exception of those for bedding out purposes—can be placed on a bed of ashes in a cold frame, and with a little care as to closing the lights early, watering, and shading, &c., the foliage will soon obtain their true colours and habit. Bronzes also require to stand in a cold frame if the best colour is desired, and mixed with the tricolors they make a very pretty effect. It must be remembered that both bronzes and tricolors are variable as to the time when they show most colour, some being best in spring, and some in autumn, but very few being at their prime during the hottest part of summer, and even those which are in good form are only made so by shading and other adventitious means. The soil we use for tricolors is composed of good maiden or fibrous yellow loam three parts, and one part thoroughly decomposed cow manure and leaf soil, or peat. To this compost is added enough sharp sand to maintain the whole in a proper state of porosity.

Tricolors should be put out in beds at least a week or ten days later than the ordinary zonal varieties, on account of their being much more tender, but at the same time it is well to remark that they are not so effective as a rule, as other coloured foliage plants, and it is far better to use them for decorative pot plants only. In only a very few places are tricolors or bronzes really effective bedded out in the open ground.

Ivy leaved pelargoniums require much the same treatment as the ordinary zonal varieties.

The varieties with scented foliage also require much the same treatment, the only difference being perhaps more sand in the compost, so that greater porosity may be maintained, as some of them have to be potted firmer than the ordinary zonals on account of their running too gross if potted loosely.

The double varieties require much the same treatment as ordinary scarlets, but they must not have too much room for the roots, or the foliage will be most conspicuous. Too rich a soil should also be avoided. For the use of amateurs the varieties marked with an asterisk are best. Where convenience exists, doubles do best struck from eyes, the same as vines are done, but as a rule there are scarcely any amateurs who can perform this part of a propagator's duties ; and to say the least some skill and much attention must be paid, or failure will be a certain result.

Cape pelargoniums are really fine plants for the decoration of the greenhouse and conservatory, and grown in from 6in. to 8in. pots, form masses of bloom that cannot easily be equalled. The culture is most simple, and as the earliest bloom is that most desired, we give our plan of obtaining it, so that plenty of bloom is to be had from March to May, and, with a little management, even later than that. In the first place we strike cuttings in March or April, and keep the young plants growing on until the middle of September, stopping back, and training into form as occasion may require. The plants at this time will be in 6in. or 8in. pots according to their habits, and of good size, the pots not being over full of roots. Water is gradually diminished after September, until the plants are dormant, and some time in October they are placed on a light airy shelf in a greenhouse where frost is excluded, but where a high temperature is not maintained. About the beginning of February some of the plants are started into growth, and a slightly increased temperature is afforded them, and by the end of the month some are in bloom. The others are not started until the end of February, and they take the season of blooming into May.

Some plants struck in July, and wintered as described above, but re-potted in spring, will take the blooming season on until the end of August, that is if the plants are grown out of doors, or rather in cold frames. These may also be bedded out, but we find they do not answer well in all places. The various kinds have a wide variation in the habit of growth, but although some will reach 4ft. in height, if care is not used, others will not be more than 9in. or 1ft. in height.

For soil we use maiden loam, enriched with a little leaf soil, and thoroughly decomposed manure, and to this is added enough sharp sand to keep the compost well open. The quality of the soil must be varied somewhat, according to the habit of the plant, and a little care must be used as to the amount of water given, so that a too vigorous, or in fact a too rapid and weak growth is not induced.

For sorts select from the following : *Scarlet zonal.*—Lord Derby, Vesuvius, Charley Casbon, Cybister, Stella, Lucius, Julius Cæsar, Dr. Livingstone, Albert Memorial, Caven Fox, Bonfire, John Thorpe. *Plain leaved scarlet.*—Punch, Tom Thumb, Aigburth Beauty, Amethyst, Boadicea, and Kentish Fire. *White flowered.*—Madame Vaucher, Mrs. Sachs, Madame F. Hoch, Purity, and White Swan. *Salmon flowered.*—President Thiers, Polly King, L'Aurore, Seraph, and Mr. Rendatler. *Oculated blooms.*— Alice Spencer, Bride, Madame Werle, and Fairy Ring. *Pink and rose coloured flowers.*—Rose Rendatler, Forget-me-not, Christine, Amaranth, Lady Louisa Egerton, Countess of Rosslyn, Amy Hogg, Violet Hill, Nosegay, Madame Barr, Delight, and Caroline. *Various colours.*— Monster, light scarlet, immense truss ; Purple Prince, bright magenta, shaded dark purple ; Marginata, ground colour, bright pink, with pink edge on a pearly white ground, very fine if slightly shaded from bright sun ; Wellington, dark maroon crimson ; Reine Blanch, white nosegay ; Phœbe, orange cerise. *Ivy leaved section.*—Green foliage : Innocence, pure white, dark maroon stripe on upper petals ; Willsii rosea, rose, very fine ; Elegans, mauve ; Peltatum elegans, bright mauve ; Alice Lee, violet crimson ; Favonier, dark purple carmine. Variegated foliage : Duke of Edinburgh and L'Elegante are the two best. *Scented foliage.*—Grandis odorata, sweet scented, like the oak-leaved variety ; Crispum, citron scented ; Filicifolia odorata, fern leaved ; Lothario, and Capitatum. These are all useful, and are scented to a greater or less extent, but it is not possible to describe the scent of either so as to be generally understood. *Double flowered.* — Scarlet : *Victor Lemoine, Goliath, *Wilhelm, Pfitzer, *double Tom Thumb, and Jewel. Rose coloured : *Marie Lemoine, Crown Prince, Madame Lemoine, and *Spark Hill Beauty. Of whites we will not mention any, for all we have seen have been white in name only, the greater part of the blooms appearing as if they had been in a plentiful shower of brick dust, as far as colour went. No doubt good whites will ultimately be brought out, but for these we must wait.

Tricolors. — Golden : Gem of Tricolors, Sunset, Mrs. Pollock, Sophia Dumaresque, Louisa Smith, Macbeth, Lucy Grieve, Lady Cullum, Sophia Cusack, Edwina Fitzpatrick, Achievement (Stevens's), Mrs. Dunnett, The Moonstone (Aldred's), Prince of Wales, Miss Goring, and Mr. Rutter. Silver : Lass o' Gowrie, Mrs. Col. Wilkinson, Mabel Morris, Charming Bride, Prince Silverwings, Velvet Cushion, Italie Unita, Silver Star, Enchantress, Mysterious Night, Lady Dorothy Neville, and Princess Beatrice. *Bicolors* (not bronze).—Yellow and green : Doctor Primrose, Golden Chain, Golden Fleece, Pillar of Gold, and Crystal Palace Gem. White and green : Castlemilk, Miss Kingsbury, Snowdrop, Daybreak, Flower of Spring, Bijou, and Mangle's Variegated. Plain yellow-leaved varieties : Robert Fish, Creed's Seedling, Yellow Christine, Yellow Boy, and Golden Beauty. *Golden bronze.*—Rev. C. P. Peach, Black Douglas, Earl of Rosslyn, Mrs. John Lee, Princess of Wales, Black Knight, Fairy Ring, Southern Belle, Harold, Crown Prince, Sybil, Rev. Mr. Radclyffe, Beauty, E. G. Henderson, Bronze Queen, Golden Banner, Crimson-crowned Canary, and Champion. *Cape Pelargoniums.*—Admiration, Black Prince, Brilliant, Brigantine, Chas. Turner, Duke of Edinburgh, Envoy, Heroine, Joan of Arc, Maid of Honour, Mr. Rassam, Pollie, Ajax, Danaë, Hector, Midas, Rameau, Yvonne, East Lynn, Formosa, Leotard, Marmion, Princess Teck, Queen Victoria, and various others.

A full list of pelargoniums, with descriptions, would occupy a large volume, so we only give a selection of those we know to be good. Pelargoniums have been greatly overdone, and although they are *the* plants for amateurs, the varieties are so many and the forms of colouring, &c., so various, that we should most decidedly advise intending purchasers to trust to no list, but to see the plants when they are in the best form, and then to purchase only what suits their fancy.

Petunias.—These are old-fashioned plants of much beauty, and at the same time very easily grown ; given the same treatment as the verbena, they form magnificent plants ; and as they are not easily approached in colour by other plants, they are really necessary in a well kept conservatory. The double kinds are really fine if well grown, and the single varieties are also very useful for basket and vasedecoration. Seeds raised and treated as half hardy annuals also give great satisfaction out of doors, as the flowers being from one to two inches in diameter, and of various bright shades of colour, from pale rose to dark purple, produce an effect not always to be obtained with other plants, especially as they bloom very profusely from July until frost destroys them.

Six good doubles are, Bonnie Dundee, purple, deeply margined with white ; MacMahon, white-veined pink ; Snowball, pure white ; Lorraine, dark purple crimson ; Marie Van Houtte, deep purple ; King of Crimsons, rich purplish crimson. Six good singles are, Spitfire, intense dark purple ; Single Beauty, lavender, dark purple centre and rays ; Othello, deep purple crimson, veined black ; Perdita, bright crimson, shaded light, with white rays ; Etoile du Nord, white, mottled with crimson and light purple ; Maggie Cochrane, purplish crimson, mottled with rosy white. Seeds saved from these singles produce very useful border plants, and, at times, a plant or two worth saving. For cultural directions see "Verbena."

Primula.—The double and single varieties of *P. Sinensis* are very useful for decorative purposes in the winter and spring months, and as they are of comparatively easy culture they do—or rather should—form a very large part of the soft-wooded plants in bloom from October to February. During the dull months of the year it often happens that ordinary geraniums and other miscellaneous plants are very chary of blooming, and then it is very handy to have plants that will bloom at that season. Doubles are far more trouble to grow than single varieties, and the treatment is different ; but the singles are as easy to grow as grass, if ordinary care is used. There are also semi-double varieties that are easily raised from seeds, and they are as easy to do as the singles, requiring the same treatment; but, as we said before, doubles proper require quite a distinct treatment.

We will take the singles first. In the first place it is absolutely necessary that the plants should be grown on steadily from the time of sowing until the time of blooming, and during the whole of the time they must not become pot-bound, for if they do they will most assuredly commence blooming prematurely, and the consequence then is that a lot of the energy of the plants is wasted, and unless care is taken the subsequent blooms will be comparatively poor. For this reason it is advisable to make more than one sowing, as by sowing at intervals a better succession is maintained. Besides, by having two or three sowings less risk is run, for if one batch is a whole or partial failure others will not be. And here let us inform our readers that it is useless to purchase cheap seed of primulas, as the great cost and labour involved in saving good seeds, and the comparatively small quantity of seeds produced in the best strains, renders the seed expensive, and a really good article is always worth a good price. The seeds that are usually retailed in sixpennyworths and shillingsworths, are very poor, if they are such as will grow, and the flowers as much resemble a good fimbriated strain as a buttercup resembles a first-class ranunculus. Poor washy things, not so good in form as a common primrose, and of no decided colours, and very weedy withal, are the seeds sold in ordinary retail trade, unless they are in sealed packets. We therefore recommend every one who grows primulas to have the seeds in sealed packets, the lowest retail price of which is half-a-crown ; but it is far preferable to have a 5s. packet of some good and well-known English strain, and if these be obtained of a good house, little fear need be entertained as to quality.

We sow seeds in April, June, and August, sowing the seeds on the surface of rather finely prepared soil, in well-drained pans, and covering the pans with sheets of glass, which are whitewashed on one side to prevent the admission of too much light. These pots or pans are then placed in a pit or frame where a temperature of 60° to 65° is maintained. Here the seeds germinate freely, and as the plants get on towards the third leaf, the whitewash is removed, and air is gradually admitted, but care is taken not to allow the sun to burn the plants, as they recover from such a check to their growth very slowly. Previous to sowing, the pots are well soaked with water, by standing them in a tub with the water reaching up to the rims of the pots only. By this means enough water is absorbed by the soil to render more water unnecessary until the seeds have germinated. As soon as the young plants have their fourth leaf they are potted off into 3in. pots, well drained and with more sand in the compost than mentioned further on. Or if it is considered desirable, the plants are pricked off into pans, about 1in. asunder, there to remain for a fortnight or three weeks. After this transplanting the plants are removed to the pit or frame from which they were taken and kept close for a few days to prevent them receiving a check, and then air is gradually admitted. When the pots in which the plants were potted singly are filled with roots, or when the plants pricked out have attained a fair size, the former are potted on into 5in. pots, and the latter into 3in. pots, and they are then placed in a cold frame, but kept close for a week or ten days to prevent the plants receiving a check. When the plants have filled the pots with roots they are again repotted, the former into their blooming pots, and the latter into 5in. pots, these latter having to be again repotted when the pots are full of roots. The plants are kept in a cold frame until well into October, when they are removed into the greenhouse, where a temperature of 45° or 50° causes them to bloom for a long time. During the whole of their growth the plants are not allowed to become dry at the roots, neither are they allowed to become infested with insects, or failure is sure to result. It is also a matter of much importance that the foliage should be kept as short and healthy as possible, as long spindly leaves cause the blossoms to be hidden in a basin as it were, instead of standing prominently above the foliage as they should do to show to the greatest advantage. To ensure this due attention must be paid to admitting air, &c., and during the hottest part of the season the plants may be with advantage stood in frames facing the north-west, as then the hottest rays of the sun will not reach them. Like most of the primulas, *P. Sinensis* and its varieties suffer much from a hot arid atmosphere, the majority of them requiring a somewhat moist atmosphere while growing. When in the greenhouse during the winter season this must be nearly reversed, as then the fullest light must be afforded, and the house must be dry, or it is not at all an improbable thing that the plants will damp off. Water must, of course, be given as required, but it will be found that less will be necessary than during the growing period.

In potting it is necessary to always supply a good amount of drainage to the pots, and to vary the fineness of the soil according to the size of the pot. Thus, in a small pot the soil should be much finer than in a larger one, and, generally speaking, more sand will be requisite in the earlier stages of growth than later on. On no account should liquid manure be given, or the probable result will be that the plants will rot off at the collars, or a disease (?) will set in and cause failure to a greater or less extent. For compost we use about three parts good fibrous maiden loam, in a good mellow state, and one part cow manure and leaf soil in equal parts, both of which are thoroughly rotten. To this is added enough sharp silver sand to keep the whole open. But in

H

this preparation of compost a little judgment has to be used, as some soils vary in texture to a great extent, and therefore it is necessary to vary the proportions used.

Although it is possible to do so, we do not advise the keeping of primulas of this section more than the one season, as they do not pay for the trouble a second season.

Double primulas of the old variety are very troublesome subjects, and unless proper accommodation for their culture exists, we do not advise their being taken in hand. Of course for market purposes they pay a successful grower, but they do not pay the amateur for his trouble. The way the plants are successfully grown is as follows: The plants are broken up in April or May, and after potting each cutting in a small 60-sized pot, they should be placed in a brisk bottom heat, with a rather moist temperature. When well rooted they should be shifted into 4in. pots, and put back into the place whence they were taken until they are well established. When this is accomplished the plants should be removed into a more airy position, and placed as close to the glass as possible without actually touching it, and a certain amount of air must be given to prevent them becoming too weak and spindly.

In potting, care must be taken that the plants are set sufficiently deep, or they will rot off at the collar. They should be buried to the base of the lower leaves, but not deeper, and if other points are properly carried out, success is almost certain. Water must be carefully and not too abundantly supplied until the roots have taken good hold of the soil, but then the soil must not get dry, although at no time should the soil be soddened. The plants may be potted on until they reach 6in. or 8in. pots, according to their strength, in which sizes they should bloom. It is also advisable to apply a slight shade through the very hottest weather, but this must not be overdone, or a great loss of strength will ensue. During the autumn and winter the plants should stand in a light airy house, somewhat near the glass, and a temperature of about 50 or 55 deg. should be maintained, combined with a medium treatment, not hurrying the plants on or letting them stand still. Stagnant moisture should be carefully avoided, and air should be admitted according to the weather, but in any case a close, heavy, stagnant atmosphere should be avoided, as it tends to render the plants more liable to rot off.

For compost use three parts maiden loam, as recommended before, one part peat, and one or two parts leaf soil, with a liberal allowance of sharp sand. If, as sometimes happens, the loam is rather poor, a little decomposed cow manure may be added; but this is a matter that can only be decided on the spot. Plenty of drainage must be afforded, or the plants are sure to rot off.

Various hardy primulas may be introduced into the greenhouse, but we do not give a list here, as few of them can compete with the P. Sinensis (Chinese primrose), the culture of which we have just described. As a matter of taste many persons might introduce a few, but to fully test the merits of hardy and nearly hardy primulas a house for them alone would be required, and therefore the consideration of the subject would be out of place in this handbook.

Pancratium.—These are handsome bulbous plants that are well worth cultivation, but the majority are really stove plants, and unsuited to the general greenhouse. There are, however, four varieties that are suitable for cultivation in the ordinary greenhouse, and they all produce handsome umbels of superb white blooms. Our favourite is, *P. crassifolium*, which until lately has been somewhat scarce. It is, however, now within the reach of all who have a greenhouse, as the price is only from half a crown to 3s. 6d. each. The pancratiums belong to the Amaryllidaceæ, and require much the same treatment as some of the Amaryllises, but we give the treatment we have found successful. *P. speciosum* requires more heat than the others, and produces its blooms in the end of the year, while the others bloom later in the season.

We have found the handsome white blooms of very great use for the decoration of vases, baskets, and in some cases hair decoration; but they are more useful for the former purpose. Like many of the amaryllids they are extremely useful, as they stand well for some days after cutting, and if a good selection of other flowers is mixed with them, the effect is both elegant and grand, that is if grandeur can be associated with cut flowers. The description of some of the amaryllids suits the pancratiums, so we need say nothing further on this point.

The way we treat them is as follows: About six or eight weeks after blooming the plants are repotted into pots of a size suitable to the size of the bulbs, in a compost of two parts good sandy loam and one part thoroughly decayed leaf soil, to which sand has been added in sufficient quantities to keep the compost open. Good drainage is afforded, so that when necessary plenty of water can be given without waterlogging the soil. This is an important point with all bulbous rooted plants, as if the soil is waterlogged they sooner or later decay, and consequently are lost. After potting the plants are kept watered according to their requirements, and are placed in a light position, and from the end of June until well into September are kept in a frame or pit with other greenhouse plants, and when brought indoors, placed in a light position where they will bloom in their season. After blooming the supply of water is diminished to ripen the bulbs off somewhat before repotting. In potting only such roots as are dead should be removed, and all young bulbs should be removed, and carefully potted either singly or three or four in a pot, according to their strength. These young bulbs, if carefully grown on, will in the course of two or three years make good blooming plants, and although at times they do not appear in large quantities, still, generally speaking, a couple of bulbs of each variety to start with will make a good stock in a few years, and superfluous bulbs are, as a rule, always saleable.

Pancratiums may also be treated in the same manner as evergreen amaryllises, and, as a rule, they do well so treated.

The sorts for the purpose named above are *P. crassifolium*, *P. speciosum* *P. maritimum*, and *P. Illyricum*, the two latter not requiring so much heat as the former. In fact, in some places they are hardy, but in the majority of cases they do best as cool greenhouse bulbs. They are all white.

Pachyphytum.—This is a succulent plant much used for bedding, and, although we do not intend giving cultural directions for all the succulents here, yet as one or two may be found useful about the house, we select some of them as we proceed. The pachyphytum is really a gem amongst succulents, and it is well worth a place in the greenhouse. The plants, being small, are admirably adapted to stand on the edges of stages, where they are brought conspicuously before the eye, but if grown for bedding purposes it will be found necessary to have a large variety, for although the plant in question is of much beauty, with its rich creamy colour and compact habit, still it is not effective by itself. A good sandy loam, or, rather, a very sandy loam, suits it as well as anything, if plenty of drainage is provided, and the plants can stand the hottest weather without losing their beauty. Like most of the succulents, they will also bear a lot of drought, but, except in winter, it is best to allow a fair amount of moisture when they are kept solely as greenhouse plants. During winter, however, they do not require water often, as too much water causes the foliage to rot off. The propagation is also very simple; by taking off the leaves, with just a small shred of the bark attached, and after laying them in the sun for a day or two to dry, placing them round the edge of propagating pans or, in fact, all over the surface, and nearly withholding water, young plants will be formed at the base of each leaf, and when these young plants are large enough to handle they can be potted off, and with a little care will do well. The tops may also be taken off in autumn and inserted singly in small pots. These, if placed on a dry shelf near the glass in a warm greenhouse, will root freely if not watered to cause them to rot off, and in spring they will be fine plants. The old stumps will break during the winter, and the offsets thus obtained will make small though useful stuff by May.

P. bracteosum is the sort we have referred to above. If seeds can be obtained fine stocks of plants can be raised from them, but seed is very scarce, and, as in the majority of cases, the plants do not bloom, there is a great difficulty in obtaining seed at all.

Pyrethrum Aureum.—See "Annuals."

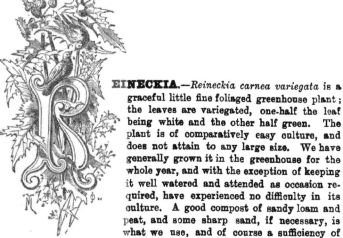

REINECKIA.—*Reineckia carnea variegata* is a graceful little fine foliaged greenhouse plant; the leaves are variegated, one-half the leaf being white and the other half green. The plant is of comparatively easy culture, and does not attain to any large size. We have generally grown it in the greenhouse for the whole year, and with the exception of keeping it well watered and attended as occasion required, have experienced no difficulty in its culture. A good compost of sandy loam and peat, and some sharp sand, if necessary, is what we use, and of course a sufficiency of drainage is requisite. The plant is easily propagated by means of cuttings inserted in very sandy compost, and placed in a gentle bottom heat. When rooted the cuttings are potted off singly into small pots, and returned to the frame until the roots have taken possession of the soil, and then they can be hardened off somewhat, and placed in the greenhouse. During winter the plant can be kept growing, and presents a pretty appearance. If in a cool house it must be treated as a perennial of doubtful hardiness, as it is hardy only in some parts of the United Kingdom. For general work it can well be done in the manner described, and doubtful as it may appear to many, appears to thrive with the treatment given.

Richardia.—See "Calla."

Rochea.—*R. falcata* is a nice, highly ornamental succulent, producing large heads of scarlet flowers, which contrast well with the fresh green colour of ferns, &c. As the plants can be had well in bloom in August, they are very useful, and if kept dwarf, can be placed almost anywhere in decorating. It is this dwarfness that renders them so useful, and therefore it is necessary to use all possible means to obtain it. It is best done by keeping the plants near the glass during their growth, and this alone will cause them to be dwarf. We have generally given the plants the same treatment as kalosanthes, and we have found it to answer very fairly, so we must refer our readers to that head for the cultural directions. *Rochea falcata* is also very useful for window garden culture, and, therefore, young plants are generally much valued.

The mode of propagation is very easy, and in no essential point varies

from that of pachyphytum. Of course, it is really necessary only that
mature leaves are used for the purpose, and that they are perfect. The
young plants should be placed as near the glass as possible after potting,
and at all times care should be taken that they do not draw up too high,
or all their beauty will be lost. With all succulents of this nature it is
desirable to maintain the plants as dwarf as possible consistent with their
habit, as bare stems are not beautiful.

ALVIA.—These are plants which, from their
beauty and easy culture, are well suited to
the wants of the amateur, and as most of
them are grown as easily as a chrysanthemum
there is no excuse for not cultivating them.
Some of the colours are very bright and attractive, and the scarlet *S. coccinea* and blue
S. patens are very fine if grown well. Indeed,
we believe that there is no blue flower to
excel *S. patens* for either purity or brightness. *S. Roemeriana* is also a nice dwarf crimson
variety, rarely exceeding 6in. in height, and
when well bloomed the plants are very pretty.
Salvias can be raised from seeds very easily, but,
when a good variety is at hand, it is the more
politic course to propagate by cuttings, as then
the plants are certain to bloom as well as the parent; whereas, with seedlings
this cannot certainly be depended on, as in nearly all cases some variation
from the parent plant ensues, and although this may be of some advantage
in perhaps a few plants, it is, generally a disadvantage, as some trifling
defect, such as taller growth, duller colour, or perhaps not quite so floriferous a habit, will quite spoil the effectiveness of a lot of seedlings.

For decorative purposes salvias come in very useful, as their cut blooms
can be worked in for many purposes, and the plants when well grown in
pots are very effective for table and room decoration, but more particularly
the latter. As bedding plants, too, they are very useful if the soil is of
the right sort, but in some soils the foliage will be more conspicuous than
the flowers, and this is not a very desirable state of things in bedding
plants.

The propagation by seeds is a very simple affair, so long as the seeds are
good; but if too old very few will germinate, and the result will be a comparative failure. In fact we have more than once received disappointment
from this cause, and should therefore advise readers to save their own

seed, or to purchase only of good firms. We have always found it the easiest plan, when raising plants from seeds, to sow them on sandy soil in well drained pots, and to place these pots in a gentle bottom heat, keeping the soil uniformly moist, but not soddened with wet. As soon as the plants are in rough leaf they should be potted off into small pots, and returned to the bed, and as soon as the roots have taken possession of the soil, the plants should be gradually hardened off, and afterwards treated as rooted cuttings.

Cuttings should be made in March, and inserted in pots of sandy soil, having plenty of drainage; these pots should then be placed in a gentle bottom heat, and if the ordinary rules for striking cuttings of this class be carefully attended to, they will nearly all do well. Of course it is only reasonable to expect a certain amount of loss; this with us is only about 5 per cent., but, where persons are not used to the work, a larger per-centage may reasonably be expected. When the cuttings are rooted they should be potted off into small pots, in a light sandy loam, and when the plants are established in their new quarters they should have treatment suited to their requirements. We do not hold with striking cuttings late in the season for winter work, but for that purpose have treated the plants as described further on.

Plants for bedding purposes should be got into 48-sized pots as soon as the roots kiss the sides of the small ones, and we have found that the compost used should be a rich sandy loam, to which has been added some leaf soil or thoroughly decayed manure. They should be kept in a genial growing atmosphere, and such an amount of water applied as would be found necessary for their steady growth. Such plants as are inclined to run up too spindly should be stopped, to induce them to break freely and form bushy plants, as these are most useful for bedding purposes. They should be gradually hardened off somewhat before planting, which should be done at the usual time.

Such plants as are to remain in pots for the season, should be placed in a cold frame in May, and as soon as necessary repotted into six or eight inch pots, and keep close for a day or two. Care must be paid to stopping and training, so as to cause the plants to assume a nice pyramidal form, and also to prevent the blooming, and the best plan to prevent this is not to allow the plants to become potbound or dry at the roots. About August the plants should be repotted into eight or ten inch pots, as may be necessary, and pinching the points of the shoots must still be adhered to to prevent the formation of bloom, but about the third week in the month this should be discontinued, or the object of obtaining bloom during the winter will be frustrated. About the middle of September the bloom buds will commence appearing, that is, if the plants are sufficiently potbound, and then it is advisable that liquid manure—preferably sulphate of ammonia—should be given once a week. About the end of September the plants should be removed to their winter quarters in a light airy greenhouse, where a temperature of about 45° can be maintained, and by watering with liquid manure from once to three or four times a week according to the season, large quantities of bloom will be obtained. In doing plants in pots, it is necessary to plunge them in a bed of ashes out-doors, from the end of June to the end of August, and it is needless to add that it is necessary to supply water in abundance during the hot weather. Frequent syringings will also be found necessary to keep down red spider, and the foliage must be wetted underneath as well as on the top. Although the foregoing is a good plan, we do not think that the plants do so well as when treated as described below.

Good thrifty plants should be chosen about the first week of June, and these should be planted out 3ft. or 4ft. asunder in rich soil in the kitchen garden, and care must be taken to get them in good form by pinching and training, as described above. A pyramidal form is the best, as it causes a greater display of bloom, and as a rule exposes the whole surface of the plant to light, a matter of much importance to plants of this description which are required to bloom in winter. During the season, the soil should be often cut down at a distance of about 8in. from the stem of the plant to sever the roots, and so cause the production of a ball of fibrous roots, a point of the greatest importance. Plenty of water is necessary during the hot weather, and syringing must not be forgotten, or in sandy poor soil red spider will be very abundant. The last pinching should be given about the first week in August, and early in September the plants should be carefully taken up and placed in well-drained pots, boxes, or tubs, so that the roots are disturbed or reduced as little as possible. The interstices should be firmly filled in with good sandy soil, and the plants well watered to settle the roots. They should then be placed in a frame and kept close for a few days, and then removed to the house where they are to bloom. Old plants from the beds, if showing plenty of unexpanded buds, can also be treated in the same way. Old plants should be cut down, potted, and wintered in a shed, or any place where frost cannot reach, and if started in the greenhouse in February will afford plenty of cuttings. When they break again they can be divided, and then make good border plants.

For sorts, S. patens, blue; S. coccinea, scarlet; S. c. pumila, scarlet; S. splendens, scarlet; S. Boliviensis verticulata, scarlet; and S. Heerii, scarlet, are the sorts best suited for house decoration in winter; and S. bicolor, blue and white; S. Rœmeriana, scarlet; and S. fulgens, dull scarlet, for bedding purposes; but, at the same time, some of the hardy kinds are very useful. In growing salvias it is necessary to give a good soil, liberal treatment, and bloom them in an airy house.

Sarracenia.—Amongst the so called carnivorous plants, the sarraceniæ hold a prominent position, and as some of them are of easy culture, we give them a place. One or two plants are very good in the greenhouse, as their presence tends to increase the interest in the place. As with a good many other things, it is, however, possible to have too many of them, and there-fore it is as well to restrict the number to a few only, unless indeed they are grown to give away. Most growers give too much heat, for from plants we have seen, and have grown in the following manner, we rather incline to a cool treatment. We have found a temperature of 40° to 45° through the winter, rising to about 70° in summer, to be quite enough to produce fine plants. S. purpurea is quite hardy; in fact we might truthfully say that it is one of the hardiest exotic plants we have, standing in a cold exposed wet bog all the year through, and luxuriating in a position which would kill hundreds of our native plants. Of course *S. purpurea* must be omitted from the following cultural remarks.

The best compost is the following : good fibrous peat, from which the soil has been taken, and chopped sphagnum in about equal parts. To this should be added a fair amount of crocks and charcoal, broken fairly small, and a liberal sprinkling of sand. In potting use either Matthews' orchid pots or pots about half filled with crocks, so that plenty of drainage may be afforded, as these plants require large quantities of water to grow them well. With the exception of *S. Drummondii alba* and *S. D. rubra*, which should be re-potted in July, all the plants should be re-potted in February, carefully removing all the old soil. Pot moderately firm in such a manner that the creeping growths are just above the compost. Water must be applied daily as the plants come into full growth, sufficient to soak the soil being given at each watering. The plants should be stood on a shelf near the glass on the south side of the house, and the shelf should be covered with about an inch of charcoal or other absorbent substance. This layer should be soaked with water once or twice a day to maintain a somewhat humid atmosphere around the plants, as it is not advisable to syringe them. As the growth is ripening, less water should be given ; and, during the time they are at rest, water applied twice a week is ample. *S. purpurea* can be successfully grown in a cool house, or in a house not heated, but where frost is excluded ; and the same general treatment except temperature, may be given as for the others. The plants of this variety can also be syringed with advantage; in fact, it is almost an aquatic.

Scale is the chief insect enemy that affects *sarracenias*, and great care must be taken that they are destroyed as soon as they appear, or most disastrous results are almost sure to follow. A sharp watch must also be kept for thrips and other insects, thrips in particular, as they also do much harm.

S. Drummondii alba, white ; *S. Drummondii rubra*, red ; *S. psittacina*, pinkish lilac ; and *S. purpurea*, purple, are all good and interesting, and are, perhaps, as easy to grow as any. For the amateur, these plants are well suited, as they are both curious and beautiful.

Solanum.—The hybrids of these are very interesting, and as they are best treated as soft wooded plants, or at least like seedling stocks, we give our method of treatment. About June we sow seeds in sandy soil, placing the pans in a cold frame. The seeds are sown thinly and evenly over the surface of the soil, and the pans are well drained, as the seed is often a long time in germinating, and consequently it is necessary to prevent the soil becoming water-logged, and thus destroying the seeds. As soon as the plants are in rough leaf we pot them off into thumbs, and as soon as the roots kiss the sides we shift into large 60's, where they stand the winter. For soil we use two parts loam, one part leaf soil, and one part rotten cow manure and sharp sand, mixed.

he plants are taken in in the early part of the winter, and placed on a shelf near the glass, not giving more water than is really necessary, but keeping them dormant. In spring, when they break, they are cut back closely, so as to make good plants, and in May they are put out into a rich open spot in the kitchen garden. Plenty of water is afforded if necessary, and the plants are pinched back in June and July, so as to cause them to make a good bushy growth. When the berries begin to colour, or about September, the plants are taken up, without injuring the roots, and placed in pots of sufficient size to hold them properly. They are then well watered, and kept close for a few days in a shaded—but not dark—frame, and thence are removed to the greenhouse, where they are very ornamental until growth recommences. Such is about the easiest mode of culture, and anyone having a house from which the frost is just excluded can grow them well.

Another plan is to put in cuttings in April or May on a slight bottom heat, and as soon as rooted to transfer them to 3in. pots. So soon as the roots kiss the sides the plants should be shifted into 6in. pots, where they are to fruit. They should remain in frames at a temperature of about 60°, and should not want for water. In June the plants should be pinched back, so that they shall be of good shape, and if required a little training may be afforded; but it is advisable to dispense with sticks and ties as much as possible, as the plants look far better if grown in a natural manner. During the blooming period plenty of air should be admitted, and every means should be taken to prevent a check. As soon as the berries are a good size some of the plants should be taken indoors, and about September the whole of the stock should be housed, when, if properly cared for and in a light sunny place, they will ripen and retain their berries for a long time.

The soil we use is good sandy loam, to which some thoroughly rotted manure has been added, together with sufficient sharp sand to ensure porosity. Good drainage is of course necessary, but these plants do not require so much as some others.

Fumigation will often be necessary to keep down fly, and outdoor plants must be syringed with some insecticide once or twice in the season.

The sorts we prefer are *S. capsicastrum* or *cerasiformis*, *S. c. variegatum*, Wetherill's hybrids, and Henderson's conical fruited solanum, all of which are really good and useful. We may add that in some parts of the country these solanums are hardy, or require only slight protection in winter, and they have a very cheerful appearance until the berries fall.

Spiræa Japonica.—This is one of those plants which, although hardy, or nearly so, yet requires special treatment if grown indoors. Its great beauty and decorative value renders it almost a necessity where plants are required for table or window decoration, and therefore we give it a place here rather than among hardy plants. The light feathery spray of which the truss, or rather spike of blooms is composed, is also very useful for mixing in bouquets, for buttonhole bouquets, and for the decoration of vases and epergnes. The entire plant, when well furnished with bloom, forms a magnificent object for the dinner table, or for a specimen for a solitary stand, while amongst other plants the pearly whiteness of the blooms and the fresh green foliage contrast well with darker and more gorgeous neighbours.

The culture is, comparatively speaking, easy, and, unless it is desired to have the plants in bloom very early, forcing need not be resorted to. The way we bloom the imported clumps is as follows: As soon as ripe clumps can be got, they are potted into five and six inch pots, while any that are extra large, and that have the largest number of blooming crowns, are potted off into seven or eight inch pots, according as they promise to cover them with foliage. A good depth of drainage is allowed, from one to three inches, according to the size of the pots. The clumps are potted fairly firm in a compost of fibrous loam two parts, leaf soil one part, and thoroughly decayed manure one part, with a sufficient quantity of sharp silver sand to keep the whole thoroughly permeable to water, as large supplies of water are necessary during growth. As soon as potted, the plants should be put in a cold frame, and about the end of November they should be placed in a house at a temperature of 45°. They should be well watered, and as soon as growth commences stood near the glass, and water given as required. Plenty of light must be afforded, and care must be taken to keep down insects. A temperature of about 50° may be maintained when the plants are in full foliage, and in this they will bloom. Other batches should be brought in at intervals of three weeks or a month until the end of March, and after that they can be bloomed in a frame.

When the plants have ceased blooming, they should still be attended to with water, &c., and in April they should be carefully planted out on a rich border facing the south, well watering them to settle the soil around the roots, and in dry weather applying liberal supplies of liquid manure and water. About the end of August watering should be gradually discontinued, and when the plants have thoroughly ripened off in a natural manner, they should be taken up and potted as we have described.

Where only a cold house exists, the plants should be kept in a cold frame until February, and then they can be brought into the house. With care in watering, &c., such as the natural wants of the *spiræa* require, very good results can be obtained, although the bloom will be late. We have, however, had the blooms finer in a cold house than where they have been forced; but, of course, the clumps used were really good.

As a matter of fact, there is no more trouble in growing *spiræas* than in blooming a hyacinth; and, indeed, we would rather grow *spiræas* than geraniums, although the former are now far from profitable in a marketable point of view. Several of the hardy *spiræas* bloom very well in a cold house or frame; but they are not, as a rule, desirable plants in a house, as thrips and greenfly are so very partial to them.

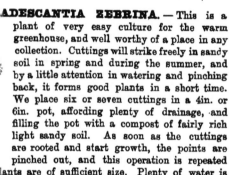

RADESCANTIA ZEBRINA. — This is a plant of very easy culture for the warm greenhouse, and well worthy of a place in any collection. Cuttings will strike freely in sandy soil in spring and during the summer, and by a little attention in watering and pinching back, it forms good plants in a short time. We place six or seven cuttings in a 4in. or 6in. pot, affording plenty of drainage, and filling the pot with a compost of fairly rich light sandy soil. As soon as the cuttings are rooted and start growth, the points are pinched out, and this operation is repeated until the plants are of sufficient size. Plenty of water is necessary. A few plants are always useful, as they form one of the gems of the house.

Tropæolum.—Among these will be found very useful plants, useful either as climbers—or more correctly, trailers—and dwarfs, very useful indeed both for in and outdoor use. For spring blooming they are unrivalled, and if sufficient heat is obtainable, combined with a light position, the culture is of the simplest, and even if there is not sufficient means at hand for early work, still a good display can be made both in and outdoors. Although the blooms are like the ordinary nasturtium, the plants are vastly different from them, both in habit and profuseness of bloom, and a few plants are very useful in every house. Vases and hanging baskets can be embellished with them most advantageously, and in the season they can be used most successfully outdoors for the same purpose. They stand heat well, provided it is not of too arid a nature, and with a little care they always look handsome.

In the first place they are propagated from cuttings, and this is the most difficult part of their culture. For winter blooming the cuttings should be struck in the early part of July, selecting healthy cuttings, and having them about an inch to two inches long. These cuttings should be placed singly in small pots of well-drained very sandy soil, and then placed in bottom heat to strike. As soon as the roots kiss the sides of the pots the plants should be hardened off somewhat, and then shifted into 6in. pots, and when these pots are fairly filled with roots the plants should be removed into nine or ten inch pots, in which they will stand through the winter. Until the end of September the ordinary cool house will be all that is necessary, but after that date a temperature of from 50° to 55° must be kept up, and even if it rises as high as 60° no harm e done. The plants should be stopped when about three feet high, and again when about double the height, and after the final potting they should be trained over the roof or from pillar to pillar in the house, allowing the shoots to hang somewhat loosely, as more bloom is obtained thus than if the plants are trained too strictly. Thorough drainage is necessary, and about three inches of crocks should be given to the 9in. pots, as it is necessary to give liberal, although not too abundant, supplies of water throughout the season. Plants for summer decoration should be struck in early spring, and then will come in most usefully for the various purposes for which they are generally employed.

The best soil is a compost of good turfy loam, free from grubs and wire worm, to which is added about one-third part of leaf soil and sharp sand, and, in fact, this is the best soil for all the tropæolums.

Among the sorts useful for cut blooms in the above section, and which are also very ornamental as plants, are, *T. Cooperi* scarlet; *T. Lobbii*, orange scarlet; and Boule de feu, which is one of the best scarlets we have. In fact, with the above three, anyone might well be content.

Dwarf plants require much the same treatment if to bloom in winter, but for outdoor work they should be struck in spring, and the following are good plants for the purpose: Yellow Dwarf, fine yellow; Lustrous, bright crimson; The Moor, dark maroon; Minnie Warren, richly variegated foliage, the variegation being pale cream; *T. compactum coccineum*, rich orange scarlet. The following trailing kinds are also very useful for bedding purposes and for house decoration, if treated as recommended above: Attraction, citron yellow, blotched on each lobe with bright scarlet; Mrs. Tredwell, very fine brilliant red; Perfection (Dean), brilliant scarlet; and Coronet, yellow.

T. tricolorum is one of the prettiest of the species, and is of very easy culture. It is a tuberous-rooted variety, having roots somewhat resembling potatoes, and bears a profusion of rich orange-scarlet flowers, which contrast extremely well with the fine green foliage. About November a compost of sandy turfy loam and peat should be prepared, and to this should be added a little sharp sand. The pots must also be well drained, and this drainage should be covered with a little moss or fibrous turf, to prevent the soil washing down amongst the drainage and so choking it. The tubers should be planted in 9in. pots, and if they are small several can occupy each pot; but if large, from one to three are sufficient. Place in a position in the greenhouse where they will not be disturbed, and the only care necessary will be to prevent them becoming dust dry. About April the young shoots will appear, and then more water may be given, increasing the supplies as the plants grow. A bundle of birch twigs inserted around the edge of the pot, or a young fir tree clear of its leaves, forms an excellent support for the foliage, and the only care necessary in training the plants is to see that they do not run into knots, but that each shoot travels fairly. About midsummer the foliage will begin to fade, and water must be gradually discontinued until the plants ripen, when the foliage should be removed, and the pots laid on their sides in a cool place until the next potting time.

There are several other varieties of tropæolum, but these we omit, as the preceding are sufficient for our present purpose.

ALLOTTA.—See " Amaryllis."

Verbena.—These are very useful for many purposes, both for bedding out and as pot plants, and it is doubtful if there are any other plants which will fulfil the same purposes. For ordinary border purposes those raised from seed are as good as any; but for pot culture they are not of much use, unless, indeed, an extraordinarily good strain is obtained. The raising of verbenas from seeds is a very easy matter—in fact, as easy as raising any half hardy annual; but, as we said before, they will not do for pot work if raised in this manner.

To obtain plants from seeds, the seeds should be sown in pots of fairly rich sandy soil, and but slightly covered with soil. As soon as large enough, the plants should be shifted into small 60-sized pots, in which they can remain until planting time, if necessary; but, where time and space allow, they can be transferred to 3in. pots with advantage, and, with once pinching, will make good useful plants for bedding. It is, of course, quite possible that something good may be obtained by this method, although the probability is but small; but, if a good plant is obtained, of course it should be saved and propagated.

In raising verbenas from cuttings, no trouble need be experienced; but, as it is necessary to have good plants from which to take the cuttings, we will give the culture from the commencement. In August a few cuttings should be struck, and planted on a border facing the south; and at the end of September these should be carefully taken up and potted. About the second week in October the plants should be stored away in a dry pit or frame from which frost is excluded, and care should be taken that they are kept dormant, and as dry as can be allowed consistently with keeping them alive. If mildew should appear, then they should be liberally dusted over with flowers of sulphur; but, if care is taken, this will not be necessary. About February these old plants should be placed in heat to afford cuttings, and as soon as these are formed they should be taken off and inserted thickly in well-drained pans of very sandy soil, which should be kept rather moist, and in a brisk bottom heat.

Another good plan to strike soft-wooded cuttings of this description is to half fill some pots with fine crocks, and on these place a thin layer of fibrous material to prevent the soil washing down amongst the drainage. Then fill the pots to within an inch of the top with rich sandy soil, and on this place half an inch of clean washed sharp silver sand. The pots should then be well watered through a fine-rosed watering can, and as soon as the superfluous water has drained off the cuttings should be inserted, just sprinkling them with water to fix them in position. The pots should then be stood in a brisk bottom heat, and in a fortnight they will be ready to pot off.

In potting, a soil composed of three parts rich fibrous maiden loam, one part leaf soil, and one part rotten cow manure and sharp sand, should be used, and the soil should be in good working order. Pot moderately firm, and replace the plants in heat for a fortnight, when they may be gradually hardened off; and should there be time they may be transferred to 3in. pots as soon as the roots kiss the sides. If the plants are for pot work they should be put into 3in. pots when well rooted, choosing only the strongest plants for the purpose. These should be treated as above until slightly hardened, and should then be transferred to a position near the glass in a light airy greenhouse. As soon as the pots are fairly filled with roots the plants should be transferred to 6in. pots, well drained and clean, and the shoots should be neatly staked out. The shoots should be five or six in number, unless cut bloom for exhibition is required, and then three will be plenty. As the pots become filled with roots, weak liquid manure should be applied about twice a week, but in no case should sulphate of ammonia be used, or the foliage will suffer. When the trusses show colour the plants should be removed to a cooler position, as they will then last for a long while, more especially if a little shade from bright hot sun is given. A dry (but not arid) atmosphere should also be maintained. These pot plants come in excellently well for table decoration, and, in fact, are as useful as any dwarf flowering plant grown.

Should fly or spider put in an appearance—and the latter will not come if the plants are properly grown—fumigation should at once be resorted to. Generally about three fumigations are required during the season. Mildew, if it does appear, should be kept under by dredgings of flowers of sulphur.

V. venosa, which is hardy on most fairly light soils, should be raised from either seeds or cuttings, but preferably from seed.

The following are good bedding varieties : Crimson King, dense brilliant crimson; Snowflake, pure white; Purple King, purple; Lord Raglan, magenta, scarlet; Scarlet Defiance, scarlet; Géant des Batailles, lurid crimson, maroon eye; Firefly, pink, crimson eye; La Grande Boule de Neige, fine white; Ladybird, flesh, purple eye; Jupiter, rich plum; Rev. S. R. Hole, pale lilac, tinted crimson. For pots the following are good, but to secure good plants for exhibition it is necessary to select from a good stock when in bloom, as fresh varieties are continually being added : Apollo, blush; King of Lilacs, lavender blue; Géant des Batailles; Foxhunter, scarlet, white eye; Rev. S. R. Hole; Princess of Wales, pink and white striped; Prince of Wales, scarlet; Richard Dean, purple, fine white eye; Thomas Harris, mulberry, white eye; Carnation, white and crimson striped; Bismark, dark maroon, white eye; Blue Boy, blue; Anatole Leovy, dark purple, shaded maroon, white eye; and Basilisk, scarlet.

VI.—COOL HOUSE PLANTS.

E now come to those plants which are quite hardy, but which are much used for indoor culture. Amongst them are many gems, and, with the exception of a few previously noticed, they can be used almost exclusively for the decoration of the cold greenhouse. We do not give too extended a list, as the plants can be added to from time to time, but we give some of the best and most easily cultivated, as these are the most acceptable to the amateur.

In growing these plants in a cold house, all that is necessary is to see that the natural state of growth is followed as closely as possible, and that the roots do not get frozen in winter or scorched up in summer. To this end it is advisable to plunge the pots in beds of cocoa fibre refuse, as this is—if kept moderately dry—a good non-conductor of cold, and being very absorbent, it answers admirably in summer to prevent scorching. In fact, it is a most useful article to have about the place, as it is serviceable for many purposes. In growing hardy plants indoors, great care must be taken to keep them clear from insects, as of these they generally have a good stock, the increased tenderness of the plants rendering them peculiarly liable to the attacks of insects of all kinds; but, if only ordinary care is used, this evil is easily kept in check, and only to the careless or lazy cultivator will insects be any real trouble.

Care will also be necessary in growing the plants, as they will be forwarded into bloom a long while before their natural season, so that it is necessary to adapt as it were the temperature of the house to the season, and also to the class of plants grown. If too high a temperature is kept up, then green fly will be more remarkable than the bloom. The same may also be said if alternate extremes of heat and cold are maintained. The chief point is to keep an equable temperature consistent with the season and the state of the plants, and to regulate the fire heat in such manner as to co-operate with the sun heat, and not to clash with it. With this class of plants it is also very necessary to admit a free circulation of air at all times, except when heavy fogs or frost may occur, and even then sufficient ventilation must be given to prevent the air becoming stagnant. Water must be supplied as the requirements of the trees or shrubs render necessary, and whether this is necessary must be left for the cultivator to decide, as no hard and fast rule can be made: but the supply of water must be regulated by the temperature and atmospheric moisture of the house, and by the amount of foliage which the plants possess, as the amount of leaf surface has much to do with the water required, the quantity requisite being to a great extent governed by the evaporative powers of the foliage. In all cases it is an absolute necessity that plenty of drainage be afforded, or otherwise the plants will, in the majority of cases, die, as the roots become rotten from their inability to absorb the water, which consequently stagnates around them.

BELIA. — These are very ornamental plants that are well suited for the cold greenhouse, either trained on trellises or grown as pot plants. The plants are very floriferous when well grown, and they are of very easy culture, growing well in a compost of peat and loam in equal parts, to which a sufficient quantity of sharp sand has been added. The care required is not much—simply watering, &c., and, in fact, treating them as hardy plants, being sufficient. Of course they will bloom earlier in the house than out of doors, but forcing is not a desirable point with them. In fact, such treatment as we have recommended to camellias suits these evergreens well.

The better of the two varieties is *A. floribunda*, which bears reddish pink blooms, and is the more floriferous. *A. triflora* does not produce its red flowers as freely as the others, and is not so well suited to house culture, but still at times it is very useful as a change.

Agapanthus.—See "Soft-wooded Plants."

Amygdalus.—Almonds are very pleasing subjects if obtained in a small pyramidal shape, and, from their great beauty when in bloom, they

form most appropriate subjects for the decoration of a medium sized
house. They are, however, not suited to a small place, as the plants,
to bloom well and be effective, should be at least two or three feet
high, and of course wide in proportion. A pot should be chosen that will
hold the roots comfortably, and the tree should be carefully potted,
taking soil that will work freely, and run into the interstices amongst the
roots. After potting, water thoroughly, and place the trees in a cold
vinery or frame for a few weeks, when they can be removed to the place
they are to occupy. We have premised that the tree has been prepared in
the open ground in a nursery, and if such is the case, if there are plenty of
good fibrous roots, there is no reason why the trees should not bloom well
the first year. A temperature of about 50° or 55° is amply sufficient to
bring the plants into bloom, and indeed a higher temperature is apt to
frustrate the object in view. Successional plants can be brought in from
time to time, as the bloom does not last for a long time. After blooming
the plants should be gradually hardened off until about the end of May,
when they should be plunged out of doors for the season. Repotting
should be done as soon as the leaves fall.

The best varieties of Amygdalus for our present purpose are *A. Persica
florepleno*, double pink; *A. P. fl. pl. alba*, double white; *A. P. caryophylloides*, double carnation striped, and *A. P. rubra*, double crimson.

Anthericum.—These are useful for cold houses, and as their culture is
simple and the price moderate they come within the reach of all. For soil
use a compost of fibrous loam and coarse sand, enriched with a little
thoroughly decomposed leaf soil, allowing plenty of drainage to the pots.
The pots should be comparatively large, but if they can be had of a deep
pattern it is far better than of a wide one. The number of roots to
be grown must depend on the size of the pots and on the size of the
specimens required ; but about three make a very good potful. Re-pot as
soon as growth commences, and keep watered as advised for lilies. After
blooming remove the pots to a bed of coal ashes and supply with water
until the plants are ripe. Keep from frost, and introduce to the house as
required. A gentle warmth will hasten the blooms a little, but if forcing
is attempted but little result will be obtained.

A. Liliago (St. Bernard's Lily), white ; *A. Liliastrum* (St. Bruno's Lily),
white ; and *A. graminifolium*, white, are all good, and well repay for the
trouble bestowed on them.

Arum.—Some of these pay well in the cold house, and the treatment
bestowed is so nearly similar to that required for *Calla Æthiopica*, that
a detailed description is not necessary. The roots must not become frozen,
or yet soddened with water during the season of rest, although it is not
advisable that the soil in the pots should become dust dry. During the
season of growth liberal supplies of water must be given, and due care
taken that the plants are not drawn up spindly. The curious spathes are
of various colours, brown, yellow, and white being the chief, and the
plants are certainly a change on the ordinary subjects one so often sees.
A house is not really necessary for the plants, as a cold frame answers as
well.

We have used the following for the present purpose : *A. albispathum* brown; *A. cornutum*, yellow; *A. crinitum*, brown; *A. Italicum*, pale yellow; and *A. maculatum*, white.

Azalea.—The hardy azaleas are very useful for the cool house, and also for those where a little heat can be had, as it readily accommodates itself to various situations, and if gradually brought into a heated structure, will bear a good amount of forcing. Plants should be well established in pots for this purpose, and the general treatment is much the same as for *A. Indica*; that is, so far as the management of the plants go. They should be re-potted annually as soon as the foliage is ripe, and either loam and peat in equal parts, peat, or fibrous loam alone can be used, provided that sufficient sand is mixed with the soil, and a proper drainage is afforded. The plants should be brought into a warm house in successional batches; and the plants for this purpose should be kept in well ventilated cold frames, so that the sudden change shall not bring the buds off. With these, as with all plants, the change from cold to heat should be gradual, or the effects will be most disastrous. In no case will nature perform its functions if excited by fits and starts, or if too sudden changes are indulged in.

The colours are very bright, and range from white through orange to red, and from red to crimson, and while some have blossoms while the stems are quite bare, others have both flowers and foliage together.

The various hybrids, and varieties of *A. mollis, A. Sinensis, A. nudiflora,* and *A. Pontica,* are very useful, and are obtainable at all hard-wood nurseries. It is, however, the best plan to select the plants while in bloom, as the colours or shades of colours are so numerous that no real idea of their appearance can be written. Suffice to say all are good, and reasonable in price.

AMPANULA.—These are best done as described in "Soft-wooded Plants," but in a cold house they will be later in blooming, and consequently will do so in a more natural manner. Pot plants should be plunged in a bed of ashes through the hot weather, but otherwise but little difference is made between these and the plants in the open ground, so far as outdoor culture is concerned. A list of good sorts is given in the previous section. ·

Canna.—The whole of the dwarf cannas are useful for pot work in this section, and they make a good show. The culture has been described in "Soft-wooded Plants," and will not be referred to here. Plenty of water while in growth, destruction of insects, and free admission of air, are the chief points in their culture in the cool house. A list of varieties is given in the section to which we refer.

Cerasus.—The cherries are very useful for house decoration if treated the same as almonds. The double varieties are the best for the purpose, having flowers like large double daisies, either white or pinkish white, according to the nature of the soil. The single varieties are of little use indoors, but are fine outside; but as the bloom is not so persistent as the double kinds, the plants are not so well suited for indoor work. The application of manure of a highly nitrogenous character requently causes the blooms to be suffused with pink to a greater or less degree; but it is better to select plants having this characteristic while they are in bloom, so as to insure—to a certain degree—its repetition. These are amongst the prettiest hardy deciduous hard-wooded subjects that there are.

C. Japonica multiplex, double dwarf pink almond ; *C. J. alba fl. pl.* double dwarf white almond ; *C. serrulata*, double Chinese ; *C. sylvestris fl. pl.*, double French ; and *C. vulgaris fl. pl.*, common double, are about the most useful of all the plants amongst the cherries, and, as we said before, they well repay for any trouble bestowed on getting them forward in the house.

Chimonanthus.—This is a very useful class of plant, of very easy culture, best suited for planting out in the borders of a conservatory. In fact, we have never seen it done well in pots, either in a private garden or nursery, and therefore cannot recommend it for pot work. The plants should be grown in a compost of loam and sand, enriched with leaf soil, and a sufficient root space should be afforded, and they should be trained against a wall, and so arranged that a sufficient space for the full development of the foliage is afforded. The same general treatment as regards watering, ventilation, &c., should be given as to other hardy subjects, and the plants will grow and bloom freely. The flowers are highly fragrant, and although not very ornamental, are yet very useful for various purposes.

The sorts we would recommend are *C. fragrans*, brown, and *C. lutens*, yellow; *C. grandiflorus*, yellow, is also very good.

Chrysanthemum.—See "Soft-wooded Plants."

Convallaria.—See "Lily of the Valley."

Crocus.—This is a class of early blooming bulbous plants that comes in very usefully in either cold or warm greenhouses, and the culture is very simple. Place from three to seven bulbs in a pot, according to the show required, and arrange the colours according to taste. Use a compost of rather rich loam and sand, and allow plenty of drainage, as the plants will require liberal watering while growing. For further treatment see "Hyacinths."

The following are good sorts for pot culture :—Albion, white, striped blue; Alfred Tennyson, dark violet, striped white; Brunel, dark shaded blue; Mammoth, white; Marquis of Lorne, dark purple; Ne Plus Ultra, blue, white margin; Prince of Wales, dark blue, edge white; Purity, pure white; Golden Yellow; Cloth of gold, golden yellow, bronze crimson stripes; and Sir John Franklin, very dark indigo.

Cyclamen.—The hardy cyclamens make very pretty objects in the cold greenhouse, and are of very easy culture, as we have previously explained. The plants do not bloom as early in a cold as in a warm house, but the treatment is practically the same. List and descriptions were given in a previous section.

ACTYLIS GLOMERATA, fol. var.—This is a useful dwarf pot plant. It is perfectly hardy, and must be brought into the house in relays as required. Either a warm or cold house suits it very well for a time, but as the plant will not last for long under glass frequent changes must be made. A compost of sandy loam suits it well, but as plenty of water is required good drainage must be afforded. Some care will be necessary to keep down green fly if the plants are in a warm house, but with this exception but little fear of trouble from insects need be entertained.

Daphne.—For treatment see "Hard-wooded Plants." D. collina, D. dauphina, D. Fioniana, and D. Indica, are the best for cold house culture, and are very sweet scented, thus rendering them very useful for bouquets.

Deutzia.—These are about the hardiest of the dwarf white flowering shrubs, and as they can be bloomed in either a cool or forcing house they are doubly useful. To have them at their best it is, however, advisable to bloom them in a temperature of from 45° to 50°, as then both foliage and flowers are well developed; but at the same time, if only a cold house exists they will do well in such an one. A compost of good sound loam, enriched with about a sixth part of thoroughly decayed cow manure, and rendered sufficiently permeable to water by the addition of coarse sand, suits them well, while the pots, which should not be too large, should be well drained. The plants should be repotted each year after blooming, and plunged in a bed of coal ashes, attention being paid to training and arranging the shoots in such a manner that an equal growth is maintained throughout the plant, so that it shall have a somewhat globular form. Remove to a frame before frosts come, and thence remove the plants to their blooming quarters. Water will be required in proportion to the growth, and an occasional dose of liquid manure will be of great advantage.

The two best sorts are D. gracilis, single white, and D. crenata flore pleno, double white, this latter being finer in the individual blooms, but less effective as a whole than D. gracilis. D. scabra is too gross a grower for the purposes to which the others are put.

Dicentra.—See "Dielytra."

Dielytra.—This is the old familiar "Dutchman's breeches," of the herbaceous border, and is a deciduous perennial. The bright pink flowers which are borne on long spikes of a graceful drooping habit are very effective when combined with other plants, and the bright and somewhat glaucous foliage contrasts well with the darker greens of the hard-wooded plants. As a rule it is not a good plan to grow the plants in pots for more than one season, it being preferable to have fresh plants each year, returning those plants which were bloomed indoors into the borders for one or two seasons, to recuperate their exhausted strength, and in their places take plants that have been in the borders for a similar term. The roots should be potted into a compost of sandy loam in well drained pots as soon as the foliage dies off, and these pots should be placed in a cold frame until introduced into the house. If grown in a warm house they should be placed in a warm light position as near the glass as possible, and a moist growing temperature should be maintained. The plants should be neatly staked and turned round frequently to equalise the growth. After blooming, the pots should be removed to a cold frame, and as soon as severe frosts are past the plants can be placed out in the borders. Successional batches must be brought in as occasion requires, and with little trouble bloom can be kept up from February to June. In the cold house the plants will flower—according to the severity of the season—from the end of March till June, and the general treatment is the same as in the warm house. Plenty of water is necessary when the plants are in full growth, and an occasional dose of weak liquid manure is an advantage. It is also necessary to keep down green fly, or the plants will be ruined.

The best sorts for pot work are *D. spectabilis*, pink ; *D. spectabilis alba*, white ; and *D. eximia*, red ; but this latter is not so easily done as the two first. *D. cucullaria*, yellow and white, does very well in a cold house, but is not so good as the others. In fact, one rarely sees it grown in pots.

Dodecatheon. — These are the American cowslips or "shooting stars," and although they prefer a cool situation in which to grow, still they can be used to decorate the cold house, provided a somewhat shady cool spot is found for them. We have grown them well with a very little trouble in frames, and in an old cold house just wind and watertight. The way our plants were done was as follows : In November the plants were taken up and potted in 6in. pots, in a compost of loam, enriched with leaf soil, and rendered porous with a sufficient quantity of sharp sand. Plenty of drainage was afforded, as it is necessary to apply plenty of water while the plants are growing. The plants were kept in a cold frame until the first week in March, and then transferred to the house, applying water as necessary. After blooming the plants were plunged in a bed of coal ashes, under a wall facing the north, but protected from inclement weather, and during the summer they were well attended to. The following year they were treated the same, giving larger pots, and the third season the plants were divided, so that they should not become too large. One thing must be remembered, these plants will neither stand hot sun nor forcing heat, and are only fit for blooming in the cold house, or frames, or to stand in rockwork, &c., as hardy plants.

Dodecatheon Meadia and its varieties are the best for pot culture, as they are the least trouble; but the other plants, if well grown, are really worth the trouble taken. *D. integrifolium*, crimson; *D. Jeffreyanum*, red; *D. Meadia*, red; *D. M. albiflorum*, white; *D. M. a. violaceum*, violet; *D. M. elegans—giganteum* of some—rose and lilac; *D. M. lilacinum*, lilac; and *D. M. purpureum longiflorum*, purple, are all good for the purposes we have mentioned, and the two first make good exhibition hardy plants.

ERYTHRONIUM.—The dog's tooth violet, as it is called, is a most useful pot plant if well grown in the cool house, and with a little care it can be also done well in a house that is heated moderately, but it is not advisable to subject it to too high a temperature. Like all the Liliaceæ, careful attention and steady growth are the only secrets in their culture, but should they be done on the fit and start principle, then success will be very far from being attained. The destruction of insect pests is also a matter of importance, and indeed a matter of necessity, as the plants will not bloom unless they are kept clean. The bulbs should be taken up in August and September, and potted, so that the plants will cover the pots, and the soil should consist of about one-third peat or leaf soil, and two-thirds sandy loam, affording plenty of drainage. Pot in soil that is in a moist (not wet) state, and stand in a cold frame facing the north, but from which frost is excluded. In December remove the pots to the greenhouse, either warm or cold, and keep the soil just moist until the foliage appears, and then apply water more liberally. After blooming remove the pots to a frame, and when the foliage ripens, stand in a bed of coal ashes, repotting again in August, or, what is better, transferring them to the borders, and potting up fresh ones.

For sorts select from *E. dens canis album*, white; *E. d. c. majus*, red purple; *E. d. c. majus roseum*, rosy purple; *E. d. c. majus album*, white, brown base; *E. d. c. passiflorum*, light purple shading to blue; *E. d. c. purpureum*, purple; and *E. Americanum*, yellow. The above will repay for any trouble that may be taken with them, the cyclamen-like flowers being very handsome indeed.

ORGET-ME-NOT. — The Myosotis is a plant of which many persons are very fond, and certainly the flowers, and in fact the whole plant, are very pretty. There is only one fault, and that is the inducement it offers to the green fly, which prefer the sub-aquatic to any other plant, with the exception of the herbaceous calceolaria. *M. dissitiflora* is the best kind for general cultivation, as it does not need such vast supplies of water as does the sub-aquatic section, and, moreover, the colour is more pleasing. The habit of the plant is also more compact and suited to the use of pots for its culture. Frames should be prepared with a moderately rich sandy soil in September, into which plants raised from seeds sown in August should be pricked out about six inches apart. Treated in the same manner as other hardy plants in frames, they will remain until March, when they can be carefully taken up with a good ball of earth adhering to the roots, and potted into 4in. pots. They should be carefully but thoroughly watered, and returned to the frame for a month, or until such time as the flower stems are thrown up, and then they should be transferred to the cold house, where, with ordinary attention, they will bloom for a long time.

Fritillaria. — These are useful plants for early blooming, and are very little trouble. They can be had outdoors, in frames, or in the cold or warm house, but they must not be forced, or the foliage will be more remarkable than the flowers. They are chiefly useful for early work, but we have seen bulbs produce adventitious blooms in October, although such blooms are extremely rare. In August, or early in September, they should be potted, four or five in a pot, good sandy loam being used for compost, and plenty of drainage afforded. Treat the same as the preceding, and good results will be attained.

F. meleagris, chequered purple; varieties of *meleagris*, of various colours: *F. Persica*, brown; *F. præcox*, white; *F. pudica*, purple and yellow; *F. tristis*, brown; and *F. tulipæfolia*, brown and purple, are all useful sorts. It is, however, the better plan to make the forms of *F. meleagris* the chief point to depend on, as they are certain to bloom well if good bulbs are had in the first place.

Funkia. — As fine foliaged plants for the cool greenhouse there are very few that can equal the funkias in the particularly soft foliage, and at the same time the bloom is not to be despised. The plants are deciduous perennials, the same as pœonies, and other plants of a like nature, and

consequently require to rest for a certain part of the year, and it is therefore the better plan to keep them in a cold frame from which frost is
excluded during the winter. In spring and early summer the plants can
remain in the house which they will help to decorate in a very effective
manner; but from the end of July, until the foliage ripens, it is the
best plan to stand the plants out of doors, and their ornamental foliage
will be useful in various places. The large ovate leaves of some of the
varieties, and the gracefully curved spikes of flowers, render the plants
very handsome specimens for flat vases, large pots, &c., and as the
beauty of the plants lies in the form and markings of the foliage, the
plants do well stood rather low on the stages, or perhaps on the ground.
It is, however, a matter of the greatest importance that plenty of light
and air be given, and also that all insects, particularly green fly, slugs,
and snails, be kept scrupulously destroyed, as if these are allowed to
prey on the plants the foliage will be anything but handsome. We use a
compost of loam, leaf soil, and rotten manure, to which some sharp
sand has been added. Plenty of drainage is also necessary, as during
growth the plants require free supplies of water.   -

Funkia Fortunei, glaucous blue foliage; *F. glauca*, broad glaucous
leaves; *F. grandiflora*, handsome foliage, highly fragrant white flowers,
which, if the plants are taken into a temperate house ere frost comes,
will continue in bloom until December; *F. ovata variegata*, leaves finely
margined with white; *F. o. aurea*, soft yellow foliage; *F. ovata*, glaucous
green foliage, pure flowers; *F. obcordata*, fine foliage and pure flowers, and
F. undulata medio-variegata, fine foliage and pure flowers, will all be
found very useful for the purposes named, and besides these there are very
many more which are useful for either in or out door decoration. The
best plan is to see the plant before purchasing; and a visit to Mr. Ware's
nurseries at Tottenham from June to September would amply repay the
intending purchaser, as he grows a large variety.

ALANTHUS. — The snowdrops are so well known that a description is unnecessary, suffice to say that a few pots in the cold house come in very handily early in the season. The culture is very simple—in fact, so simple that the only thing to be surprised at is the scarcity of these lovely blooms just after Christmas. All that is necessary is to pot the bulbs, about five in a large sixty-sized pot, using a somewhat rich compost of sandy loam and leaf soil, to which some sharp sand has been added. The bulbs should be potted as soon as they can be had, and then stood in a cold frame until the end of November, when they should be taken indoors and kept just moist until growth commences, when more water should be given. It is also necessary that a light airy position should be chosen for them, and it is an advantage if the house is kept at a temperature of from 35° to 40°. After blooming the bulbs can either be turned into the ground or thrown away.

The best sorts are *G. nivalis*, *G. nivalis fl. pl.*, and *G. plicatus*, all of which are white tipped with green.

Geranium.—One or two of the geraniums can be used sometimes in the cool house, or they can be grown in a cold frame, and transferred to the house when in bloom. The plants are perfectly hardy, and bloom very freely in their season; but as they can be made to decorate the cold house so much the better, and as the colours are of very pleasing shades they tend to improve the appearance of the place greatly. The culture is very simple, simply repotting when the growth commences, using a compost of leaf soil and sandy loam, and potting moderately firm. A fair amount of drainage must be afforded, or the plants will not thrive. In no case is it desirable to introduce the plants to a heated house, as the plants will not thrive well in such a place. Another good plan is to carefully lift the plants when showing bloom, and then pot them up, keeping in a shady place for a few days, and then introducing to the house.

Some of the following can be used for cold house work :—*G. albidum*, white ; *G. angulatum*, purple ; *G. Ibericum*, blue ; *G. nodosum*, purple ; *G. phæum*, black ; *G. pratense*, blue ; *G. roseum*, rose ; *G. sanguineum*. blood red ; and *G. Vlassovianum*, red.

YACINTH. — Very few persons who have a greenhouse would care to have the hyacinth absent, and as the plants are alike useful in both heated and cold houses, their value is so much the greater. Comparatively speaking, the culture of the hyacinth is very simple, but at the same time it is necessary to observe some rules in their culture, which rules, although very simple, are very important. The hyacinth is useful for a great many purposes, chief amongst which may be pointed out table and room decorations, the decoration of the greenhouse, and for various uses as cut bloom. One London decorator we are acquainted with uses over 25,000 hyacinths each season, and although many colours are used, white, blush, pink, red, blue, and yellow are the chief colours used. As he does not grow anything but hard-wooded stock himself, and as the bulbs are consigned to the rubbish heap when done with, this shows plainly that he cannot grow the plants so cheaply as he can purchase. The first point to be observed in the culture of the hyacinth is to have good sound bulbs. Not a parcel of rubbish that is to be had at mock auctions and fifth-rate seed shops, but good sound bulbs that are worth the money paid for them. Good sound heavy bulbs should be selected, and the bulbs should be clear from offsets or protuberances, and what is equally as important, there should be only one crown. In fact, a hyacinth should be like a fine onion, clear in the skin, and smoothly and well proportioned, at the same time the bulbs should be heavy for their size. In the second place, rich sandy soil should be provided for their nourishment and for the full development of the blooms; and, lastly, a sufficient time for the production of roots should be allowed before they are brought to the light, or only very indifferent results will be obtained. A compost composed of one-half good loam, one-third good leaf soil, and the rest manure and sand, will suit the bulbs well, and cause them to produce large spikes, if it is a sort that will do so. The bulbs should be obtained as early in the season as possible, and a portion including some of the white Roman should be potted up at once, giving plenty of drainage, and using the compost mentioned above. The pots should be then plunged in a bed of coal ashes or cocoa fibre refuse, covering the bulbs to a depth of six or seven inches. The other bulbs should be stored in a cool place, and potted up from time to time, and treated as the first batch, and these later lots will make good successions to the first ones. After the bulbs have been under cover for about five or six weeks they can be taken out and placed in a frame or greenhouse, and kept moist. The flower spike will then soon throw up, and the plants should be kept near the glass, so that all the light that can be obtained is afforded them. A temperature of 50° will bloom the bulbs well in the early house, and if plenty of water is afforded the plants when they are growing vigorously fine spikes of bloom will result. The successional batches must be brought forward from time to time, and treated the same as the first lot.

Some good bulbs for pot work are: Amy, bright rich red; Meyerbeer, bright red; Mrs. Beecher-Stowe, delicate shaded rose; Ariadne, rose shaded with pink; Circe, carmine; Norma, delicate pink; Von Schiller, deep salmon pink; Tubiflora, blush white; *Alba maxima*, pure white; Blanchard, pure white; Grand Vainqueur, white; La Candeur, white; Couronne de Celle, blue, light centre; Grande Vedette, pale porcelain blue; Baronne Van Tuyll, blue; Brunette, rich blue; Chas. Dickens, pale shaded blue; Nimrod, light blue; General Havelock, black purple; Mimosa, black; Anna Carolina, yellow; Heroine, pale yellow; Ida, good clear yellow; La Pluie d'Or, primrose. The yellows are not nearly so good for pot culture as other colours, but they make a change in the appearance of the plants. We mention no doubles, as they are, as a rule, not worth the room they occupy, unless they are specially grown, and this is scarcely worth troubling about, unless exhibition purposes are studied.

RIS —Some of the bulbous irises are worth growing in pots for the decoration of the greenhouse, but more particularly for the decoration of the cold house, as there the colours come very pure, and the markings are very distinct. Great care must, however, be taken that insects are kept down, and that the plants are kept as near the glass as possible, so that they do not become drawn, for if such should happen, or should the plants become infested with fly, they will not bloom, and unless they bloom the plants are useless in a decorative point of view. The general treatment is the same as for fritillarias, and if the directions for the culture of these plants are followed, a good show of bloom may be reasonably expected. Some of the evergreen irises may be bloomed in the cold house, or in a cold frame, if the roots are carefully taken up and potted in pots sufficiently large to hold the clumps without damaging the roots, using good sandy loam for soil, and affording plenty of drainage. As a rule, however, it is not safe to try to force the herbaceous sorts, as they will not stand being over-excited, but in the cold house they can be had in bloom very easily.

Amongst the bulbous sorts the varieties of *I. xiphioides* have the largest flowers, and those of *I. xiphium* are the earliest. The following varieties of *I. xiphioides* are very good, and are really worthy of being well culti-vated: Brutus, reddish purple; Damon, pure white; Gloriosa, pale blue and white; Grand Vainqueur, rosy lilac, La Beauté, lilac, Lord Palmer-ston, purple; Miss Barclay, white splashed with violet; Mungo Park, dark violet; Penelope, white mottled with lilac; Pourpre Blenâtre, rich purple. Of *I. xiphium*, the following are really good; white, yellow, rich violet purple, and blue. There is no advantage in having named sorts, as, if the bulbs are had to the colours named, no advantage will accrue by purchasing named ones, the only difference being in the price. *I. pavonia major* (peacock iris), beautiful white, with sky blue blotch on each petal; *I. Persica*, white, blue, and yellow; *I. reticulata*, deep blue, and golden yellow; *I. Susiana* (Chalcedonian iris), broad petalled blush tinted brown flowers, netted with dark lines; *I. tuberosa* (snake's headed iris), rich violet, tinted glossy black flowers; *I. primula*, various; and *I. suavolens*, various, are all good for our purpose, if grown in a manner consistent with their various habits. The chief points are, to treat as nearly as possible as hardy plants, to give plenty of air, and to keep free from insects.

JAPAN MEDLAR. — The Japan Medlar (*Eriobotrya Japonica*) is a very handsome large foliaged evergreen tree that almost rivals the *Ficus elastica* in stateliness of appearance. The plant, which is of doubtful hardiness, requires an ordinary greenhouse temperature to make it appear at its best, and then it has its leaves from eight to fourteen inches long. We have always raised the plants from seeds, and, as the only point was to obtain fine foliage, our treatment was as follows : As soon as seeds or fruit could be had in the shops, they were sown singly in three-inch pots, and placed in a cold frame. When frost set in the plants were taken into the greenhouse and kept moderately dry. In spring we repotted into five-inch pots, and in June plunged in the borders out of doors, taking care the plants were not starved for water. They were wintered as before, and in spring re-potted into eight-inch pots. The plants were then kept in the conservatory altogether, or stood out the same as oranges during the summer. A small shift was given each year until the pots got large, and then an annual top dressing, and supplies of liquid manure while the plants were growing was found sufficient. Plants obtained from a nursery, properly prepared for the purpose, will bear yellow fruit about the size of a small apricot, and these are both useful and ornamental. They, however, require to be a good size for this purpose, and therefore it is only in large conservatories where they can be fruited.

ALMIA.—This useful class of American plant is well suited for the cool house. The flowers are very pretty, much like some of the rhododendrons, and the treatment given to those plants will suit Kalmias. With care the plants will bloom well each year, but for our part, we prefer plants freshly lifted, for these generally answer best. The plants that have bloomed indoors can also then be planted out to prepare for indoor work again when required. A soil composed of peat and sand is necessary, and firm potting must be the rule. For treatment see " Rhododendrons."

The sorts most suitable are K. glauca and K. latifolia, both of which are very pretty, and repay for the trouble taken with them.

Kerria Japonica, fl. pl.—This old fashioned plant is very good for bringing into bloom early in the season, and there is very little trouble in doing this. Suitable plants should be chosen as soon as the leaves fall, taken up carefully, so as to preserve all the roots, and put up in pots of sufficient size to hold them comfortably. Good sandy soil should be used, and the pots should be well drained, but with the exception of these points no further special directions are necessary. The plants can either remain in a cold house, or they may be gradually introduced to a warm one, where the flowers will be freely produced. The blossoms which are yellow—buttercup colour—are formed somewhat like a double daisy, and contrast admirably with the white cerasus, but they require wiring to be of use as cut bloom.

AURUSTINUS.—See "Viburnum tinus."

Leucojum.—These are early blooming bulbous plants, of easy culture in the cold greenhouse, and are of a somewhat similar appearance to the snowdrop, but they are much taller, and the form of the blooms is different. The culture is the same as for *Anthericum*, using a free sandy loam for soil, and affording plenty of drainage. The plants are not well suited to other than the cold house, and therefore forcing should not be attempted.

The sorts we have grown are *L. æstivum*, *L. pulchellum*, and *L. vernum*, all of which are white.

Lilium.—See "Soft-wooded Plants." Several of the other lilies can be tried in a cold house; *L. speciosum*, *L. Humboldtii*, and *L. Leitchlinii*, and some others being suitable for the trial; but, as a rule, unless the house is large, but little success will be obtained.

Lily of the Valley.—The lily of the valley, or *Convallaria majalis*, is a plant that is in much demand during the early part of the season, but it is one that can rarely be found grown in a proper manner in the hands of the amateur. It must be remembered that the plants will not bear forcing, as the term is generally employed, but a little coaxing must be resorted to if the plants are required early. A compost of leaf soil and mellow loam in equal proportions, to which has been added a sufficient quantity of sharp sand to render the whole sufficiently permeable to the water that is applied, suits the plants very well for the time they are in the pots, for, after they have ceased blooming, they must be turned into the open ground. Whether prepared clumps or single crowns are used, it matters but little in the results obtained if the treatment is of a rational character, and, indeed, many persons are of opinion that the single crowns, if carefully selected, are the best. Suffice to say that we have found but little difference in the two methods of preparing the roots. As soon as the roots can be obtained, they should be potted into four or six inch pots, according to the display required and the size of the roots. The crowns should be just covered with soil to the depth that they are covered when growing naturally, and after potting the plants may be stood in a dark and moderately warm place until the shoots get about three inches long, when they should be gradually introduced to the light to get the colour into the foliage and to open the blooms of a good size and colour. The plants may also be potted up and placed under the stage in the greenhouse, and when started removed to the light, to grow

K

and bloom. In the cold house but little trouble is necessary, as the plants will only bloom about a week or so before their natural season here. A temperature of about 45° is quite high enough if a good head of flowers is desired, but an additional five degrees may be allowed as the foliage becomes fully expanded, as the flowers will open more freely in a temperature of about 50°. Water must be given as required; but it must be remembered that while plenty of water is necessary at some stages of the growth of the plants, if too much is given the soil will become waterlogged and totally unfit for the growth of plants, and as a natural consequence the plants will fail, and probably rot off. After blooming the plants should be turned into a border of maiden loam and leaf soil in about equal parts, and plenty of water should be given through the hot dry weather. Fresh lots of crowns must be potted each year if a good lot of bloom is required, as the plants rarely bloom the second season in pots.

The varieties used are—*Convallaria majalis*, single white, the best for ordinary work; *C.m. flore pleno*, double white; *C. m. rosea*, rose; *C. m. foliis marginatis*, and *C. m. foliis striatis*, both having variegated foliage, and bearing white flowers.

IMULUS.—See " Soft-wooded Plants."

Muscari. — The grape hyacinths are pretty bulbous plants, of dwarf growth, blooming rather early in the season, and in the cold house making a nice show, at times being about a month earlier than their fellows out of doors. The colours range from white to purple, and the colours are of very pleasing tints. The culture is rather simple, as they will do well if treated in the same manner as *Galanthus*. The plants must not, however, be kept too wet, as they are liable to decay, and it is also necessary that plenty of drainage be afforded for the same reason. A rich sandy soil, or a compost of sandy loam, and a little thoroughly decayed leaf soil, to which some sharp sand has been added, suits the plants well, and as they are not so good in pots the second year, the chief point is to obtain the best possible the first season. After blooming it is a good plan to plant the roots in a prepared border of rich sandy soil, and let them have a season's rest, and then they can be taken up and potted again, when a large increase will also be obtained. The bulbs are, however, cheap, and unless there is plenty of room outdoors, it is not worth the while to trouble about saving the bulbs with a view to potting them again.

The varieties are—*M. botryoides*, blue; *M. b. album*, white; *M. b. carneum*, flesh; *M. b. pallidum*, white; *M. comosum*, purple; *M. c. atrocœruleum*, dark blue; *M. c. monstrosum*, blue; *M. moschatum*, blue and yellow; *M. pulchellum*, blue; *M. racemosum* and *M. r. major*, blue.

Myosotis.—See "Forget-me-not."

ARCISSUS.—The polyanthus narcissus (*N. Tazetta*) and the jonquil (*N. Jonquilla*) are both extremely useful for decorative purposes, and stand forcing well. They are also most useful for use in the cool house, as the extremely bright coloured flowers and fine scent render them objects of general admiration. The culture varies but little from that given to hyacinths, but, perhaps, the culture had better be described. In the first place, it is desirable that the bulbs—foreign by preference—should be had as early in the season as possible, and it is then a good rule to divide the bulbs into two lots, the first to be potted off at once, and the others to be kept in a cool place until the middle of October, when they should be potted up. When potted, the bulbs should be placed in a dark place, or *under* a bed of cocoa fibre for a few weeks—say from four to six—and thence they should be removed to the warm or cold house as occasion or season should require, and if placed in a light position near the glass, the plants will bloom well, and throw up spikes of bloom without drawing to too great an extent. The amount of water required will of course depend on the state of growth of the plant, as we have frequently mentioned before, and aëration will depend on the weather, but where it is possible to admit air with comparative freeness the plants will thrive much better. A good rich sandy soil is requisite, and plenty of drainage will be necessary, as the plants will fail should the soil become water-logged or sour, and therefore all necessary

K 2

precautions should be taken to prevent this. As the bulbs are only good for one year's pot work, as soon as they have done blooming they should be planted out in a sheltered border, or in the fronts of rhododendron and other beds, where, after a season's rest, and if left undisturbed, they will from time to time produce very acceptable blooms for bouquets, &c.

The sorts or varieties we have found to answer best are Grand Soleil d'Or, yellow, orange cup; Queen of the Netherlands, white, yellow cup; Grand Primo Citronnier, white; Grand Monarque, white, pale yellow cup; and Lord Canning, yellow. Paper white, pure white, and the early Roman double white and yellow are all so easy to grow that anyone can grow them. We have not grown, but we have seen Bazelman major, a fine white, and Bouquet Triomphant, in fine form; and perhaps the above will be as good a selection of the *N. Tazetta* section as can be had for amateur use. Of jonquils, the ordinary double yellow, single, and Campernelli are the three best, and grown as above directed they are sure to give satisfaction.

XALIS.—Many of the oxalises are useful in the cold house, and the culture is very simple. In fact, we may say that the whole of the oxalises are useful in the cool houses that are common in most places, but as there is such a vast number of them, from fifty to nearly a hundred kinds, according to various botanists, we shall not give a list of sorts here. Suffice to say that in all nurseries where herbaceous plants are grown, and in many places where pot plants are to be had, more or less varieties can be had, and persons living near the metropolis can see large collections at the various large nurseries; where herbaceous plants are made a speciality, from thirty to seventy kinds can generally be seen growing. We have given a list in a previous section, and all the plants there mentioned can be grown in the cold house. A compost of two-thirds good mellow loam and one-third leaf soil and sharp sand in equal proportions will do the plants very well, provided plenty of water is given during the growing season and the plants are allowed plenty of light and air. A season of rest must also be allowed, and as this will nearly approach the time of rest that is natural to the plants when in the open ground, due allowance must be made accordingly. See also "Soft-wooded Plants."

ERSICA. — The double peach in its red and crimson form is very handsome, and as it is suitable for either a large or small house it is generally useful. It requires much the same treatment as the almond, and does well with the cultivation recommended for that tree.

The varieties are—*P. vulgaris fl. pl.*, double red; *P. v. fl. pl. alba*, white; and *P. v. fl. pl. sanguinea*, crimson.

Plumbago.—This plant can be grown as a pillar or wall plant in any place where the frost can be kept out, and will produce a good amount of bloom, although the bloom will not, as a rule, be so fine or so plentiful as in a warm house. The general treatment is the same as described in "Hard-wooded Plants," and so need not be again described.

P. Capensis, sky blue; *P. Europæa*, blue; and *P. Larpentæa*, blue, are the sorts useful for the purpose.

Polygonatum.—The Solomon's Seal is a fragrant early blooming plant that pays well either for forcing, or in either the warm or cool greenhouse, and the culture is most simple. All that is necessary is to secure good clumps in the autumn, and to pot them in a compost similar to that advised for the preceding, affording plenty of drainage, as at the time the plants are growing freely they require an abundance of moisture. The plants should be well watered after potting, and they can then be placed in heat or otherwise as may be required, and as soon as they start growing they must have a light position near the glass, so that they shall be prevented from drawing up weak and spindly. The flowers, which are as a rule produced in axillary clusters, are of a greenish-white colour, and emit a pleasant perfume, particularly in the early part of the day. After blooming, the plants should be planted in a rich border to have a season's rest and recuperate themselves. Plenty of water is necessary during the growing season, and even in the season of rest the plants—if kept in pots—must not become dust dry, or the stems, when produced in spring, will be of but small value.

The varieties that are useful for pot work are—*P. Japonicum*, *P. J. argenteum striatum* (variegated foliage), *P. multiflorum*, *P. m. florepleno*, *P. m. aureum striatum* (variegated foliage), *P. roseum*, and *P. verticillatum*, all of which bear whitish-green or greenish-white flowers, with the exception of *P. roseum*, which has rose-coloured blossoms.

Primula.—The primroses are quite a host in themselves, and where there is only a cold house, or a house from which the frost only is excluded, they fill up a great gap in the supply of bloom, as many blossom as early as the end of February out of doors, and under shelter they may reasonably be expected to bloom at least a fortnight—if not three weeks —earlier. As the family is so large, we cannot afford space for a description of each kind, but must be content with general remarks only.

P. *Sinensis* and its varieties will thrive in a light house where frost is excluded, as will any of the hardy varieties, but it must be remembered that in all cases where plants are in pots it is absolutely necessary that such means shall be provided to protect the roots from frost as shall be necessary. The best sized pots in which to grow primulas are four and six inch, according to the natural habit of growth of each plant, and as the plants are very impatient of too much root moisture, care must be taken that the drainage holes in the pots are sufficiently large to admit of the free passage of superfluous water. The plants being in some cases rather deep rooting, the pots should be deep, rather than shallow for their size. In all cases it is necessary to supply plenty of drainage to the pots, and also in the case of some of the alpine varieties to place some broken sandstone amongst the soil, so that a certain amount of coolness and moisture shall be maintained during the hot weather. A good general compost consists of two parts good mellow fibrous loam, not sifted, one part thoroughly decayed leaf soil, and sufficient sharp clean sand to insure the requisite amount of porosity for the free passage of the superfluous moisture. If possible, the house should face the north-east, as, during the summer, if the plants were permanent occupants, the sun would otherwise be too powerful; but if there is plenty of frame room, any house would be suitable, as the plants could be removed to frames facing the north during the hot weather, or from the end of May until October, when they could be returned to the house. This latter would also be about the best plan that it would be possible to devise to secure the blooms at their best. As much air as possible should be admitted at all seasons, or the plants will become drawn and practically useless. Insects, but more particularly green fly, which will be sure to put in an appearance, are very injurious, and it will therefore be found necessary to fumigate as soon as the first one appears, so that no damage may be done; for, as they attack the tenderest parts of the foliage, they soon destroy the heart, and consequently the bloom—if not the whole plant —of any plant which they may attack. Slugs and snails, although doing more damage individually, are not so much trouble to exterminate and discover as the fly, for while the former leave a slimy trail to show their presence and whereabouts, the latter work so insidiously that only close examination will discover their presence as a rule.

Amongst the kinds that may be grown in the cold house the following are very good, but as there is such a large number of primulas, it is far the better plan to go to a large nursery and select such as suit the particular tastes of the various purchasers. The varieties of the common primrose (P. *acaulis*)—but more particularly the double varieties—are very useful and pretty, and as they can be taken up and bloomed in the house, and then returned to the ground, they should be largely used for this work. *P. acaulis fl. pl.*, pale yellow; *P. a. alba fl. pl.*, white; *P. a. lilacina fl. pl.*, lilac; *P. a. lutea fl. pl.*, deep yellow; *P. a. purpurea fl. pl.*, purple; *P. a. rosea fl. pl.*, rose; and *P. a. rubra fl. pl.*, deep crimson, are the best doubles of the *acaulis* section. *P. auricula* contains many good things, especially the alpine varieties, and a dozen or two of good seedlings would not be a bad investment. *P. a. nigra fl. pl.*, is a good double black, and *P. a. lutea*, and its double variety, are good yellows, while the hybrids are legion. *P. Altaica*, purplish crimson; *P. Candolleana*, purple; *P. cortusoides* and its varieties, are good tall primulas of rather robust habit. *P. erosa*, lilac; *P. minima*, rose (about the smallest of the family); and *P. verticillata*, yellow, may all be grown, but they require much care to do them well, unless a house is devoted to them alone.

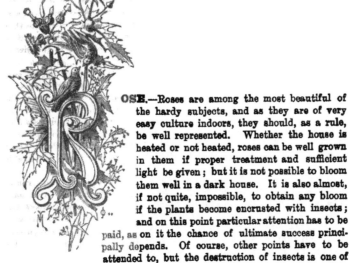

OSE.—Roses are among the most beautiful of the hardy subjects, and as they are of very easy culture indoors, they should, as a rule, be well represented. Whether the house is heated or not heated, roses can be well grown in them if proper treatment and sufficient light be given; but it is not possible to bloom them well in a dark house. It is also almost, if not quite, impossible, to obtain any bloom if the plants become encrusted with insects; and on this point particular attention has to be paid, as on it the chance of ultimate success principally depends. Of course, other points have to be attended to, but the destruction of insects is one of the most important, as, however good the other treatment may be, if the insects are not kept down, no good results can possibly be obtained.

It is desirable that roses to be bloomed indoors should be well established in pots before they are brought in; and, indeed, it is better if they have been grown in pots a couple of seasons before housing, as then they do far better than if grown in pots for one season only prior to housing. The method of potting and growing in pots will be found fully described in

Mr. Prior's "Rose Growing for Amateurs." * It is necessary in growing roses indoors that plenty of drainage be afforded, and also that a rich and porous soil be used, as the amount of water that has necessarily to be given is apt to turn a close soil sour, and to render it unfit for the use of plants.

Roses can also be profitably employed to cover the interior of the roofs of conservatories or greenhouses ; and for this purpose they can be planted out either in inside or outside borders in the same manner as vines, or they can be grown in large pots or tubs. The best plan, however, is to plant them out in a cool house, where light and ventilation are well provided, and then by judicious treatment a splendid harvest of bloom will be obtained with but little trouble.

According to whether the plants are required early or late, so must the time vary as to when they are brought indoors, and due allowance must also be made for the temperature of the house. In no case should the plants be exposed to frost, but previous to bringing into the house they should be kept in frames, and then they will be found to thrive far better when taken indoors.

· Carefully prune the trees and introduce them to a house where the temperature is of about 45° to 50°, and keep the soil just moist until the plants break, and then apply moisture according to the growth, and also outside weather ; if bright sunny weather more moisture is requisite than when cloudy dull weather prevails. The breaks or shoots should be reduced to from four to twelve of the strongest, according to the size of the plants, and these should be carefully trained out so that both light and air are freely admitted to all parts of the foliage. Great care must be taken to prevent mildew, but should it appear flowers of sulphur should be at once applied and syringed off with water of the same temperature as the house, at the end of twenty-four hours ; or Ewing's mildew composition should be applied. Green fly must also be removed as soon as it appears, and this is best effected by the use of a small brush, say a stiff camel's hair pencil. Plenty of light is an absolute necessity, and air should be given more or less on every favourable opportunity.

When the plants cease blooming they should be removed to the frames until such time as they can be safely plunged outdoors, and great care must be taken throughout the growing season to cause them to make fine ripe wood, as on this the next year's bloom depends. In all cases it is absolutely necessary to remove all insects, to keep the plants regularly and uniformly supplied with a sufficiency of moisture, and to treat as recommended above. Roses are essentially hardy plants and must be treated as such.

Amongst the sorts that are of most service in the house are—Maréchal Niel, bright yellow ; Celine Forestier, deep canary yellow ; Devoniensis,

---

* "Rose Growing for Amateurs: being Practical Instructions for the Successful Culture of Roses, with Selections of the Best Varieties Adapted to the Requirements of the Amateur in Town or Country." By W. D. Prior. Price 1s. 6d.

creamy white; Gloire de Dijon, buff, orange centre; Niphetos, white, pale straw yellow centre, buds very useful; Safrano, bright apricot, like the last, very fine in the bud; Souvenir de la Malmaison, blush, flesh centre; Victor Verdier, deep carmine; Senateur Vaisse, dazzling red; Prince Camille de Rohan, deep lurid crimson; Madame Victor Verdier, cherry rose; Madame Gustave Bonnet, pure white, shade carmine; Jules Margottin, glossy pink; Géant des Batailles, crimson; Baronne de Maynard, pure white; and Madame Plantier, pure white, are all useful for the above purpose, and as we have grown them ourselves for the same purpose, we can recommend them with confidence. The fairy roses also come in very useful, and require the same treatment. For all further particulars on roses, see Mr. Prior's book on the subject.

ALVIA.—These plants, as a rule, are hardy, or so nearly hardy as to do well in any place where frost and excessive moisture can be kept from them. The general cultivation of the plants has been described in a previous section, and can easily be adapted to the cold house. The plants will not, however, bloom in winter, but during the summer and autumn months, rendering the house very attractive with their bright blooms. As with many other hardy plants, insects will be somewhat troublesome, but with a little care but little damage will be done to the plants, and, therefore, there is no reason to fear on that account. The names of suitable sorts have been given under "Soft-wooded Plants."

Sarracenia.—*Sarracenia purpurea*, a hardy American pitcher plant of much interest, can be grown in the cold house very easily, and, in fact, it is well suited to such purpose in those parts of the United Kingdom where it cannot be grown outdoors. The treatment has been given previously in "Soft-wooded Plants," and need not be referred to here. Great care must, however, be taken that green fly is not allowed to obtain a footing on the foliage, or the plants will produce only deformed leaves, and consequently the main point of interest will be lost. At Glasnevin the plant stands outdoors in frost and snow, and, according to some folks, seems to like the severe weather, but, as with all other hardy plants, if grown indoors, care must be taken that the pots do not become frozen, or the damage done to the roots, which are, as a rule, just inside the pot, and not protected by the soil around, will be very great. As one of the so-called carnivorous plants, this *sarracenia* is well worth growing.

Saxifraga.—One of the saxifrages, *S. sarmentosa*, is very pretty as a hanging basket plant, and is, moreover, very easy to grow. The chief point is to keep it well supplied with water while it is in full growth, and to use a compost of about two-thirds sandy loam and one-third leaf soil and sharp sand mixed. A good sprinkling of broken sandstone or brick should be added to the compost, and plenty of drainage should be afforded. Provided the plants are kept well provided with water, and have an occasional dose of liquid manure when in active growth, they will make fine plants in a very short time. Re-potting once a year as soon as they have bloomed will keep them in good fettle for many years. The plants are easily propagated from the numerous offsets, simply pegging them down on a pot of soil being sufficient. The colour of the flower is rosy white, or its general appearance leads to that opinion.

Scilla.—Squills do very nicely for cold house work where early bloom is required, and they can also be used in the warm greenhouse, but as they do not do so well in the latter as in the former, it is perhaps the better plan to devote them to the latter class of house only. The culture is of the simplest, potting the bulbs the same as crocuses, and using the same kind of soil, and, in fact, treating in the same manner as recommended for those plants. Their habit and pleasing hues of colour render them very useful as small decorative plants, and if the blooms are wired and mounted like the hyacinth, they work in well for table decorations and for bouquets, but more particularly for buttonhole bouquets.

S. bifolia, dark blue; *S. nivalis*, pale blue; *S. Siberica*, blue; *S. Peruviana*, blue; *S. P. alba*, white; *S. verna*, blue; *S. nutans rosea*, rose; and *S. bifolia rosea*, rose, are all gems for the cold house.

Snowdrop.—See "Galanthus."

Solomon's Seal.—See "Polygonatum."

HALICTRUM.—Of the rather large variety of thalictrums one is very useful in either the hot or cold house. *T. minus* is a plant having foliage resembling to a great extent the maidenhair fern. In the plant we more particularly desire to introduce to our readers—*T. adiantoides*—this resemblance is still greater, and where ferns cannot be done well it is extremely useful, as the foliage is well adapted for the same uses as those to which the fronds of the ferns are put. The flowers of *T. adiantoides* are white, and those of *T. minus* are pale yellow; but the flowers are of no value compared with the foliage. The plants should be potted up as soon as the foliage is ripe, and they can be kept in a cold frame during the winter if desired, or they can be taken into the cold house at once. In the warm greenhouse, if the plants are introduced during the season of rest, they should first occupy a cool shelf near the glass, and as growth commences they should be removed to a warmer part of the house, but they should be kept as near the glass as possible. The object to be attained being the production of fine, healthy, hard foliage, due attention must be paid to such little details as will be found necessary in practice; and, above all things, some amount of air must be allowed on all favourable occasions, both to harden the foliage and to obtain a good colour. Water must be given as it is found necessary from the state of the plants; for while they are in an almost dormant state very little moisture is required, whereas when in active growth they require more liberal supplies of water. A compost of sandy loam and leaf soil, rendered sufficiently porous by the addition of some sharp sand, is necessary. In all cases good drainage must be afforded, as the plants do not thrive in soil that is water-logged. In the cold house the treatment is practically the same as the preceding, except that the plants coming into growth but a short time before their natural season require only the ordinary treatment for hardy plants.

The most suitable sorts for pot culture are *T. adiantoides* or *adiantifolium*, white; and *T. minus*, pale yellow.

Tulip.—The tulip is one of those bulbs which, like the hyacinth, is of universal cultivation, and is also of universal use. To a certain extent the culture is very easy, provided the plants are not started too early in the season. As most persons are aware, the bloom of the tulip starts from the interior of the bulb, which at the same time divides into a number of young bulbs. Unlike the hyacinth, the bloom of the tulip derives the greater part of its nourishment direct from the soil, consequently a rich compost must be provided. As the bulbs are very cheap, it is scarcely worth the trouble of saving the bulbs over for the second season, and therefore it is only necessary to provide a soil for the present. We have grown large quantities of tulips for both home and market use, and have, as a rule, used a compost of two-thirds good mellow loam and one-third rotten cow manure, to which should be added enough sharp sand to render the soil freely porous. Plenty of drainage must be afforded, and a little crushed animal charcoal mixed with the soil will intensify the colour of red and scarlet flowers. The bulbs should be put in in batches from the end of August until about the middle of November, placing about five bulbs in a 4in. pot. These bulbs should be treated in the same manner as hyacinths, so far as regards covering for a few weeks, to induce the production of roots. The plants should—when taken from the bed—be gradually brought forward to the light, and a temperature of from 45° to 60° should be afforded, regulating the supply of root moisture according to the growth of the plants. Plenty of light is absolutely necessary, and a somewhat moist atmosphere is an advantage, as a dry atmosphere conduces to the more rapid production of the green fly, which is particularly partial to these plants. The several batches must be introduced at several times, so as to obtain a continuance of bloom. Great care must be taken to destroy, or rather to prevent fly, and we have found Fowler's insecticide more advantageous to use than tobacco or fumigation. Another very good plan is to prepare some boxes in the same manner as the pots, and to place the bulbs in them about a couple of inches asunder, just covering with soil. These boxes, placed in a warm house close to the glass, and kept well supplied with water, supply a large quantity of dwarf plants for various decorative purposes, especially for vase decoration and for the ornamentation of the dinner table.

In the cold house the cultivation of the tulip is very simple: potting the bulbs, and standing them back till they commence growth, when they should have the full benefit of both light and air, and the same rules as to watering, as given above, should be applied.

For very full instructions for tulip growing we would refer our readers to Mr. Fish's book on "Bulbs and Bulb Culture."*

For sorts for pot culture the following are most suitable, their earliness is given approximately in the order in which they stand, singles: Duc Van Thol, cinnabar red, orange border; Duc Van Thol, in varieties of rose blush, scarlet, white and yellow; Artis, bronze, crimson; Alida Maria, tipped and flaked cerise, white ground; Canary Bird, rich yellow; Bride of

* "Bulbs and Bulb Culture : being Descriptions both Historical and Botanical of the Principal Bulbs and Bulbous Plants Grown in this Country and their Chief Varieties; with Full and Practical Instructions for their Successful Cultivation both In and Out of Doors." By D. T. Fish. Part I.—Snowdrop, Bulbocodium, Sternbergia, Crocus, Colchicum, Tulip, and Hyacinth. Part II.—Anemone, Narcissus, and the Lily. Price 1s. each. London "The Bazaar" Office, 170, Strand, W.C.

Haarlem, white, bordered with crimson; Feu d'Angers, scarlet; Golden Prince, golden yellow; La Belle Alliance, bronze scarlet; Queen Victoria, pure white; Silver Standard, white striped cerise-crimson; Vermillion Brilliant, scarlet. Doubles: Tournesol, scarlet and yellow, and the yellow variety; Duc Van Thol, red, edged pale yellow; Gloria Solis, bronze crimson, orange border; La Candeur, good clear white; Rex Rubrorum, bright scarlet; and Agnes, a bright scarlet dwarf.

Tussilago.—The variegated coltsfoot (*T. Farfara foliis variegatis*) is a handsome plant, producing fine leaves, very beautifully margined with a band of rich creamy white. The flowers are yellow, and of no particular beauty or interest, and, in fact, are not nearly so ornamental as the dandelion. The leaves, which are from four to six inches broad, lay flat on the surface of the pot or soil, and do not often rise more than from four to six inches above the level. As a low plant for the front of stages, or to stand along the front of a group of plants, this is one of the best, as it is both conspicuous and ornamental. The culture is very easy; pot each crown in a well drained four inch pot, using a rich sandy compost, and treat in the manner described for polygonatum. If the plants are not required to remain in the house throughout the whole season, they can be used outdoors, either as an edging plant, for which purpose they are well suited, or for placing in clumps of three or four in the borders. The other tussilagos are practically useless for all but the botanical collection of plants.

IBURNUM TINUS.—This, the laurus-tinus, is a good plant if it is done in the proper manner. The best plan is to take up plants, thickly set with bloom buds, about the end of September, or early in October, pot carefully in sandy loam, and after watering thoroughly, place in a cold frame or vinery at rest, where air can be freely admitted, and the plants will bloom freely at least a fortnight earlier than those outdoors. A temperature of about 46° will forward the plants somewhat, but a forcing temperature should be avoided. Treat the same as rhododendrons after blooming.

Violet.— In contradistinction to the bedding violas, the sweet scented violet (*V. odorata, vars.*) is most useful on account of its scent.

In fact, in some of the varieties this scent or odour is so great as to cause only a few flowers to fill a room with perfume. When properly grown the plants are but small trouble, but they, as a rule, are less trouble if in the cold house than kept in the ordinary greenhouse. In the first place, it is necessary to select stout firm runners in April or May, but preferably in April, and to place them under handlights on a moist shady border. Wiry runners, or those produced from pot plants are practically useless, and therefore much care is necessary in the selection of the plants from which the runners are obtained, as also in the runners themselves. When the plants are rooted they should be placed out about 6in. or 8in. asunder, according to the habit of growth, taking care that the soil of which the border is composed is of a rich light character, and that it faces north or north-east, and is kept moist. It is also necessary that, in preparing the border, deep digging should be one of the points that is strictly looked after, as a deeply dug soil conduces greatly to the well-being of the plants. Careful attention as regards watering, &c., is also necessary, and by the end of September fine plants for potting will be obtained. These should be carefully taken up with a good ball of earth adhering to the roots, and potted into 4in. or 6in. pots, according to the size of the plants, taking care that plenty of drainage is afforded. The pots should receive a good soaking of water, and be placed in a shaded frame facing the north for a few days, until the plants have recovered from the check they received when shifted. Thence the plants may be removed to a light airy shelf in a greenhouse, kept at a temperature of about 45°, where, if due attention is paid to watering, aëration, and the destruction of insects, the plants will bloom nearly the whole winter and spring.

In the cold house, all that will be found necessary is to prevent the pots becoming frozen, and to pay attention to the above points of culture, of course preparing the plants as previously described. As a rule, the single varieties are best for pot culture, but if fine blooms are desired the double kinds are preferable.

Of sorts, the common white violet, *Viola odorata alba*, is perhaps the sweetest; and the Czar, a fine long stemmed blue, is the best scented blue, but the whole of the following are good : *V. odorata*, blue; *V. odorata alba*, white; *V. o. a.*, *fl. pl.*, double white; *V. suavis* (Russian) blue; *V. s. alba*, white; *V. s.*, *fl. pl.*, blue; and the varieties of *V. suavis*; *Devoniensis*, blue; the King, blue; the Queen, white; and Marie Louise, white; *V. o. Neapolitana*, pale blue, is good; and probably the new double white Belle de Chatenay will be useful for the same purpose as the above, and from blooms we have seen we consider it to be one of the best violets there are, provided it is of a sufficiently floriferous habit.

Violet, Dog's Tooth.—See " Erythronium."

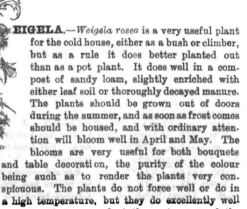

WEIGELA.—*Weigela rosea* is a very useful plant for the cold house, either as a bush or climber, but as a rule it does better planted out than as a pot plant. It does well in a compost of sandy loam, slightly enriched with either leaf soil or thoroughly decayed manure. The plants should be grown out of doors during the summer, and as soon as frost comes should be housed, and with ordinary attention will bloom well in April and May. The blooms are very useful for both bouquets and table decoration, the purity of the colour being such as to render the plants very conspicuous. The plants do not force well or do in a high temperature, but they do excellently well in a cool or cold house. If rather cramped at the roots, so much the better do they bloom, and either in pots or borders this should not be lost sight of. The same general treatment applies as to other hardy deciduous plants, aëration, &c., having to be seen to in the ordinary manner.

VII.—CLIMBERS.

BUTILON.—*A. vexillarium* and *A. v. igneum* are well suited for pillars or trellises. For treatment see "Hard-wooded Plants."

Acacia.—Some of these are also useful for pillars and trellises, the best for the purpose being—*A. dealbata, A. longifolia magnifica, A. lophantha, A. pubescens,* and *A. verticillata.* For treatment see "Hard-wooded Plants."

IGNONIA.—These are handsome climbers, of great use in comparatively large houses, and in such give great satisfaction when well done; but if neglected, and the foliage rendered unsightly by the attacks of insects, are but of little beauty. The great point in the culture of all climbers is to obtain free, and at the same time sturdy, growth, giving due attention to training, pruning, &c., or the plants soon exceed all limits. Like all free-growing plants, bignonias do best planted out in the borders, and if in suitable soil they soon make a fine show, the fine heart-shaped leaves setting the bloom off to the greatest advantage. *B. radicans* does well in a large cool conservatory, and in many places it answers fairly out of doors in a warm situation, and on a warm sheltered wall they grow and bloom well, and are therefore generally termed hardy in catalogues; but in many instances the term is delusive, as they do well only in the warmer parts of the British Isles. The sorts that are useful for our present purpose are *B. Australis*, *B. Capensis*, *B. capreolata*, *B. grandiflora*, *B. speciosa*, *B. Tweediana*, and *B. venusta*, all of which are good, that is, good for large houses. The best plan is to plant out in the borders of comparatively light loam and leaf soil, affording plenty of drainage, and taking care the soil is in a sweet and fresh condition.

Bougainvillea.—This is one of the most useful climbers there is, either for comparatively cool or for warm conservatories. During the summer it does well in a cool greenhouse. It can be grown in pots, and in the borders, but it certainly does best in the latter, as the plant is essentially a very gross rooter, and therefore requires plenty of space in which to extend. Strict training and pinching is not a great advantage either, as it does not tend to induce the free production of bloom; indeed the best plan is to allow the plants to ramble freely over the roof of a moderately high house, or along the upper portion of a back wall, and they will then bloom profusely for several months in the year, always providing that the proper attention is paid to feeding, and the plants are in a

L

properly prepared medium. In preparing a border for the reception of
bougainvilleas, the first point to be considered is the drainage, which
it is necessary to thoroughly secure. This is best done by laying in a
quantity of brick rubbish, about 6in. in thickness, and communicating
with the drain belonging to the greenhouse or conservatory, by which
means all sourness and unfitness of the soil is obviated. The bed should
be excavated to a depth of 2ft. or 3ft., according to the soil and position.
For soil use rough turf, loam, and fibrous peat, about two parts of the
former to one of the latter, and about one-fourth to one-sixth part of
sharp gritty sand, according to the quality of the other soils, heavy loams
requiring more sand than that which is more friable. Some cultivators
use manure in the compost, but this we do not recommend, as it tends
rather to cause the soil to become stiff and impervious to air, which, to
say the least, is very undesirable, as such a condition is directly opposed
to the well-being of any plant. We would rather advise the liberal
application of liquid manure, as this supplies all the necessary food,
without destroying the porosity of the soil. As a rule these plants do
not answer for pot culture in the greenhouse, as for this kind of treatment
they require stove heat, which cannot be given in a greenhouse. When the
plants cease blooming each year, say November or December, they should
be closely spurred in, the same as with vines, and all weak leaders should
be removed, so that strong wood is only left. Scale and mealy-bug are the
only insects to be feared, and these can easily be kept down by hand
picking.

For sorts choose B. *glabra*, B. *speciosa*, and B. *splendens*, which are all
good.

ALAMPELIS (or ECCREMOCARPUS) SCABRA. — This is a useful evergreen climber, and is well worth cultivation in suitable positions, as it looks well, and is of comparatively easy culture. It is of free growth, and soon covers a large space, and therefore is very useful in many situations. The same cultural remarks apply to this as to *Cobœa scandens*, which is treated further on, and therefore it is unnecessary to enter on the subject here.

Cereus.—For culture see "Epiphyllum" and "Cactus." The best sorts are *C. flagelliformis* and *C. McDonaldæ.*

Chorozema —See p. 38. The best variety for pillars and trellises is *C. spectabilis.*

Clematis.—In this family we have a class of plants which is useful, and good in all greenhouses or conservatories alike. The bloom of some of the varieties is simply magnificent, both as to size and colour; and when trained on a wall or on a balloon trellis the effect they produce is more easily imagined than described. Of course large effects cannot be expected from small plants, and to produce large plants it is necessary to give liberal culture. The majority of the clematises are quite hardy, and should therefore receive plenty of air, and but little excitement from too great a heat, or the shoots exhaust the roots to too great an extent, and therefore, after a time, the plants become less floriferous and useful. For general purposes it is, therefore, preferable to have a well-lighted house for the cultivation of the clematis, and care should also be taken to avoid a too close atmosphere, a well-ventilated house being a *sine quâ non*. As the blooms are produced on the ends of the current year's shoots the mode of cultivation should be such as will allow the plants to be well pruned back each winter, and also the situation chosen should be suitable for this purpose, or a vast amount of bare stems will soon be obtained. The secret of success lies in liberal culture and close pruning; when we say close pruning we mean spurring the shoots in to two or three eyes. For soil use three parts good sandy loam and one-fourth well rotted manure, thoroughly incorporated. To these may be added about an eighth part of broken sandstone, or broken bricks passed through a ¼in. sieve, so that the requisite porosity may be maintained, as clematises dislike a wet, heavy soil, and, in fact, soon die out in such. If the plants are put into the borders they should have 6in. of drainage, and 18in. to 24in. of the above compost in which to grow. During the period of growth liberal supplies of liquid manure should be given, and by cutting back the shoots when they cease blooming two or three successive lots of bloom can be easily obtained. A house that has a temperature of 40° to 50° is the best, and whether the plants are trained on the roof, or on a back wall, the above rules should be observed.

The following are good for house cultivation : *C. aristata, C. indivisa lobata, C. Jackmanii, C. magnifica,* C. Thomas Moore, C. *Standishii,* C. Lady Bovill, C. Mr. F. C. Baker, C. Albert Victor, C. Lucy Lemoine, C. John Gould Veitch, *C. rubella,* C. Star of India, and C. Lady Caroline Nevill. All but the first two are hardy, and have very fine flowers, and all or any of them are well worthy of cultivation.

Clianthus.—This is a greenhouse climber of great beauty, but from its great liability to the attacks of red spider, it has got into disrepute amongst amateurs and gardeners who do not take a real interest in their work. Now it is an easy job to keep down spider if it is not allowed to get a firm footing on the plants, but let it once get fairly at home on the foliage, it is almost an impossibility to be rid of it. The only way to keep down red spider is to syringe daily throughout the growing season with clean water. Scale sometimes attacks them, but careful hand-picking, and sponging with Fowler's Insecticide, will keep this unwelcome visitant at bay. The best plan for an amateur to pursue is to obtain plants from a nursery in the fall of the year, and keep them in a greenhouse until April, when the plants should be examined, and if the roots are moving they should have a 2in. shift, using good fibrous sandy loam and sand for compost, or, if this is not attainable, peat and sand. The compost should not be sifted, but should be broken up by hand, and compressed firmly in the pots. After potting, the plants should be placed in a pit with other young hard wooded subjects, and kept close for a few weeks, turning and syringing the plants daily. Training must be attended to regularly if it is desirable to keep the base of the plants well furnished, as the wood when old is very liable to break off. If it is desirable to keep the plants in pots they can be either trained out on sticks or on a trellis, either flat or balloon-shaped, or they may be planted out as pillar or wall plants, but from their liability to the attacks of spider the amateur will probably do them best in pots. Remove the points of the leading shoots and attend to watering at the roots, and the treatment is complete for the season. Winter as before and give a 3in. shift in April, attending to watering and syringing as before, and as they will probably bloom during July or August, the leading shoots should not be stopped. After blooming the shoots should be cut back and the plants be treated as before. The next season give another 3in. shift and treat as before, and a good head of bloom will result. If only moderate sized plants are required, instead of re-potting remove the top 3in. of soil from the pots and fill with the previous compost, to which a fifth part of rotten manure has been added; apply liquid manure once or twice a week, and with this treatment the plants will last for years.

For sorts, *C. puniceus* (the glory pea of New Zealand), and *C. magnificus* and *C. Dampierii* are all that can be desired.

Cobœa.—This is a family of free growing climbers that is suitable for either greenhouse or conservatory, and also for summer use out of doors. It is very free growing, and during the season its free growth renders it peculiarly useful for covering the roofs of ferneries or other places where shade is a *sine quâ non*, as it only requires a circulation of air to maintain it in good health, and as it is not particularly liable to the attacks of insects, it is, to say the least, a desirable plant for the purposes mentioned. The variegated form is well suited for giving brightness to bare walls, or for arches, porches, &c., while, like all the family, the general gracefulness of outline renders it an object of admiration. The cobœas are readily raised from seeds in spring, a little bottom heat alone being necessary if the seed is new; but old seeds are, as a rule, very unreliable. A free, moderately rich soil is necessary, and the plants do best if planted out, but, at the same time, they do very well in large pots. In autumn the long shoots can be pruned back, and fresh growth will be made in spring. In fact, these are about the handiest plants there are for covering. The flowers, which are large, bell-shaped, and purple in colour, are noticeable for their size, but are not very decorative, and are useless for cutting, but still, as a part of the plant, are worthy of notice.

The sorts are, *C. scandens, C. s. pendulæflora,* and *C. s. variegata.*

ICUS.—*F. repens* and *F. collina* are two good wall creepers, and soon cover a rough wall or rockwork, and as they have good hard glossy foliage, they look well, and form an agreeable background for bright flowering or foliaged plants. For treatment see " *F. elastica* " (p. 45.)

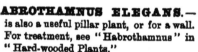

ABROTHAMNUS ELEGANS.—is also a useful pillar plant, or for a wall. For treatment, see "Habrothamnus" in "Hard-wooded Plants."

Hibbertia volubilis is a good pillar plant, and the bloom is very handsome. It is, however, not so much grown as it should be, although it deserves a place wherever there is room. It is a plant that requires plenty of root room, and may either be grown in large pots or planted out, care being taken to provide good drainage, a point that is too frequently neglected. We have grown it in peat and loam, both together and separate, always providing a sufficient quantity of sand to maintain the soil in a healthy porous condition, as in no case will any plant do well in a close sticky soil hard-wooded plants particularly. If insects attack the plants they must be got rid of at once, or they soon cause the plants to become unhealthy and unsightly, and so obtain it a bad name.

Hoya.—This plant is remarkable for the waxlike appearance of the foliage and flowers, and which causes it to be much sought after. It is one of those plants that give comparatively little trouble, but which always look well if kept clean. Even if no flowers are obtained the foliage is far prettier than that of many of the plants that are grown for their foliage alone, the peculiar brightness and waxy appearance being very beautiful, and if we consider the appreciation it generally receives it stands pre-eminent as a wall climber. It can either be planted out or grown in good sized pots, according to the convenience of the grower, but in neither case must it get dry during the growing season, or the leaves will have a rusty appearance that does not improve the look of the plant. For soil use peat and loam in equal parts, with enough sand to keep the whole porous, and do not overpot, as there is no advantage derived from so doing. The temperature of the house must not sink below 40°, and the plants should not be exposed to full sun during the very hot weather. Training should be carefully attended to, and water should be applied when necessary.

For sorts, *H. carnosa* stands first, and if one plant is not enough, add *H. c. variegata*—a variegated form of the preceding—or *H. bella*.

ASMINUM.—These are, like the preceding, useful for walls and trellises, and being pretty free bloomers, are suited for permanent plants against walls, &c. Being of a not too robust growth, these can be grown successfully in pots, and while young may be trained on trellises affixed to the pots, either flat or balloon shaped. The blossoms being more or less odoriferous, they are very desirable for cut blooms. The plants are best purchased from a nursery in autumn, and kept in the greenhouse until about March, when they should be repotted, or planted out as the case may be, using good sound peat, or two-thirds peat and one part loam, and a sufficient quantity of sharp sand to ensure the proper porosity of the soil. A minimum heat of at least 40° must be maintained to keep the plants in thorough order, and while plenty of ventilation is maintained when necessary, the ordinary temperature of the house will be sufficient for the plants. Water must of course be given as necessary, and the syringe must be used occasionally both for the sake of cleanliness and to keep down red spider. Training must be afforded as required, and shoots that unduly take the lead over the general growth of the plants should be stopped.

For sorts, select from J. Azoricum, J. gracile, J. grandiflorum, J. odoratum. We have also seen the hardy J. revolutum grown well in a cool house, but it should be treated as a hardy plant during the summer, when, with careful treatment, it will bloom freely early in the season.

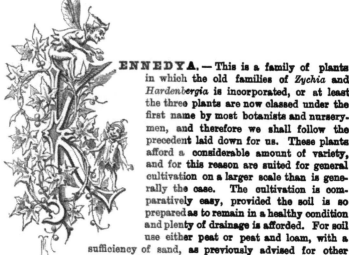

ENNEDYA. — This is a family of plants in which the old families of *Zychia* and *Hardenbergia* is incorporated, or at least the three plants are now classed under the first name by most botanists and nurserymen, and therefore we shall follow the precedent laid down for us. These plants afford a considerable amount of variety, and for this reason are suited for general cultivation on a larger scale than is generally the case. The cultivation is comparatively easy, provided the soil is so prepared as to remain in a healthy condition and plenty of drainage is afforded. For soil use either peat or peat and loam, with a sufficiency of sand, as previously advised for other plants, potting pretty firmly. Water must not be given more than is required, neither must the soil be permitted to become dust dry at any time, or serious damage will be done. A warm greenhouse or conservatory suits them best, but still, if the minimum temperature in winter is from 40° to 45°, they do very well. The attacks of insects must be kept down, as advised for other plants, or the foliage will become unsightly.

For sorts, select from the following : *K. australis, K. coccinea, K. Comptoniana, K. digitata, K. inophylla, K. i. variegata, K. lilacina, K. monophylla, K. m. variegata, K. ovata, K. o. alba, K. o. purpurea, K. o. rosea, K. pannosa, K. rubicunda,* and *K. r. superba.*

APAGERIA.—This is a very fine climber or roof plant, where there is plenty of room for it to grow, and as its handsome bell-shaped blooms are produced freely, it is of a very ornamental character. To do it well it, however, requires to be put out in a prepared border, where plenty of room is afforded, although decent plants can be done in pots if care is taken. They are plants that dislike much sun, or a dry arid atmosphere, therefore the best plan is to grow them in a moist shady house, or on a wall that is somewhat shaded, and as a rule the north wall of a house suits them well, that is, if the long rambling shoots are allowed to ramble at pleasure, but if it is trained out in a stiff formal manner, it does not display its blooms to any great advantage. We think the best plant we ever saw, or rather the best half dozen plants, were grown in an old vinery, where the roof was glazed with glass six inches square only, and the laps were filled up with dirt. In fact, it was essentially a "dark" house, which few cultivators would care to possess. But for all that the plants produced on an average about 2000 blooms each year, and they were much admired by visitors, who prized a few cut blooms very highly, as they retain their beauty for nearly a month, if the water in which they are kept is changed from time to time. To obtain the full amount of flower, lapagerias should ramble at their own sweet will and pleasure, the only training given consisting of the leading of the shoots in the direction it is desired they shall go. It is nearly hardy in the southern and midland counties, and at Messrs. Pince's nursery, in Devonshire, it flourishes against a wall and blooms profusely. The method of cultivation in pots is much the same as in borders, except that the plant is more unmanageable, and where it is possible we should advise the use of a border. The same treatment applies to pots as to borders. In all cases plenty of root room must be afforded, and if the plants are tried in pots large ones must be used. In the case of cultivation in the border, the stations for the plants should be prepared as follows: In the first place excavate the soil to the depth of three feet, and about four feet square or a space of about the same capacity, the depth in all cases being the same. A good exit for superfluous water must be afforded, either by a drain or by a layer of rubbish, that will afford an exit for the water, though preferably by a drain. At the bottom of the site place a layer from six to twelve inches thick of broken porous bricks, and on this place turves of fibrous peat, not broken in any way, and fill in the interstices with very coarse sand or broken potsherds, that will pass through a quarter inch meshed sieve. Fill in the hole with lumps of peat and loam, adding a small portion of sharp sand from time to time as the work proceeds, so that a sufficient porosity of the soil is kept throughout. The soil must be lightly trodden, and then the place is ready for the reception of the plant. A good strong free grown plant is necessary to start with, and this should be carefully planted without disturbing the roots. When planted give a good watering to settle the soil around the roots, and as soon as the plant begins to grow freely water must be supplied in greater abundance. The best time to plant is when the plants commence growth, as they then take to their new quarters more readily. The chief insects which attack lapagerias are thrips and a small white scale, both of which can be kept down by applying Fowler's Insecticide at a strength of about 6oz. to the gallon of clear water. Care must be taken not to break the leaves, which are very brittle at the axils, and faded or dead leaves do not enhance the beauty of any plant.

The sorts are, L. alba, L. rosea, and L. rosea splendens. The white one is, however, rather expensive, being from £3 3s. to £5 5s. each for moderate sized plants, whilst big plants fetch larger sums.

MYRSIPHYLLUM.—This elegant climber is one of the plants which no amateur should be without, especially if he has any taste in vase or other table decorations. For various purposes in the greenhouse it is also of great value, its extreme neatness rendering it useful for various purposes where larger and more striking plants are quite out of place.

The myrsiphyllum is very extensively used in America, where its beauties are far more appreciated than they are here; and, in fact, a friend who has written us from Boston, U.S.A., says that large houses are there devoted to this plant alone, and that immense quantities of the cut plants (we can find no other term) are sent to Philadelphia and New York. The way they grow it in America is as follows : from July to September the roots are planted (indoors) in prepared beds of light rich soil, from a foot to 18in. deep, and with a good amount of drainage below. One or two good waterings are given, and the plant is soon started, and grows rapidly away, so that in three months it is ready for cutting; that is if it has been properly hardened off during the latter part of its growth. Each vine is trained up a single string, and when the time arrives it is cut, and the string being severed at top and bottom is slipped out, leaving the vine perfect. After this first cutting, more heat is applied, and treatment being given as before, in about three or four months the crop is again ready. During June and July rest is induced by nearly with-holding water and by maintaining a cooler atmosphere; and then it can be started early in August, to finish off by Christmas. During the whole period of growth plenty of water must be given, and clear liquid manure must also be applied about twice a week, the plants being such gross root feeders that this is absolutely necessary.

We have grown *Myrsiphyllum asparagoides* in pots, and by the method recommended by a friend who has travelled in the States. Our plan is the same as that given above, so far as soil and time of planting are con-cerned; but, as the plants are in pots, variations have to be made. In the first place, we plant from four to six roots in a pot, and treat as before described, but apply liquid manure when the plants are in full growth at least three times a week. The growth is gradually hardened off when it has attained the height of from four to six feet, and consequently is then ready for use for decorative purposes. The chief rules for the culture of this plant are warmth, liberal culture, plenty of water, early and con-tinuous training, and hardening off before cutting the vines for decorative purposes.

The sorts we grow are as follow : *M. asparagoides, M. longifolium, M. variegatum,* and *M. gracillimum,* all of them being very useful for baskets, &c., but, with the exception of *M. asparagoides,* of little use for cutting.

ASSIFLORA.—Passion flowers belong to a class of plants that well repays for liberal culture, but, like the last subject, they require plenty of room in which to extend their growth. To obtain the best results the plants must grow pretty freely, and must not be starved or stunted, or an interminable crop of insects will take the place of bloom, a consummation not devoutly to be wished for. Where care is taken of the plants, however, very little trouble will be experienced under this head, for a full flow of sap is adverse to the comfort of insect pests, slugs and snails perhaps excepted, but these rarely attack greenhouse roof climbers, although at times they make a meal of a promising young shoot at the base of a plant. These plants, like the lapageria, require properly prepared stations, but they need neither be so large nor so deep, so long as drainage is well provided for. For the different varieties the soil requires some little variation as regards the quantity of sand used, but in other respects they will all do in the soil we mention. A good layer of broken bricks or pots must be placed in the bottom of the hole, which must be filled up with equal parts of rough fibrous peat and loam, to which some sand and broken charcoal has been added. Press it moderately firm, but do not tread too hard, as the roots require a free root run. Well water the plants in at first, and during the growing season abundance of water will be necessary. Training must be attended to as necessary, and the plants must be kept clear of insects if they chance to appear. The wood of the passion flower requires to be well ripened off by the admission of plenty of air, and then profuse blooming will result.

For sorts, use a selection from the following : *P. Bellottii*, *P. Campbellii*, *P. cærulea*, *P. c. racemosa*, *P. c. racemosa rubra*, *P. fragrans*, *P.* Comte Nesselrode, *P.* L'Imperatrice Eugenie, *P. Newmanii*, and *P. palmata*, all of which are good.

Plumbago.—*P. Capensis* and *P. Zylanica* make good pillar or wall plants if properly treated, as described in " Hard-wooded Plants."

OLANUM.—*S. jasminiflorum* and *S. j. variegatum* are two very good climbers for wall or trellises, and are interesting in appearance. The culture is not very difficult, and although these plants do best in the borders, still they can be done very well in pots. In any case plenty of drainage must be afforded, and a pretty fair amount of root room. The soil should be loam and leaf soil in about equal parts, and a good dash of sharp sand to keep the soil open and sweet. Water should be given freely during the growing season, and during the season at which the plant is at rest the soil should be allowed to become moderately (but not dust) dry. Insects of all kinds must be kept under as previously described' and the same remarks also apply to training.

ACSONIA.—These plants, which are closely allied to the passion flowers, do well with the same general treatment, both as to culture and training, &c. Of course with these, as with the passion flowers, variations will have to be made in some minor details, but these will be readily seen. The flowers of some of the tacsonias are very beautiful, and will commend themselves to the attention of most cultivators, where they have plenty of roof room, such as a large warm conservatory or a light greenhouse, and we should advise their use amongst passion flowers.

For sorts select from the following: *T. Buchananii*, *T. ignea*, *T. manicata*, *T. mollisima*, *T. sanguinea*, and *T. Van Volxemii*.

Tecoma.—This is also a plant that requires plenty of head room, and a large amount of border in which to extend its roots. It is practically useless in a small place, but where it has plenty of room it is a good thing. For soil use good fibrous peat, three parts, and sound fibrous loam, one part, with a good admixture of sand. Plenty of drainage must be afforded, as during the season liberal supplies of water must be applied. The young shoots should ramble at will, and not be trained to any formal pattern. For the domes of large conservatories, and similar positions, the tecomas are very useful; but, as we said before, they are of little use for small places.

For sorts, the following are good: *T. Capensis*, *T. jasminoides*, *T. j. alba magna*, *T. j. rosea*, and *T. j. splendens*.

VIII.—ANNUALS.

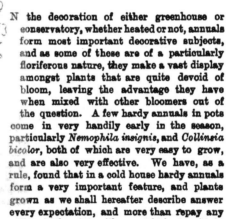

N the decoration of either greenhouse or conservatory, whether heated or not, annuals form most important decorative subjects, and as some of these are of a particularly floriferous nature, they make a vast display amongst plants that are quite devoid of bloom, leaving the advantage they have when mixed with other bloomers out of the question. A few hardy annuals in pots come in very handily early in the season, particularly *Nemophila insignis*, and *Collinsia bicolor*, both of which are very easy to grow, and are also very effective. We have, as a rule, found that in a cold house hardy annuals form a very important feature, and plants grown as we shall hereafter describe answer every expectation, and more than repay any trouble taken with them. The chief point with annuals is to obtain plants that are fully developed, and to gain this, as long a season of growth as possible must be accorded them. Whether we take greenhouse annuals proper, or hardy annuals, great care must be observed to prevent the plants being starved, as such starving tends to an early maturity, and consequently the blooms are either to a large extent abortive, or they are small and stunted, while the plant itself is so diminished in size, injured in constitution, and the foliage is so small and distorted as to leave much doubt as to the identity of the plant itself. Insects are also very objectionable for this reason, as well as from the mechanical harm they do in devouring the foliage, and, as it were, destroying the lungs of the plants.

The chief points in growing annuals are slow and steady growth, giving sturdy and firm habit, and with those plants which are from any reason too slender or weak to support themselves, a careful training and supporting by artificial means. Great care is also necessary to ensure a sturdy growth under glass, and the best means of preventing the plants drawing to an undue extent, is to afford them as much air as possible, and to keep them as near the glass as their individual habits will allow. We give cultural directions below.

Hardy annuals are only of real practical utility for early work, *i.e.*, until about June, and therefore it is necessary that they be sown in the September previous. The way we grow hardy annuals for this and some other purposes is as follows: In the second week in September seed is sown of the various plants we require to stand the winter, and the seed beds are well attended to until the plants are large enough to handle. Some beds of poor and rather sandy soil should then be prepared, so that the glass of the lights do not stand above 6in. or 7in. from the soil. Into these beds the plants should be transplanted, having them about three inches apart each way, or with very slender things two inches will be enough. After planting, the beds should have a good soaking of water, and the lights should be kept closed for a few days, but after a week the lights should be off on every favourable opportunity, and open at all times, except in frost or fog. The plants must be prevented from becoming frozen, and the supply of moisture must be so regulated that there is no rotting off during the winter months, and insects must be kept in check. At the same time, if fumigation is resorted to, great care must be taken that the foliage is perfectly dry, or the results will be most disastrous, the smoke having a great tendency to destroy the foliage when it is damp. About February or March, according to the situation of the garden and earliness of the season, the plants should be carefully taken up and potted in four or six inch pots, using a good rich sandy compost, and affording a fair amount of drainage. The soil should be in a moist but not wet state, and, after potting, the plants should stand for a day or two before watering. If, after potting, they are taken into a greenhouse at a temperature of about 45°, and there placed in a light position near the glass, kept watered, and otherwise attended to, they will soon come into bloom, and when fully out can be removed where they are required. Successional batches can be taken in as needed, and after the middle of April they may either remain in the frames or be removed to the cold house as desired.

The following sorts are useful for the above purposes, and, grown as described, will not fail to give satisfaction: *Asperula azurea setosa*, blue; Candytuft, the purple and crimson varieties; *Clarkia pulchella, var.*, Tom Thumb, rose; *C. p. var.* Tom Thumb, *alba*, white; *Collinsia bicolor*, lilac and white; *C. multicolor*, crimson black and white; *Coreopsis nigra nana*, dark red; *Erysimum Perofskianum*, orange; *Gilia minima cærulea*, blue; *Godetia*, The Bride, white and crimson; *Godetia Whitneyi*, blush and crimson; *Godetia*, Lady Albemarle, carmine.

Nemophila insignis, blue; *N. i. grandiflora*, blue; *N. i. marginata*, blue and white; *N. atomaria cœlestis oculata*; blue with black centre; *N. discoidalis*, black; *Saponaria Calabrica*, pink; *Silene pendula compacta*; rose pink; *Viscaria oculata nana*, pink; and *V. elegans picta*, crimson and white.

Half hardy annuals, unlike hardy annuals, will not stand the winter in frames, but such sorts as are sown in autumn must be kept in pots or in store pots through the winter. Take lobelias, for instance, it is rarely that anyone can obtain the plants of a sufficient size if sown in spring, but if sown in August, and pricked off into store pots or boxes, they can be wintered well, and in spring when potted off they make fine plants. Some things, such as marigolds, ageratum, one or two of the amaranthuses, Euonide bartonoides, tobacco, perilla, ricinus, &c., if sown in the end of August, and kept in a light house during the winter, do much better than if sown in spring; at the same time it is, however, as a rule, too difficult an operation for the majority of amateurs. There is, of course, a little difficulty in keeping annuals in a house, as they require plenty of light and air, and not too much moisture, while the compost should be light and fairly rich. A temperature of about 40° is also necessary, but many degrees higher or lower will cause the plants to run up dwindly or else fog off, either of which renders the trouble taken of no avail. Where plants are kept in the manner described above, they should be potted off in March and gradually hardened to plant out in May.

The best plan for amateurs to adopt is to sow the seeds of the various half hardy annuals in heat in January, and gradually grow the plants on in warm frames, or in a greenhouse until April, when they should be transferred to the frames to harden off preparatory to planting out in May. By doing this, good results are obtained without the trouble of keeping through the winter. Well drained seed pans or pots should be prepared in January, using a compost of rich light soil; these pans should be well watered and set aside for some hours to drain. The seeds should be sown evenly and thinly over the surface of the soil, and then covered with their own thickness of fine sandy compost. When placed in the position they are to occupy, each pot should be covered with a sheet of glass, and in a short time the seeds will appear. It is not advisable to water the pots overhead, but the better plan is to stand each pot in a tub of water reaching to the rim of the pot only, and when the water soaks through, the pots should be stood aside to drain, and then returned to their places, unless there is plenty of drainage at their own spot, when they can be put there as soon as they are removed from the tub. When the seeds have fairly commenced growth the glasses should be gradually removed, and the heat gradually diminished, at the same time admitting air to the plants in proportion to the rate at which heat is taken off. When in rough leaf they should be potted off into single pots, or two or three in a pot, according to the size of the plants and the purpose for which they are intended. If for indoor use they should be put into small 60-sized pots, and thence transferred to 4in. pots when the roots kiss the sides of the pots; but if for outside work they should—with the exception of such things as ricinus—

M

be stood where they are to occupy until planted out. Plenty of drainage
and a fairly rich and light soil are necessary for the well being of the plants,
whether grown in or outdoors. The general treatment is the same as for
half-hardy soft-wooded plants if grown indoors, therefore we shall not
refer to it further here.

For sorts of half-hardy annuals select from the following, those
marked with an asterisk being most suitable for house decoration:
Abronia umbellata, rose; *Acroclinium roseum*, rose; *A. roseum
album*, white; *Ageratum* (see "Soft-wooded Plants"); *Alonsoa
Warscewiczii compacta*, scarlet; *Amaranthus tricolor, bicolor*, and *melan-
cholicus ruber*, fine foliage plants; *Arctotis brevis capa*, orange; *Asters
of sorts (to be sown in March); * *Begonia sedeni Victoria*, various colours ;
* *Clintonia pulchella*, purple and yellow; *C. pulchella alba*, white; Convolvulus of sorts, various colours. *Datura ceratocaulon*, pink and white;
D. chlorantha fl. pl., white; the daturas are very fine for borders ;
Eucnide bartonioides, yellow; *Fenzlia dianthiflora*, rosy lilac; *Gaillardia
amblyodon*, deep red; *Helichrysum brachyrincham*, yellow; *Helipterum
Sandfordii*, yellow; ice plant, white; *Ipomœa Learii*, violet and blue; *I.
rubro cœrulea*, sky blue; *I. r. c. alba*, white; these three are fine for
greenhouse work, other Ipomœas are useful · for outside decorations;
marigold, in variety; *Martynia fragrans*, crimson; * *Mesembryanthemum
tricolor*, crimson and white; *M. t. album*, white, both useful for hot
situations; *Nemesia versicolor compacta*, various colours; *Nicotiana virginica*, pink; *N. grandiflora purpurea*, purple; *N. macrophylla gigantea*,
pink; *Nycterinia Capensis*, white; *Perilla Nankinensis* and *atro purpurea
laciniatus*, bedding foliage plants; *Phlox Drummondii*, various; *Portu-
lacca*, of sorts, stands heat well; *Rhodanthe*, of sorts, various;
Ricinus, various coloured foliage; *Salpiglossis atro purpurea*, purple;
S. coccinea, scarlet; *S.* dwarf scarlet, scarlet; *Schizanthus*, of sorts;
stocks, of sorts; *Tagetes signata pumila*, yellow, excellent for bedding
purposes; *Waitzia aurea*, yellow; *W. corymbosa*, various; Zinnia, of
sorts, various colours, most useful for bedding purposes. The above do not
comprise some for which we shall give special treatment.

Tender annuals differ from the preceding, inasmuch that they require to
be grown under glass for the greater part, if not for all the time of their
existence. Balsams, cockscombs, and such like are tender annuals, and as
they well repay any trouble in their culture, we shall give separate instructions for their growth. The chief points to be seen to are a light
house, in which to grow the plants, and a careful system of attention by
which the plants will be kept as stocky as possible, as long lanky plants
are not good to look upon.

We will now give cultural directions for the various half hardy and
tender annuals referred to above, which are especially worthy of attention.

STERS are much esteemed for conservatory decoration when in pots, but our advice is, "don't grow
pot asters in the pots, grow them in the open
garden." We have seen them grown, and grown
them in pots ourselves, and never have we come
across such good specimens as those from the open
garden. A bed of fairly rich good soil should be
prepared in the kitchen garden, taking care that it is
free from wireworms, and also that it is deeply dug. The
seeds of aster should be raised in a cold frame in
March or April, and when large enough, transplanted into the beds about
18in. asunder each way. Attention in the way of weeding, watering, &c.,
must be afforded, and when the first bloom opens, the plant should be
carefully taken up with a good ball of earth adhering, and transferred to a
pot sufficiently large to hold the roots comfortably. The whole of the
plants should be served in the same manner as they become ready, and as
soon as they are potted they should be removed to a frame facing the
north, and kept shaded from sun, and should also receive liberal supplies of
moisture. In from three days to a week of potting they can be taken to the
place they are to occupy. We leave the choice of sorts to the intending
grower, but perhaps the pyramidal varieties are best. A reference to any
catalogue will give a wide selection of colours and varieties.

ALSAMS.—A well grown balsam is a plant of
which the grower may be well proud, but it is
rarely that it is seen in good condition. The
general fault with plants grown by amateurs is
the long stem and poor blooms, blooms that are
not even semi-double being very common, and,
except where balsams form the one hobby of the
grower, it is rare to see the camellia flowered and
other varieties in good form. A good balsam bloom
should be quite as double as a camellia, and to show to
the greatest advantage should appear like one in the
arrangement of the petals. The great difficulty in starting the culture of
these plants is obtaining good seeds, and unless the intending cultivator
knows anyone who makes a fancy of balsams, or unless he can obtain
first-rate plants, some time will probably elapse ere a good fixed strain of

flowers is obtained. Seeds should only be saved from the finest and most perfect flowers, and although the quantity must of necessity be small the quality will be good, and this is what is of most importance. Only the best blooms on a plant should be reserved for seed, and if it is desired to have the seed extra good, only the blooms selected for seed should be allowed to remain on the plant.

The cultivation of the plants is very easy, and provided the seeds are right the results are sure to compensate for the trouble of culture. About the third week in March seeds should be sown on properly prepared pans of sandy rich soil, and placed in a gentle bottom heat, say about 65°, and as soon as the first rough leaf appears the plants should be potted off into 3in. pots, being careful to keep them close down in the pots, *i.e.*, let the seed leaves be close to the soil. As soon as the roots kiss the sides of the pot re-potting should be resorted to, and this should be repeated until the plants are in 8in. or 10in. pots. During the whole of the time the plants are under glass they should be kept as near the light as possible, and be frequently turned around, so that they do not draw to one side and become unsightly. Careful training must be given to the plants, or at least to such as are required in fine form. Disbudding is also necessary to such plants as are wanted at their best, removing all bloom from the main stem and base of the branches until the plants are of sufficient size, and then the buds at the tops will bloom almost simultaneously, and cause the plants to be really splendid objects. The buds that will be formed afterwards will cause a continuance of blossom for a long time; in fact, for some months, if the plants are liberally supplied with liquid manure. Instead of growing under glass the whole of the time, they may with advantage be done in the following manner, the same rules as to potting, training, &c., being applicable. By this method an advantage is gained, for although the plants will not be extra large they will be very hardy, and fit to stand about in places out of doors where required; and, being hardy in a comparative sense, they will be able to stand many little hardships, want of water alone excepted. About May the plants should be transferred to a frame where the heat is not above 50°, and the plants should be kept in a steady growing state, admitting air as required, and not omitting to supply water as necessary. They should be kept growing on steadily, disbudding and training as above mentioned. About June the plants should be fully exposed during the day, and when all danger of frost is over the lights may be kept off altogether. These should bloom in whatever size pots they are in at the end of July, and, if ordinary attention has been paid them, they will be very fine. In all cases plenty of drainage must be allowed, as the amount of water required is immense. Insects must also be looked after sharply, especially fly, slugs, and snails, one of these often destroying several specimens in a night.

For varieties the following will be found very good : Camellia flowered, rose flowered, both containing various colours ; Solferino, striped blooms, and Emperor, spotted, both kinds having various coloured grounds. The first is, however, generally esteemed most by lovers of fine flowers.

OCKSCOMB.—Before giving cultural directions for this plant (*Celosia cristata*), we may as well remark that it is of no use trying to cultivate it without heat, and many amateurs are without this requirement. Cockscombs, to be of real use, must be dwarf in stature, and the heads must be as large as can be obtained, so as to present as great a mass of colour as possible to the beholder. To the general reader we say buy the plants in full bloom, but where it is really desired to grow them great pains must be taken to obtain the proper conditions for their growth. A good cockscomb should be not more than nine inches high, and it should be quite that width over the top of the bloom, if not more. The bloom should also be as wide or thick as possible, and whatever the colour it should be at the same time clear and dense. The foliage must be kept quite green, and a sufficiency of leaves should occur on the stems, or the plants will have a very poor and bare appearance, far from pleasing to look at. The first point in growing these plants is to have the seeds sown at the proper time, and on this point different growers vary in opinion. It is, however, necessary to sow the seeds some time in March or April, using pans of well drained, rich, sandy soil, on which to sow the seeds.. Seeds of a good strain should be obtained, and if it is possible to obtain seed from a gardener who has it about three years old, so much the better, as the plants raised from such seed are not so much inclined to run to leaf as are new seeds. Where dependence can be placed in the seed, even if it is four or five years old, there is no harm done, but in such cases it is better to sow rather early, so that if one sowing fails there may be time to get in another without endangering the crop. After sowing the pans should be placed in a hot-bed, with a night temperature of about 65°, rising to about 70° with sun heat. A moist, but not stagnant, atmosphere should be maintained, and, as soon as the seeds germinate, they should have plenty of light and just a trifle of air, being careful that the soil in the pans does not become dry, or the plants will be ruined. The pans must be kept near the glass, and, as soon as the plants are large enough to handle, they should be potted off into small 60-pots, being careful to keep the seed leaves close to the soil, as the object that is desired is dwarfness. The pots must be placed in a position close to the glass, in a frame where the same conditions are maintained as above mentioned, allowing a rise of 5° or 6° in the day-time. The plants should be grown on as quickly as possible, taking care to keep the soil rather dry, but, of course, not dust-dry, and, as soon as the heads show so that the best formed ones can be selected, these latter should be re-potted into 4in. or 5in. pots, giving a good soaking of water ere re-potting, and allowing a few hours for the pots to drain.   After potting the plants should have a position close to the glass, the pots should be plunged to the rims in a bed of ashes or cocoa fibre on a hot-bed, just sufficient water, but not too much, must be given, and more air must be admitted.   It is, however, necessary that the surface temperature does not fall below 65°, or a check will be given that will probably retard the growth of the heads.   If the heads are required large another shift must be given before they are too large or much developed, and from 5in. to 8in. pots should be used for this final potting.   The same rules as to keeping close to the glass, &c., must be observed, and, when the pots become filled with roots, liquid manure should be given about twice a week.

We have found the following to be a good compost for these plants, if due care is taken in potting.   Three parts rather light loam, pulled to pieces, but not sifted, except for the seed pans, one part of thoroughly decayed cow manure, to which has been added a good dash of sharp sand. In potting, the soil must be pressed pretty firm around the roots of the plants, but not too hard, or the water will net run off.   Too loose potting, however, will cause the plants to run too much to leaf, consequently it is necessary to choose the medium course.

Of varieties crimson Tom Thumb and Sutton's prize Dwarf are good crimsons.   There is also a yellow variety, and a variety having heads striped with crimson and yellow alternately ; but, as a rule, the scarlets are best.

Calceolaria.—See " Soft-wooded Plants."

Celosia.—Unlike cockscombs, celosias have large plumes of bloom, and form pyramidal masses of colour.   The plants attain a height of from 2ft. to 5ft., and in some strains they have a graceful pendant habit, which renders them particularly beautiful when they are well grown.   Like cockscombs, they do not really answer unless a moist warmth is kept up, and, like them, they must be kept near the glass, and have plenty of room for their free development.   With all the celosias frequent syringings are also necessary to keep down thrips and red spider ; but, if grown in a moist frame, less trouble will be experienced on this head.   The seed should be sown in the same manner as cockscombs, and the treatment should be the same until the first potting.   After this the plants should have frequent shifts until the blooming pots are reached, those for the largest plants being 12in.; but they can be bloomed from 6in. pots upwards.   A moist genial atmosphere must be maintained, and the plants must not suffer from drought, or the foliage will be lost. As soon as the plants become too large for the frames, they should be transferred to a span roof greenhouse, allowing plenty of room for the circu- lation of air and free admission of light, and plunging the pots in cocoa fibre, to maintain as equable a temperature of the soil as possible.   As soon as the blooming pots are filled with roots, copious supplies of liquid manure should be given, and, where necessary, stakes should be placed to the plants to keep them upright under the weight of plumes.   Such little matters of routine as we have frequently mentioned before will also require to be seen to, and the plants will be well worth the trouble taken with them.

The sorts of *Celosia pyramidalis* that are to be recommended are *C. p. aurea*, yellow; *C. p. coccinea*, scarlet; and *C. p. purpurea*, purple.

GERANIUM.—Although not generally treated as annuals, both Cape and zonal pelargoniums are very easily grown as such; and, if the seeds are only saved in a fair manner from good plants, a fair show can be had late in the season. We do not advise the use of seedlings in preference to plants raised in the ordinary manner, as they are too late for bedding-out purposes, and, at the same time, no certainty can be held of their producing flowers of the same floricultural merit. There is, however, the chance of obtaining plants of sufficient merit to keep and propagate, and these will, of course, be in proportion to the quality of the seed. Some special features may also be obtained, which will render the plants worth cultivation independent of their floricultural merit; thus, a very dwarf, or floriferous kind, may be very useful for some particular work, like one we raised. This was a pink, the colour of Christine. The flowers were no better than the old phlox, but, as the plants did not exceed four inches in height, and the blooms were produced in great profusion, it made a fine edging plant, but no money value was attached to it— in fact, it was not worth a penny for sale. From some other seed we raised one—the only one of any use in over six hundred plants—that sold for £10 to a nurseryman, who exhibited it and took a certificate of merit, plainly showing the incertitude of raising these plants from seeds. We have also raised many tricolours of much use for ordinary work, but not sufficiently good to name, and a few have received certificates; but from the trouble it requires we doubt if it is a profitable speculation, unless it is the sole hobby of the grower. With the Cape pelargoniums, if the seed is saved from good plants, there is generally enough variety in the seedlings to render the work profitable from an amateur's point of view, although in a monetary sense there would probably be a loss if the plants were grown for sale. It is the best plan to carefully hybridise the flowers from which the seeds are to be obtained, as then it is almost certain that some plants will be produced that are worth saving. Another point with seedlings of the Cape and zonal sections is that tall standard plants can be obtained very easily, and even if the blooms are not models of perfection, still the plants render it possible to decorate large masses of shrubbery, &c., in a very pleasing manner.

For the zonal varieties the best plan is to sow in the greenhouse in January, and to grow on gradually until about June, giving the same treatment as described in "Soft-wooded Plants," but as soon as the plants reach 4-in. pots they should not be re-potted again. During July and August they will come into bloom, and any worth saving can be either re-potted or propagated; but unless a good place for their culture exists, they had better be kept in the 4in. pots until the succeeding spring. Such plants as are of no use may be destroyed ere winter comes, but they will make a little show for a time. Seed of tri colours and other variegated varieties should be sown in February, and receive such treatment as we have previously advised. If the leaves are of good form, and when held between the eye and the sun the zone in the leaf appears of a dark rich chocolate or crimson, the plants should be saved, for, even if they do not show colour the first season, they will do so eventually; and it often happens that those which are longest in breaking colour are the best. The plants of all the zonal class that are considered worth saving should be cut down in the following March or April, according to the accommodation that is at hand for their culture. After they have started into growth they should be repotted into good soil, and treated the same as ordinary plants.

Cape pelargoniums should be sown about June, or the end of May, if the weather is fine, and the plants should be grown on and treated the same as ordinary stock for spring blooming, using a little more sand in the soil than for those struck from cuttings. Saved with ordinary care the seeds will produce stock worth growing; but if the seeds are saved from carefully hybridised flowers, the results will be, as a rule, very good, although it is not probable that many plants worth naming will be obtained; but still there is a chance of such being got. But if one improved seedling is obtained in two or three hundred, it is very good work. We may add that a good stock of pelargoniums may easily be raised from seed, and if once this plan is started, the amateur will rarely leave it off willingly.

UMEA **ELEGANS.**—See "Soft-wooded Plants." This is a very useful plant, but it does best as a biennial, the soil should be a light fibrous loam mixed with sand; plenty of water must be given, but the drainage should be ample.

CE **PLANT.**—See "Mesembryanthemum."

Ipomœa.—Amongst the ipomœas some of the prettiest climbers for the conservatory will be found; and they are very useful, as both bloom and foliage are very pretty. The blooms, which are somewhat like the convolvulus in form, are of various colours, and as the shades vary more or less in the different colours, it often happens that a fine show is made, and if a little trouble is taken in hybridising the different varieties, excellent results are almost sure to follow. It is, however, desirable not to save seeds from dirty coloured flowers, such as brick reds or muddy coloured blues, but in all the shades of colour, clearness should be aimed at. The culture of the plants is very easy, and, in proportion to the beauty of the plants, may be said to be about as profitable as anything that is grown. Ipomœas require plenty of root room, and do best in a border in the house; but where this cannot be afforded, large pots or boxes are necessary for the well-being of the plants, so that a sufficient run for the roots is afforded. The plants are useful trained over trellises, or on pillars, or in fact anywhere, provided sufficient light is afforded, but if the roof is overhung with vines, it will be useless to try to grow these plants. The time of sowing will depend much on the accommodation for growing, and according as the seeds are sown early or late, so will be the period of blooming. Where convenience exists, it is well to sow as early as can conveniently be done, and sow two seeds in a small 60 sized pot. As soon as the roots kiss the sides of the pots, re-pot into 4in., and when the roots kiss the sides of these, they should be transferred to where they are to bloom. Plenty of drainage must be afforded, and the soil in the larger pots should not be sifted, but broken up small with the hands. We have found a good compost to consist of equal parts of fibrous loam, rotten manure, and leaf soil, with enough sharp sand added to keep the whole well open. Plenty of water will be necessary during the growing season, and a rather moist atmosphere suits the plants best.

For sorts, select from *I. coccinea*, crimson; *I. Learii*, violet and blue; *I. rubro cærulea*, sky blue; and *I. r. c. alba*, white. There are several others, but we curtail the list so as not to include doubtful varieties.

ESEMBRYANTHEMUM.—It is very often necessary to grow these for decorative purposes, as they will stand the sun so well; we give directions for their culture. The perennial kinds can be raised from seeds, but we do not, as a rule, think that it is advisable to do so, as more certain results can be had from cuttings; but still they can be raised in the manner hereafter described, if it is thought desirable. The ice plant and one or two others which are best treated as annuals, do well if grown as under, and they are certainly fine plants in their particular section. In most cases where the ice plant (*M. crystallinum*) is used for garnishing there is but poor foliage, *i.e.*, foliage deficient in crystalline beads, to use a common expression, and as a rule this is caused by too shaded a place for them to grow in. For our own part, a place fully exposed to the sun, but where a somewhat moist atmosphere can be maintained, would be chosen for the purpose of producing fine foliage, at the same time starving the roots of the plants somewhat. For the ordinary run of plants we sow the seeds in a warm house in February, using well-drained pans of sandy soil. The seeds are sown thinly, and but slightly covered with soil, a sheet of glass being placed over the pans, as previously described for other seeds. The pans are then placed in a warm sunny position and not allowed to get dry, but at the same time they are not kept too wet, or the seedlings would rot off. As soon as large enough to handle, the plants may be potted off into small pots, and as soon as these are filled with roots the plants should be shifted into 3in. or 4in. pots, in which they can remain for the season. A compost of two parts good loam, one part leaf soil or thoroughly decayed cow manure, and one part sharp sand, crushed mortar, and crushed charcoal in equal proportions, will be found to answer well, giving an inch of drainage to each pot. See also under "Soft-wooded Plants."

For sorts from seeds, and treated as annuals, we have found the following to be the best : *M. crystallinum* (ice plant), white ; *M. tricolor*, crimson and white ; *M. t. album*, white ; *M. cordifolium*, purple ; and *M. c. variegatum*, rosy purple, yellowish foliage.

Mimulus.—See " Soft-wooded Plants."

NICOTIANA.—Tobacco, although most suited for outdoor decoration, is still worthy of a place indoors, if it can be had in bloom in the winter or spring months ; and, as the plants are of stately appearance, they contrast well with the more dwarf stock of the soft-wooded plants that usually occupy the house of the amateur horticulturist. The seeds can be sown in April in a greenhouse in the ordinary manner, and as soon as the plants are large enough to handle they should be potted off into small pots, and from these they should be transferred into 4in. pots. As soon as these become full of roots it is necessary to pot off into 6in. or 8in. pots, and in these the plants will remain. The plants should be kept in a fairly shaded position, so that they do not show bloom until September or later, and about the end of September they should be removed into a light house, where the temperature is not lower than 45° in winter. Great care must be taken that the foliage is kept clear from insects, for if the green caterpillar that is so common in the latter part of summer once obtains a good hold of the plants, the foliage will be spoiled and the whole beauty lost. For soil we use equal parts of loam, leaf soil, and cow manure and sharp sand, mixed ; giving plenty of drainage, and supplying such water as is necessary.

The best sort for the purpose is *N. macrophylla gigantea*, a good rosy pink ; but at the same time *N. Virginica*, pink ; and *N. grandiflora purpurea*, purple, are very good. As most persons know, the fine foliage of the above tobaccos renders them very useful for various bedding purposes.

PETUNIA.—See "Soft-wooded Plants."

Phlox Drummondii. — When it is nicely grown this phlox forms as pretty a pot or low vase plant as can be desired, but unless some care is taken it is rather difficult to grow. In the first place it is of the greatest importance that the soil used shall be both rich and fairly porous, and also that good drainage shall be afforded ; and, although the plants will last the whole season bedded out, still, in pots, they will not last more than a month or so. The seed should be sown on a gentle heat early in the season, and, when sufficiently large to handle, they should be potted off into 4in. pots for single plants, or three plants in a 6in. pot. The soil we used is composed of two-thirds good fibrous loam, and one part thoroughly decomposed cow manure, to which is added sufficient sharp sand to keep the whole open. Plenty of drainage must be afforded, as the plants require a fair amount of moisture when growing freely. The same after treatment as afforded to petunias, &c., will answer very well for these plants, but they must be prepared and bloomed in frames before they are introduced to the house.

A packet of good mixed seed will produce a large variety of blooms, and unless it is desired to have expensive varieties, will answer all practical purposes. We therefore do not give a list here, but there are more than twenty names given in various catalogues, and in some cases (but not always) the plants come true to colour.

Portulaca.—The portulacas are very useful plants for either in or outdoor cultivation where the situation is warm and dry, and where there is plenty of sun. The succulent nature of the plants render them very useful for poor soils when used for bedding purposes, the colours being very bright and varied, while by keeping the plants pegged down, the bed will be one mass of bloom and lively green foliage, and if the colours are kept separate, large masses of orange, purple, white, and crimson will easily be obtained, but planted from mixed seed they will not look amiss ; in fact, some persons prefer this plan. Nice plants in 4in. or 6in. pots come in very usefully for various decorative purposes, and if large flat stages in the conservatory have to be covered, these form one of the best plants to use largely. The seeds should be sown thinly on broad mouthed pans or boxes, using sandy soil, and allowing plenty of drainage, but being careful that the soil does not become dry, or the seeds will fail. A gentle bottom heat is a great advantage in raising the seeds, as the plants come up quickly and well in such a place. When large enough they should be potted off into small pots, and be placed on a light shelf near the glass in a warm greenhouse. As soon as the pots become filled with roots, the plants should be shifted into the blooming pots, either 4in. or 6in., as desired. For soil we use a compost of good loam one part, decayed leaf soil one part, and coarse sand and broken sandstone or crocks together one part, potting the plants fairly firm, and applying water as may be requisite. A light warm but airy place will suit the plants well, and too much water must not be given if it is desired to have the finest show of bloom, but at the same time the supply must not be stinted sufficiently to cause the foliage of the plants to turn yellow.

Various named sorts exist, but, for all ordinary purposes, a packet of double and single mixed will be amply sufficient. We, however, give some names: P. alba, white; P. alba striata, white and scarlet; P. aurantiaca, orange ; P. aurea striata, orange and crimson; P. caryophylloides, striped; P. Thellusonii, crimson; P. T. splendens, rosy purple; and P. Thorburnii, yellow.

Primula.—See " Soft-wooded Plants."

RHODANTHE.—As summer decorative plants the rhodanthes hold a deservedly high place, as they are light and elegant in habit, and of pleasing colours. The flower is what is termed an everlasting, and like other plants of this class can be advantageously used for winter bouquets, provided they are cut and dried in a proper manner. For various bouquets the blooms also come in useful, and in buttonhole bouquets nothing looks prettier if combined with other blooms in a judicious manner. The blooms being rather pendant or drooping, combine well with more erect subjects, and the colours also have the same advantage. The culture is very simple, so simple indeed that it is a matter of surprise to us that this plant is not more extensively grown by private persons. With some of the metropolitan nurserymen the case is, however, different, as they find these plants very profitable, Mr. Maller, of Tottenham, alone selling from 10,000 to 15,000 each season, according to the space he can devote to them. The seeds are sown in February and March successionally, using well drained wide mouthed pans for the purpose, and for soil, having a light rich compost, rendered porous by the addition of a fair quantity of sand. These pans should be placed in a moist gentle bottom heat, and when large enough, the plants should be potted off five or six in a 4in. pot, using good, light, rich soil, and gradually inuring the plants to the greenhouse, which should be light and cool, or they will become drawn. If fair treatment is given the plants will flower in May and June, well repaying for the trouble bestowed on them. The same ordinary treatment as is given to other plants is all that will be necessary.

For sorts, use *R. Manglesii*, rose; *R. atro-sanguinea*, crimson; *A. maculata*, rose and yellow; and *R. maculata alba*, white, all of which are very pretty and useful.

Ricinus.—The castor oil plant is very useful in the sub-tropical garden, and in the conservatory as a fine foliaged plant, and as it is of easy culture there is no reason why it should not be grown for both purposes, where space permits. The culture is of the simplest, as the plants will grow in any ordinarily good soil, and when grown in pots a fairly rich free compost is all that is necessary, provided a good drainage is afforded. The seeds should be sown on a good bottom heat in March, and in the greenhouse in June, if plants are required late in the season for indoor use, as they look better in a brisk growing state than when fully grown, if they are required for house decoration. We prefer to sow the seeds singly, in small pots, and when large enough to pot on into 4in. pots, whence they can be permanently potted off into 6in. or 8in. pots, as may be preferred, but at the same time they do best in the larger pots. The earlier sown plants should be shifted into the greenhouse as soon as the first pair of leaves—not the seed leaves—are fully expanded, and can be grown on steadily, so as to be good plants to put out in June, while the second batch can be grown on in the frames, or outdoors until the end of September, when they can be taken indoors. It will be found necessary to give liberal supplies of water, and an occasional dose of manure in a liquid state. In other respects the treatment is the same as for the tobacco plant.

For sorts, use *R. communis major*, buff; *R. sanguineus*, red; *R. variabilis splendens*, various; and *R. viridus*, green. As companion plants to cannas and other stately subjects, the ricinus are very fine.

SCHIZANTHUS.—These are handsome half-hardy annuals of easy culture, suitable alike for both outdoor and greenhouse decoration, bearing an abundance of bloom, and of bright colour and rather tall habit, rendering the plants very useful in their season. When well grown, either singly in 4in. pots, or, what is better, three in a 6in. pot, the plants are very effective, and the colours being very showy, the plants form very noticeable subjects. The seeds should be sown on a gentle bottom heat or in the greenhouse about March, or even the middle of February, but we have found March early enough for all practical purposes, although, to suit special places, the earlier time of sowing might be useful. The seeds should be sown on fairly rich light soil, rendered sufficiently porous by the addition of such a quantity of sharp sand as may be necessary for the purpose. As soon as the plants are large enough to handle they should be pricked off singly into small pots, and gradually hardened off, so that they can be removed to the cold frame about the end of April. As soon as the pots are filled with roots the plants should be shifted into their blooming pots, taking care that they have sufficient drainage, and that the soil is rich enough to sustain them in good foliage. When the weather admits, they should have full exposure, and should be treated as other pot plants; as the pots become filled with roots, weak liquid manure should be applied each alternate watering, and when the bloom buds show colour, the plants can be removed into a cool light conservatory to bloom. Seeds may be saved on the best plants, but it prolongs the bloom to keep the seed vessels picked off, as the effort used in producing seeds soon exhausts the vigour of the plants.

For sorts, select from *S. Grahami*, scarlet and orange ; *S. grandiflorus oculatis*, purple and rose ; *S. pinnatus*, rosy purple ; *S. retusus*, rose and orange ; *S. albus*, white and orange ; *S. papilionaceus*, spotted ; and *S. oculatis pyramidalis*, violet.

Stocks.—Stocks, both intermediate and ten-week, are almost necessities in the greenhouse during the early part of the year, on account of their perfume, and, as the blooms of the double varieties can be mounted with but little trouble, they perfume a bouquet very nicely at any time without causing any unpleasant after effects, as is the case with some other perfumes. The culture is much the same, whether the ten-week or intermediate varieties are chosen, except that the former are sown in spring and the latter in autumn. Ten-week stocks should be sown in gentle heat in January, and successionally until the end of April, and so soon as the plants have their rough leaves they should be potted off, and when the weather becomes sufficiently mild they can be transferred to the cold frames. When the pots get fairly filled with roots a shift into 4in. pots should be made, and any of the plants which show single flowers may be destroyed at once, unless the strain is very prolific of double flowers. Care must be taken to keep the plants as close to the light as possible, to prevent their becoming drawn, or the beauty will be wholly destroyed. Where they are to be used for bedding out only they should be turned out of the small pots and planted rather thickly about the end of April, or early in May, if the weather is sufficiently open, choosing a nice open spot for the bed and using rich soil for the purpose.

The best ten-week stocks are those supplied in collections from Germany, but at times it is possible to obtain a good strain of home-grown plants, but as there is no real certainty of their turning out good when obtained from this source, it is by far the better plan to go in for German seed at once.

Intermediate stocks have to stand the winter to obtain the best result from them, and the treatment is, of course, somewhat different to that given to the ten-week varieties, insomuch as the winter treatment is concerned. The seeds should be sown in the latter end of August, and as soon as the plants are large enough they should be potted off singly into 3in. pots. Here they will remain for the winter until about the end of February, when they should be transferred into 4in. or 6in pots. The plants must be wintered in cold frames, from which frost is excluded, but to which air is admitted at all favourable opportunities. During the winter they must be kept as dry as can be consistently allowed, and the frame in which they are kept must also be dry, or they will rot off, and so the whole labour will be lost. As the plants commence growth in spring, water must be applied as required, and they should be turned round occasionally to keep the growth level. Plenty of room must also be given to allow them to develop fully, or they will have an appearance the reverse of elegant. For soil we find that in the earlier stages of growth a good maiden loam passed through a ¾in. mesh sieve, and enough sand added to render the whole freely porous, answers well; and for the blooming pots nothing answers better than three parts maiden loam and one part thoroughly decayed manure, to which is added enough sand to render the soil permeable to the water that is given. The soil for the blooming pots should be passed through an inch·mesh sieve only, as too close a soil is not good for the plants; but, of course, it is at the same time necessary to use a sufficient quantity of finer soil to fill the interstices, as the roots will not permeate the larger portions alone.

Various strains of intermediate stocks exist, some being good and some very inferior, and, therefore, it is desirable that only the best shall be used. The colours are scarlet, white, and purple, which should be very clear and pure, but at times a dull-coloured strain finds its way into the market. The East Lothian varieties are a fine selection if obtained true, but risk always attends the purchase of seed unless a good firm is dealt with.

The colours and shades of colour in the ten-week varieties are very varied, but the best are scarlet, crimson, and purple, the others, unless the strain is exceptionally good, being very dingy. The only plan, therefore, is to purchase of a first-class seedsman.

AGETES **SIGNATA PUMILA.**—This plant takes the place of the yellow calceolaria on soils where the latter will not grow well, and we therefore give it a place here. It should be sown on a gentle heat in March, and when large enough potted off singly into small pots, and gradually hardened off to plant out at the ordinary bedding season. We cannot say much for the plants when grown in pots, but in the beds or borders they answer their purpose very well. The colour is bright yellow.

IX.—RAISING SEEDS.

ESIDES annuals, there are a large number of
plants that can be raised from seeds, and,
as they are often difficult to raise, it will not
be amiss to give a few hints on the subject.
In the first place, the pot or pan on which the
seeds are to be sown should be about one-third filled
with crocks, and the soil should then be filled in to
within about half an inch of the top, and gently
compressed by tapping the bottom of the pot on the
bench. The pots should then be stood in a tub of
water, up to the rims, until the water soaks through to
the surface, and should then be set aside to drain.
When drained clear of all superfluous water, the
seeds can be sown on the surface, and a covering of
fine soil placed over them; this covering of soil not
to exceed the thickness of the seeds themselves. With
very small fine seeds it is not desirable to cover at
all with soil, but rather cover the pot with a sheet of glass,
and keep shaded until the seeds germinate. In fact, with all but the
larger seeds, it is desirable that a sheet of glass be laid over the pot or
pan in which seeds are sown, as by this means undue evaporation is
prevented, and a more equable moisture both in the soil and atmosphere is maintained. These points are particularly important in the
case of old seeds, or those where from any cause the germinating powers
are feeble, such as is the case in seeds ripened under adverse conditions, or which have not ripened on the plant, although they have
attained their full size; indeed, too much care cannot be taken to insure
the proper conditions under which the seeds will germinate. While on
this subject we may as well mention that there are but few seeds that
will germinate properly under a temperature of 45°, and for the majority
of comparatively hardy plants that are raised under glass a temperature
of from 50° to 60° is most advantageous to the raiser. With greenhouse
plants generally the seeds should be subjected to a heat of from 50° to 75°,

according to the class of plants; and in palms, acacias, and some other hard seeds, a temperature of from 75° to 105° will not be too much, provided that a moist atmosphere is at the same time equally maintained.

Watering is a very important subject where seeds are concerned, for, unless this is done properly and in a consistent manner, the seeds will either rot in the soil or else the plants will fog off ere they attain to sufficient size to pot off. It is useless to go slopping water around indiscriminately; far better leave the soil dry, as then the soil would not be destroyed if the seeds or plants were. What is required is sufficient judgment to tell when water is required, and to know how to apply it. Where large quantities of pots are used for raising seeds, it is a good plan to keep a large square washing-tray, but where only a few are used an ordinary tub is sufficient for the watering process. The way to apply water is to stand the pots in water to the rims, and to allow them to remain so until the water has soaked up to the surface of the soil; by this method the whole of the soil becomes thoroughly moistened and the tender plants are not wetted, a matter of some importance. It is important to add that the water should be of the same temperature as the house, or the roots will be chilled and the plants will, consequently, receive a more or less severe check.

The soil in which seeds are raised should be of a sandy, friable nature, so that when the plants are raised from the soil for the purpose of repotting, there will be a quantity of the soil adhering to the fibrous roots; but, at the same time, it is absolutely necessary that the soil shall be of such a nature that it breaks up freely without injuring the roots of the plants. On these points, however, the best medium is only attained by a little practice, and if a whole page were written on this subject but little practical service would be done.

In potting off the seedling plants, care should be taken to shift them ere they become too large, and, for a few days, they should receive as nearly as possible the same treatment as before, and then they can be gradually brought round to the treatment they are to receive for the future. In no case should violent changes, either of soil or temperature, be indulged in, and the treatment should always be as consistent as possible with the recognised methods of culture.

X.—PROPAGATION.

ROPAGATION is one of the most difficult parts of plant culture, and, unless proper conveniences exist, there are only a comparatively few plants that can be readily propagated by the general amateur. In nature, plants are most generally increased by means of seeds, offsets, and stolons or runners; but in an artificial state cuttings, layers, and root division are resorted to, and to meet the exigencies of trade these modes of propagation are carried on to such an extent that the plants become partially exhausted by the rapidity with which they are multiplied, and their inability to become sufficiently matured before being propagated from. If we take the ordinary scarlet pelargonium as an instance, the plant as raised from the seed is very robust, and with the general run of plants will attain a height of 5ft. or 6ft. if a little care is taken; but let the plants be of sufficiently high merit to create a demand, and it will be a lot of trouble to cause one of the young plants to attain a height of 2ft. or 3ft. This we have practically tried when raising large standard plants, it being far easier to graft good varieties on the top of seedling stems than to attempt to raise standards on their own bottoms, while seedlings do best on their own roots, simply because they are not exhausted by undue multiplication.

Such plants as can be propagated by layers, do not generally deteriorate in so great a degree as those raised from cuttings, and the deterioration is very much slower, but still in time the habit of the plants is in more or less degree changed.

Where the plants propagate themselves by off-sets or stolons, but little deterioration ensues, but still there is the tendency to deteriorate in a florist's point of view. In fact, the propagation of any kind of plant, if it has been improved, or in any way altered from its natural form, not-

N 2

withstanding the care with which it is done, tends to cause the plant to revert in a greater or less degree to what it was naturally. Excessive propagation tends to weaken the plants to a vast extent, and therefore where possible it should be avoided. It is far better to have double the number of stock plants than to risk the loss of quality caused by over propagation.

In striking cuttings it is necessary that a free sandy soil be used, and that the pots be well drained, also that the pots are clean. The cuttings should be made of a moderate length only, and should be cut close below a leaf, using a sharp smooth-edged knife. The cut should not be slanting, but should be directly across the stem, so that the smallest possible wound is made—with the exception of cuttings made from deciduous shrubs in winter. With soft- wooded plants of a sappy nature, it is advisable that a few hours should elapse between the making and inserting of the cuttings; but with such things as fuchsias, verbenas, and other plants of a like nature that have to be struck in bottom heat, the fresher the cutting is the quicker will it root; at least such is our experience. The soil in which cuttings (with the exception of succulents) are inserted should be fairly moist, or in a good state for ordinary potting, and on the top of the soil a half inch of sharp, dry, silver sand should be placed, which, as the dibble is removed, and the cutting inserted, fills the space between the cutting and the soil, and so tends to cause a more certain result. After the cuttings are inserted it is a good plan to water the pots to settle the soil around them, and after that the watering must depend on the requirements of the plants, as no fixed rules can be made on these points, the amount of water required wholly depending on circumstances ever which the grower alone has sole control.

As to the varieties and species of plants to be raised in heat; these can only be ascertained by practice, as some persons can raise plants best in heat, while others do them better in the ordinary house, and hints on the subject are given with the ordinary cultural directions. Where the matter is not mentioned with hard-wooded subjects, it is better to purchase young plants from a nursery.

Layering consists of pegging a shoot or shoots of the subject to be increased into a pot of soil, or into the borders out doors, as the case may require, first making a slit in the under side of the shoot.

Runners of plants should be pegged down on the surface of a pot of soil, and when well rooted the connection with the parent plant can be separated. For this process the ordinary soil and treatment afforded to the parent plant are all that is necessary, except that the supply of moisture must be carefully looked to, so that the plants are not rotted by an undue supply.

Offset and division of the plants, as a rule, is very s i ple, treating the plants thus obtained in the same manner as old plants with the exception of not allowing them to bloom, and paying more attention to watering, &c.

Striking cuttings in water and similar devices we do not hold with, but still they are at times practised with more or less success; but, as a rule, the young plants thus obtained do very poorly, as the roots are very fragile, and get much damaged in potting off. We would rather lose half the cuttings in the ordinary methods of propagation than strike the cuttings in water, and have such enfeebled plants as to be of no service when grown. In no case is it at all advisable to use methods that tend to enfeeble the plants, as from experience we find that amateurs generally have enough trouble with the most robust and healthy subjects, leaving out those which are rendered difficult of culture by unfair propagation.

The temperature in which cuttings emit roots varies, but for general purposes a temperature of about 60° will be found the most useful, unless, indeed, bottom heat is required, and then from 65° to 85°, according to the subjects, will be found desirable. Care must always be taken that too great a heat, or too moist an atmosphere, is not maintained, or the results will not be of the most satisfactory kind. Of course, with stove subjects that luxuriate in a moist heat, the conditions under which the cuttings are struck must be somewhat similar, but with the ordinary stock of the greenhouse great heat and moisture are quite unnecessary so far as good work is concerned.

It is useless to attempt to strike plants of the ordinary character in an arid atmosphere, as the plants rarely strike ; and if—as should be the case —the foliage is left on the cuttings, the undue evaporation caused by such a method will cause both foliage and stem to shrivel up, and so defeat the end desired.

So soon as any kind of cuttings are well rooted it is generally desirable that they should be potted off, and this operation should be carefully done, or the roots will be damaged, or, in some cases, wholly destroyed, which, of course, means the partial or complete destruction of the plants ; in fact, the loss of part of the roots at this part of the plant's existence is felt for a long period afterwards, and with slow-rooting plants it frequently causes failure. Too great care cannot possibly be taken to keep the roots intact if real success is desired. Where plants are rooted in heat, the soil used for repotting should be of the same temperature as that from which the plants are taken, and the plants should be replaced in heat for a few days until the roots have taken hold of the new soil, or the chill given consequent on the change to a cooler temperature will almost inevitably cause a severe check, from which it is possible they may not recover until too late. All plants raised in heat should be gradually hardened off, so that all checks are avoided.

XI.—INSECTS.

HE destruction and prevention of insect pests is of more importance than is generally credited, and often engrosses more time and causes more trouble than is supposed. There is not the least excuse for having plants covered with insect pests of any kind, as they are all amenable to proper treatment; and it must be always borne in mind that a crop of insects most decidedly means a vast quantity of unprofitable work, and work that could be easily avoided if the proper method of doing things were only taken. It is not of the least use relying on clearing off the insects in one lot, should they become too numerous, "because a few cannot do much harm," as that is just where the mischief lies; for those two or three scale, or aphides, or red spider, multiply and grow very numerous, and what could have been done in half an hour a fortnight ago, takes five or six hours now, and a lot of damage has been done besides.

Where it is really desired to grow plants worth looking at, it is absolutely necessary that all insect pests should be destroyed when they first appear, and close attention should be given to this matter, for on the absence of insects the future of the plants depends. If an aphis or other insect is seen, crush it at once; or should a slug or snail leave his slimy track across a leaf, or on the floor of the house, hunt till his death can be safely registered; and if ferns or orchids appear to be eaten, do not rest until every wood-louse, beetle, and cockroach is exterminated, as it is a certain fact that where there is one now in a short time there will be hundreds. No sentimental feelings should be allowed to get the better of us in this work, for sentiment and good plants will not go together. The live and let live policy is no good in plant growing, as it does not work well, neither is it satisfactory so far as the esults go.

Amongst the insects that are injurious to pot plants may be enumerated aphides, thrips, red spider, scale, caterpillars, wood-lice, and the ordinary slugs and snails; while weevils, wire worms, julus, and maggots also attack some plants. The first three are perhaps the most troublesome, as they are so prolific, though in a collection of hard-wooded plants scale is very troublesome, but still if they are taken in time a little care will soon eradicate them. Wireworms and julus are not so easy to be rid of, as they are in the soil, and are not always suspected until the mischief is done, and then the matter is past recall. Maggots in cutting pots at times do much damage, but they are easily managed. Woodlice are perhaps the most troublesome of all the larger insects, as there is great difficulty in persuading them to come and be killed. In fact, once get a stock of them and they remain for ever. We will take the insects we have named in rotation, and give some remedies that have been found useful for their destruction, premising that all insecticides are used with due care and discrimination.

APHIDES.—Of these there are two that claim especial attention—the green fly (*Aphis rosæ*), and the black or cherry fly (*Aphis cerasi*)—both of which have to be combated at one time or another. Everyone knows the green fly, which seems to have an indiscriminate taste for feeding on all succulent foliage, and which if taken in time is easily kept under. There is this to remember, however, and that is, the harder the foliage on which the aphides feed the harder it is to destroy them.

Fowler's Insecticide, if applied as directed on the bottles, is a good remedy, and one that does not injure the plants. It is also not objectionable so far as appearance goes.

Gishurst Compound is another very good insecticide for hard foliaged subjects, but it has to be washed off after twenty-four hours, or the foliage will be much stained. It is also not advisable to apply this article to plants having hairy or woolly leaves, or to plants having tender foliage, as the results will frequently be not very desirable.

Tobacco water made from the liquid expressed from "pigtail," "ladies' twist," and similar tobaccos, and sold by most large seedsmen, is very useful for many subjects, but must not be applied to tender foliage or blooms, as it leaves a stain. The strength is about a quarter ounce to the gallon of water, applied in the evening and washed off in the morning following.

Pooley's Tobacco Powder is a very useful dry application, and should be always at hand. It is the waste tobacco from the large factories, and is mixed with lime and a small quantity of assafœtida, but not enough to make the use of the powder offensive. In this state it is sold duty free, and is consequently much cheaper than snuff, and quite as effective. The powder should be dredged or sprinkled on the plants through a small dredger—a penny tin pepper-box answers admirably—and washed off with the syringe the next morning. If allowed to remain on too long it is apt to disfigure the plants, but with ordinary care it is one of the safest and most easily applied insecticides there is.

Fumigation with tobacco, tobacco paper, cloth, or any of the numerous preparations of tobacco that are in the market, is also a sure method of dealing with these pests, but it smells badly, which renders fumigation particularly obnoxious where ladies have the handling of plants. Where plants are in full bloom it is also very dangerous to use tobacco smoke, as it takes all the blooms off; therefore, before fumigating any plant house, it is necessary to remove all plants that may be in bloom—a task that cannot always be performed. The whole of the plants in the house should be fairly dry at the roots, and the foliage should be quite dry when fumigation has to be done, and care should be taken that there is no water on the foliage of the plants, or there is a great probability of the foliage being badly spotted, so spoiling the beauty of the plants and injuring them as well. When all is ready, two or three pots should be prepared by placing some well-lighted charcoal in the bottom of each, and on this the fumigating material in a damp state should be placed. The material should have been previously prepared by tearing into small pieces, and it should be just damp enough not to flame, or the consequences will be disastrous to the plants around. Care must be taken that the pots do not burst into a flame after they are lighted, but otherwise no further attention is requisite. The necessary amount of smoke is difficult to determine accurately, but it is better to give two or three fumigations on successive nights than to overdo the matter in the first fumigation. Of course it is desirable, or rather necessary, that all the glass in the house is in good condition, and that extra large crevices are stopped up with moss or other material, so that the smoke shall be kept in the house as long as possible, or it will only be waste of time and material to attempt to fumigate the place. The morning after fumigating, the plants should be thoroughly syringed, and plenty of fresh air should be admitted to clear off the bad smell, and reduce the bad effects on the plants, if there is any chance of such effects occurring; and in fact the place should be thoroughly cleaned out. Where the plants are badly infested with fly, at least three fumigations on alternate evenings will be necessary to destroy the young broods, but if taken in time one fumigation will be sufficient. Where the expense is not objected to, one of Dreschler's or Tebb's fumigators will be found to far supersede the use of pots; or if the matter of a guinea is not objected to, one of Brown's patent fumigators will render the process of filling the house with smoke a not very unpleasant matter, as the operator can stand outside with the machine and fill the house with smoke both rapidly and well with no further trouble than turning a handle. In fact, for the amateur there is no machine to beat Brown's, as no inconvenience need be experienced with it.

Other methods of destroying aphides besides those we have mentioned are in use, but they are not so useful to the amateur. If a few plants only are infested, they can be fumigated under a box; but the use of some insecticide will be found preferable as a rule.

ANTS.—In the greenhouse the presence of ants is a source of unmitigated nuisance, and unless stopped in time, the insects will work a lot of mischief. The damage done is chiefly mechanical, and the plants are not in any way injured in the manner that aphides or red spider causes injury, but the soil in the pots is disturbed, and the plants are seriously injured by that means. As a rule, the plants die, or, at least, become much injured by the water passing through the pots by means of the ant runs, instead of going through the whole of the soil and moistening it, and, therefore, some means must be taken to destroy the producers of this evil. Where there is plenty of dry rotten wood, virgin cork, or other light dry material in which they can work, the large black ants are liable to put in an appearance, but, as a rule, the small black ant is the one that is most to be feared. The red ant, too, will sometimes be found, but not so often as the black ones, and, as the same methods can be used for the destruction of the whole family, it matters but little which attacks have to be guarded against.

Where the ants have taken up their head-quarters in pots, the best, and, indeed, the only plan, is to plunge the pots in water for ten or twelve hours, and so drown the insects. In this it is necessary to use some discrimination, as balsams and plants of a similar nature would not do well if this treatment was often repeated, and hard-wooded plants at rest would in many cases start into growth prematurely, and thus perhaps the cure would be worse than the disease. As, however, in the greenhouse proper, the plants and the ants commence active life together as the weather becomes warm, this flooding will not in many cases do much harm, but still some amount of judgment is necessary, as at times failures do occur.

Our favourite plan, although a dangerous one, can easily be applied to all cases not in pots, and as we never have a failure we give it here. To half a pound of fine sugar add an ounce of white arsenic, and mix intimately with about a pound of medium oatmeal, keeping the whole dry. To use, spread small portions about the places the ants frequent, and in a very short time they will all disappear. Two ounces of white arsenic boiled in about a half-pint of water, to which is added, after the mixture is boiled, a quarter pound of treacle, and allowed to cool. To use, dip a sponge or piece of bone in the mixture, and place near the haunts of the ants, or sprinkle the mixture around the hill or infested place, and the ants consuming it, die in great numbers. It is needless to state that these preparations of arsenic are deadly poison, and should be used only when other remedies fail. Great care should also be taken that the packages or bottles containing these mixtures are labelled "poison," and kept in a secure place.

Other plans are to lay shallow saucers of oil near the runs of the insects, in which large numbers will get killed—of course changing the saucers sometimes. A sponge soaked in weak sugar water and placed in their runs will collect a great many, and if the sponge is taken up two or three times a day and thrown into very hot water a large quantity can be killed. A marrow bone is also a very good trap, scalding the insects to death when a large number has congregated together; and there are also some other traps of a similar nature.

Boiling water poured down the runs and nests of the ants is of much use in destroying these pests; but perhaps the best and simplest plan is to see that no accumulations of soil exist in out-of-the-way places, and that all the brickwork, flooring, and woodwork is in sound condition, and free from crevices in which these ants can make their nests. In no case can carbolic acid, chloride of lime, or other offensive agents be used in the greenhouse, as such do more harm than the ants themselves.

CATERPILLARS.—Caterpillars and grubs of various kinds sometimes attack the foliage of the various plants, but the attacks are more particularly confined to those plants which have large succulent leaves, such as pelargoniums, and on these their depredations show to great advantage, or rather disadvantage. The common butterflies do great damage amongst collections of tricolour geraniums and other plants of a like nature, and therefore it is a matter of good policy to keep them from entering the house if possible. This is best done by using tiffany netting, or Haythorn's netting, over all the openings; but where this cannot be done it is advisable to destroy all the butterflies that can be caught. Next to this, constant attention, so far as examining the plants and destroying the caterpillars go, is all that can be done, and this hand picking is the only real remedy. There is no application of any real service, and therefore it is really useless to go further into the matter. Hand-picking and constant attention is the only remedy, and unless this is done the foliage is sure to be punctured and eaten.

MAGGOTS.—It frequently happens that in cutting pots a large white maggot puts in an appearance, and, in some cases, it does a great deal of damage. There is only one remedy for these maggots, and that is to bake the sand before using it. As, however, it is, as a rule, only in dirty sand that the maggots appear, cleanliness is one of the first requisites, and it is only by having clean washed sand that the best results can be had. If the maggots appear at any time, there is nothing left but to take the cuttings out and bake the sand. There is no application that can be safely applied to the pots for the destruction of these insects.

RED SPIDER.—The red spider (*Acarus tellarius*) is one of the worst insects that can get into a house, and at the same time is one of the most difficult to eradicate. When the conditions under which they thrive best is known, it should be an easy matter to prevent the appearance of the spider from obtaining any great headway; but at times the plants require an atmospheric condition that is favourable to the spider, and then it is that various remedies have to be employed to destroy it. A dry, arid atmosphere, combined with dryness at the roots of the plants, will be almost certain to cause the red spider to put in an appearance, and out. doors, in very hot dry weather, the insects also appear, and thence gain an entry into the house. Some plants are more liable to the attacks of spider than others, and special treatment has to be given in such cases, but with the ordinary stock plenty of clean water applied with the syringe to both surfaces of the foliage, and applied pretty often, will be found as good a cure as any. We have no faith in insecticides, but there is no harm in trying them if it is desired to spend plenty of money over the matter.

Where it is not convenient to use the syringe sulphur can be dusted over, or rather under, the foliage and blown off with a pair of bellows in a few hours, and in many cases this will be an effectual cure, but care must be taken that the foliage is not injured by the sulphur. To this end it is desirable that the full sun should not be allowed to reach the foliage while the sulphur is on, as the fumes given off would, perhaps, do injury.

Another good plan where there is much spider is to paint the hot water pipes with a mixture of sulphur and clay, and then to warm the pipes to a nice heat, about as warm as the hand can bear comfortably, as if the heat is too great the plants will suffer from the fumes. In fact, this process should only be attempted by persons who are conversant with fumigating with sulphur, or serious effects may be caused.

A modification of the above is to heat some bricks in boiling water, and when nearly at the boiling heat they should be taken into the house and sprinkled with flowers of sulphur. On no account must the bricks be placed under tender or delicate plants, or should they be placed so that the streams of ascending fumes impinge on any climbers on the roof, or the foliage will be seriously damaged. In no case must the bricks be heated in a fire.

Where practicable, the cold water cure is, however, the best, and gives the least trouble, and therefore it is the safest in the hands of the amateur. The sulphur remedies require care to use safely, and in unpractised hands often do more harm than the red spider.

SNAILS AND SLUGS.—These are often introduced in the pots in which close-growing plants are grown, and it is therefore obvious that too great care cannot be taken to ensure the cleanliness of both pots and plants. In all cases before introducing pots into the greenhouse or conservatory they should be examined carefully, especially in the drainage holes, to see that neither the black nor white slugs are concealed about them; and the plants should also be looked over to see that they are clear from insects, as one or two slugs or snails will do damage to the extent of several pounds amongst valuable plants. Faulty brickwork, badly-arranged ventilators, and dirty houses, all tend to render it more difficult to exclude slugs and snails, and therefore these points should be carefully attended to, on the reasoning that prevention is better than cure. Hand picking is the only way by which the number of these pests can be reduced, and we always make it a rule that if a trace of either slug or snail is seen, it should be traced to the end and the insect destroyed. There is no application that will destroy or deter these insects in the greenhouse, but outdoors soot and lime are useful.

Heaps of wet bran laid about will attract the slugs, as will also cabbage leaves, and, in fact, any rubbish will attract them, thus pointing out the necessity of great cleanliness in and about the houses.

SCALE.—This is a very troublesome insect when once well established, and great care is necessary where it exists, as it soon spreads to other plants, and renders them comparatively valueless. There are two kinds of scale—the brown and the white—that are common, although there is, according to some authorities, a large variety, various trees having their own especial scale insect; but this we will not discuss.

Suffice to say, that the brown scale is all that the amateur can wish for without having a dozen or more hanging around. Scale renders the plants unsightly, and does an immensity of damage, so that it is a matter of urgent necessity that it should be destroyed ere it gets established, or the house will never be clear. Of course, if taken in time, before there are many insects on the plants, but little harm, comparatively, will be done; but woe to the neglectful gardener who just lets the plants alone because "there are only two or three" scale on them. We can assure our readers that nothing is more prejudicial to the appearance of the plants than this mode of doing work, and it should be, therefore, most carefully avoided; and anyone who takes the destruction of insects in hand before they have had time to become established—especially in the case of scale—will find that the battle is won, whereas if they have once the upper hand, only a losing war can be waged against them.

The methods of destroying scale are not numerous, and they are very simple as a rule, albeit rather tedious. In the first place, all the insects must be cleaned off, and then the stems of the plants should be washed with tobacco water, to which soft soap has been added in the proportion of two ounces to the gallon. After cleaning the plants, the surface soil of the pots should be carefully cleared off to the depth of from a half-inch to an inch, and fresh soil added to fill up the vacancy thus caused. If the scale again appears, the process must be again repeated, not allowing them to attain too large a size before commencing operations against them.

Another plan is to apply weak size water with a syringe to plants such as oranges, camellias, and similar smooth-leaved plants, and washing off with lukewarm water forcibly applied with a syringe after twenty-four hours. On no account must this be applied to hairy-leaved plants, or where there would be great difficulty in its speedy removal, for in such cases the remedy is as bad as the disease. The first is the better plan for the amateur to adopt.

Thrips.—These are perhaps one of the worst pests with which plants can become infested, as they are both very small and tenacious of life, while they multiply to a prodigious extent in a very short time. No plant that they are at least partial to long escapes their attacks, and therefore it is very desirable that, as soon as they appear, some steps should be taken to destroy them. The general cause of their overrunning a house is, plants are purchased containing more or less of their number, and thence they spread to other plants before they are noticed. It is necessary to use some thorough methods of destruction with them, and, whether fumigation is applied or some liquid insecticide is used, it is necessary that it shall be repeated more than once, or in a few days the plants will be as badly infested as before. Fumigating for three alternate nights is, as a rule, a good remedy; but it is necessary that no plants are in bloom in the house, or the bloom will all fall off.

Fowler's Insecticide is a good application, if repeated on three alternate evenings, and, where it is possible from the hardy nature of the plant to apply it, tobacco water made from the liquid previously mentioned is good.

Simpson's Antidote, Gishurst Compound, and various other insecticides are of use for destroying thrips, and, therefore, we need only add that constant attention is the chief point to be seen after.

WIREWORM.—These are one of the greatest nuisances that it is possible for a gardener to be plagued with, especially in the case of the grower of carnations, pinks, stocks, and similar plants. There is no application that can be applied to the soil for the destruction or eradication of these wretches, and all that remains is to pull the soil in pieces by hand, or to bake it, a process we object to, as it drives off some of the more useful chemical constituents of the soil.

In the preparation of all soil likely to contain these insects, it is desirable that it shall be carefully pulled into such small pieces as will not conceal the insect, unless, indeed, it be almost invisible; and when caught each worm should either be divided or else consigned to a fiery grave. If it is considered more desirable to bake the soil, this operation should be done in such a manner as not to destroy the fibres in the soil, but it must be continued for such a time as to render the soil dust dry, and dry up any wireworm that is concealed therein. The same treatment applies to julus, but these are not very often present. In no case must soil be boiled, as is often recommended, as boiling destroys the texture of the soil, entirely unfitting it for the growth of plants.

WEEVILS.—These sometimes give trouble where vines are grown, and they are not easily caught. The only effectual plan being to spread a sheet of paper or a white cloth under the infested plants, and at night to come out with a light and shake the insects off and crush them. If, however, ordinary care in the destruction of the common insects of the house is persisted in, weevils of no kind will trouble the amateur, that is if the place is kept clean; but, as we said before, unless cleanliness is maintained a clean bill, as regards insects, cannot be returned.

WOODLICE.—These do much harm to ferns, tubers, and various of the ordinary greenhouse stock, paring or rasping off the outside cuticle, and then eating their way into the interior of the stems, &c. Woodlice are a sure accompaniment of dirt and decay of all kinds, and the cause removed the stock soon dwindles away. Various methods are employed to destroy these pests, but only with partial success, as they seem to bear lives free from all allurements whatever. The best plan that we could ever find to succeed in practice was to fill a pot full of dirty moss, to which a few crumbs of potato were added, and leave the pot in one of their favourite haunts for a few days, and then take it up and drop the contents into a pail of hot water, so ridding the place of large numbers each time of operating.

Another plan is to place potatoes, scooped out in the centre, about their haunts, and to shake the woodlice into a pail of hot water each morning; and, indeed, almost any root will answer for this purpose, and a fair-sized turnip is a good trap when several fair-sized holes are bored in it.

A very effectual trap is to obtain some dry horse droppings, and to mix a few potato parings amongst them; place in shallow boxes in dark places, and once a week empty the whole into a fire or a pail of boiling water, by which means vast quantities will be destroyed.   Pouring boiling water around the crevices where they mostly congregate is also effectual, but the best plan is to stop all cracks and crevices in brickwork and wood, to have sound clean floors, thoroughly lime-whited walls, and to keep a few toads about the place.   Thorough cleanliness is the greatest enemy of woodlice.

MILDEW.—Although this is not an insect, or the effect of insects, yet we give it a place here, as it has to be largely combated in badly ventilated or badly managed houses.   It is simply the result of a warm, moist, and *stagnant* atmosphere, and if this is not maintained mildew will rarely appear   In a well-ventilated house mildew is not often troublesome.

Ewing's composition is a good cure for this disease, as is also flowers of sulphur applied one day and blown off the next.   With care, however, the plants will easily be kept free from mildew, and where our directions are carried out not one of the pests mentioned above will give much trouble.

XII.—MONTHLY CALENDAR.

S perhaps many of our readers will find a calendar of operations useful, we give it for one year, so that our little book shall be complete in respect of managing a greenhouse such as we generally find in the hands of amateurs. We commence from August, as that is perhaps the commencement of general greenhouse work, and it and the following months are certainly the most convenient for starting a greenhouse. Propagating soft-wooded plants of various kinds, the completion of the hardening-off process on hard-wooded plants, and various other points, all combine to make these two months the commencement of the season, as it were, so that by starting with these months we shall keep the calendar in its proper order.

We shall endeavour to make the hints we give here applicable to all houses that come under the head of greenhouses; but, of course, stoves and forcing houses will be excluded, as they do not come within the scope of our present work.

As, however, it is not possible to give directions for the greenhouse held by any particular person, our readers will have to adapt the directions as to management in such a manner as will meet their particular requirements; and, therefore, we only give general descriptions of management here. The selection of subjects must also be left to the individual tastes of the owners, as the various plants do not suit everyone alike. One word of advice we will, however, give, and that is, do not have too large an assortment of plants, and do not try to grow plants that require much heat in a house not suited to them. It is far preferable to grow a few suitable plants well, and have a good display from them, than it is to attempt too much and fail with the lot. Never attempt too much, but advance by degrees.

AUGUST.—The first point to be considered this month is the propagation of bedding plants of various descriptions, as the season has advanced quite far enough for the purpose. The modes of propagation having been before described, it is not necessary to enter into the matter further here, but we will give a few hints that may be useful. For the majority of plants the best pots with which to strike cuttings are those that are rather flat for their height, and which are about six inches in diameter; when filled one-third or half full of crocks, these are the most useful so far as size is concerned. We prefer round pots in the ordinary green-house, although, as a matter of course, some space is lost by their use; but the advantages gained more than counterbalance this loss of space sustained, as the freer circulation of air and more equable temperature that is obtained by this method well repays for loss of numbers in the plants, less loss occurring through damping or fogging, as it is called. Of course, so far as the saving of room is concerned, square seed-pans, or boxes made for the purpose of wintering cuttings, are best; but, in the hands of the amateur these tend to embarrass rather than assist, as such a large quantity of plants are lost by fogging as a rule. The method of heating is also a great consideration, as, in the majority of houses erected, the hot water or other heating apparatus is not fitted to use with growing a large quantity of plants in boxes.

Cuttings of the majority of half hardy bedding plants will root freely in the open air; but if a frame or two are empty, it is a good plan to stand the pots in these, as then shelter from excessive rains can be provided. In no case is it wise to allow too great a quantity of water in striking cuttings intended to stand through the dull, damp days of winter, as plants that are full of sappy growth are very liable to fog off; it is, however, necessary that *sufficient* moisture be allowed, or the cuttings will shrivel up instead of rooting.

The soil in which cuttings are placed should also have some share of attention, lest some undesirable results should follow. Great care must be taken that worms, woodlice, and maggots, &c., are most conspicuous by their absence, and that there are no chips of wood, half-rotten leaves, or other rubbish present that may be likely to cause fungoid growth. For this reason, claret and other boxes made of poplar are most unsuitable for storing cuttings for the winter, because, as a rule, fungi of a most ob-jectionable character, or rather the mycelium of the fungi, put in an appearance and destroys the cuttings. At least 25 per cent. more cuttings should be put in than the number of plants required, to allow for possible accidents.

This month is a good time to thoroughly clean all houses intended for the reception of plants, and also to mend the glass, and re-putty, and, in many instances, re-paint the roofs of the houses, as drip will do more harm than cold. When dry the paint should have a good glossy or shiny appearance, but it should not be put on too thickly; two thin coats are better than one thick one. The cleaning process should embrace all parts of the house, the stages should be washed down thoroughly, walls limewhited, flues cleaned out, water pipes cleaned of dirt and rust, valves and air pipes cleaned and put in thorough working order, and the furnace and boiler put in repair.

Another, and an important point, is to see that ventilators and sash lines are in really good order, and if the least doubt exists as to their strength, they should be at once replaced with new ones. In fact, it is necessary that the place shall be put in thorough repair in all parts, as a sash line breaking, or a pipe or flue fouling on a frosty night, will often destroy the majority of the plants in the house; and, at the same time, a dirty house will produce such hosts of insects as to cause really serious damage.

Some of the earlier azaleas and camellias may now be got in, being very careful that the foliage is dry and that the pots are clear of slugs and other obnoxious insects; but all the later stock must be kept out, giving such protection from heavy rains as may be necessary. All hard-wooded stock must have as much air and exposure as their habit requires, but heavy rains must be kept off. The pelargoniums cut down last month should now be shaken out, and re-potted into smaller pots. Chrysanthemums should be placed in their blooming pots, and receive such supplies of liquid manure as may be necessary. Cinerarias should be divided and potted in small pots, and young plants should have a shift, if necessary; some seed may also be sown. Roman hyacinths and some other bulbs should be potted up, and all bulbs for early blooming should be kept in the dark for a few weeks, so that the roots shall obtain firm hold of the soil ere the foliage starts. Annuals may in many cases be sown to stand the winter, for early work, and a sandy friable soil should be chosen for the seed beds. They must also be transplanted before they become too large.

Where vines or other roof climbers exist great care must be taken to keep them in a sound, healthy state, and free from insects and mildew, or the results will be serious to the plants that have to be introduced into the house shortly. In short, every means must be taken to keep the place in the most perfect order and the plants in the best condition, all details of tying, removing dead flowers, and other little items being most particularly carried out.

SEPTEMBER.—This month is generally a very busy one so far as the greenhouse is concerned, as all arrears of work has to be got up, and a vast amount of fresh work to be done. Amongst this work is the continued propagation of bedding plants, and this must be carried out as briskly as possible, for if left until too late much trouble and risk will be incurred. As it is, some things will root more readily by having a gentle bottom heat applied to them. In fact it is a good plan where soft wooded plants only are grown to put the fire on for a few nights when the plants are first put in; but if there are vines or hard wooded plants in the house, this cannot be done with impunity. In all cases a plentiful circulation of air must be maintained, and water must be given as it is found necessary; but it is especially necessary that too much be not given, or the plants will become sappy and unfit to stand the winter. The same rule applies to hard wooded plants, enough water should be given, and no more, and the circulation of air should be fully attended to. Great care must be taken that the drainage of the pots is perfect, and that both plants and pots are free from noxious insects.

O

The whole of the hard wooded stock must be got into their winter quarters before the end of the month, taking into account the state of the weather as to the date on which they shall be taken indoors. Great care must be taken that there are no worms in the pots, and that the drainage is perfect, or results the reverse of pleasant will be obtained. Care should also be taken that the green slimy growth on the pots, which is not infrequently found in the case of pots not plunged in ashes, should be washed off carefully, and the pots allowed to dry ere taking them into the house. All plants liable to the attacks of scale should be carefully looked over to see that they are quite clear from this pest, and particular attention must be paid to searching for slugs, snails, and caterpillars, as they often do much damage.

This is about the best time to purchase a stock of hard-wooded plants, where such purchase is required, and some little skill will be found necessary here. In the first place, it is requisite that the plants shall be well-grown young plants, and that they have been grown on in a proper manner without check, or they will not be of very much service. They should also be quite free from insects, and therefore a close examination is necessary. If, however, the plants are bought at a good nursery, and a fair price paid, but little trouble need be anticipated on this account.

In the general work much has to be done, and unless done at the proper time will not be so good for the plants. Primulas, calceolarias, and cinerarias require especial attention at this season, as well as other plants of a like nature. Particular attention is also necessary with those plants which are being prepared for winter blooming, as a day's neglect often ruins the plants for the purpose for which they are intended. Any late Cape pelargoniums should be ripened off if the bloom is over, and then headed down. A good batch of cuttings should also be got in for use in summer, to succeed those potted off. Chrysanthemums may still be shifted into larger pots where it is considered necessary, or liquid manure can be applied regularly; and in places where the room is limited this latter plan is best. Mignonette may be sown to stand the winter, but it does best in frames for this purpose. A batch of Dutch bulbs should be got in, and plants in pots, such as weigelas, which should have ceased growth, if such is not the case, should be induced to ripen by partially withholding water, but still giving enough to keep the plants in proper condition.

The aim of the gardener at this season should be to obtain a compact sturdy growth with all plants that are intended for winter blooming, and to avoid such treatment as will tend to have a reverse effect. Nothing is more injurious than to draw up the plants in a weak attenuated habit, as in such cases the bloom obtained is of the poorest, both deficient in quantity and substance, and should the bloom be cut for bouquets or table decoration, it soon falls to pieces, and even if gummed it soon withers and becomes useless. Where it is desired that good results should be obtained, it is necessary that a slow, steady, healthy growth be maintained.

Grapes should be ripened off as soon as possible, and cut and stored in a dry fruit room, or the moisture from the plants will soon cause them to become a mass of corruption.

OCTOBER.—It is still advisable to continue introducing such soft-wooded plants as it may be desired to save during winter, and cuttings of geraniums and similar plants must be got in as soon as possible, if it is desired to strike more of them at this season. As a rule it will be found requisite to use a little bottom heat in striking these late cuttings, but still in many cases it pays to do them even as late as next month, but where possible the early-struck plants are best, as they cost less in striking, stand better through the winter, and bloom better and form more useful plants in spring. Where very large quantities are required, and labour is limited, it frequently happens that time does not allow of a sufficient quantity being got in in due season, and therefore extraordinary methods will have to be adopted to obtain sufficient stock. Old plants of zonal pelargoniums can be taken up, and cut in closely, putting as many as can be got in into 6in. pots, and these old stools will make a good lot of plants in the early part of the year, besides affording a good batch of cuttings, which will strike readily in March. The tops which are cut off now will also afford a lot of good cuttings, which, as we mentioned before, will strike readily with a little bottom heat. All the bedding plants which it is desired to save should be taken up before they are injured by frost, and care should be taken that they are not kept too wet after potting. Cuttings of shrubby calceolarias may also be put in now, as well as next month, care being taken that the cuttings are not frosted, or infested with green fly. Before putting in the cuttings the frames should be carefully examined to see that no slugs or snails are in them. Where, from the dampness of the climate, or the severity of the weather, it is found that annuals do not stand the winter well out doors, they should now be pricked out in frames, and while air is freely given too much moisture must be excluded.

Hard-wooded plants should now be in a proper condition to stand the winter, and care must be taken not to get the pots water-logged, or the damage will be very great. Insects should be carefully looked for, and in no case should their presence on these subjects be passed by lightly.

Pelargoniums must be induced to become dormant by Christmas, and plants requiring much the same treatment must occupy a similar position as regards the care bestowed on them. It simplifies matters to a great extent to have plants requiring similar treatment close together, and also allows of a better disposition of the plants in bloom in the house. Chrysanthemums will be the *piece de résistance* for the next six weeks or two months, and therefore it is desirable to arrange them to the greatest advantage, and also to pay as much attention as possible to prolonging the time of blooming. Scarlet geraniums, and other plants, will, of course, be making some show, but not to the extent of that produced by the chrysanthemums. Some of the hardy plants will also be making a little display, and mignonette should be well in bloom, if the three varieties are properly grown. In a short time some of the earlier primulas and

o 2

cinerarias will be making some display, and, if time and care is bestowed in the right direction, a fair amount of interesting blooming plants will now show their beauty.

Successional batches of Dutch bulbs should be got in, and these should be kept in a dark place for a few weeks, as previously recommended. Where large plants are required, primulas and cinerarias can have another shift; but, after 4in. or 6in. pots are reached, unless the house is large, it is not well to pot on as, the plants do not show well in a small house if the pots are too large, as large pots cannot well be hidden on too upright a stage. Some more seeds of cineraria and calceolaria may be sown if very late plants are desired and the house is suitable for the purpose.

Great care must be taken to keep down insects, and to remove all mildewed or rotten vegetable matter, as these evils cause a lot of trouble during the damp winter months. A free circulation of air must be maintained, and a temperature of about 45° kept up; but rain or thick fog must not be admitted into the house.

Where vines are ripe enough, they should be pruned, and the rods tied along the front plate of the house, so that as much light as possible shall be admitted. Cleanliness should also be the order of the day.

NOVEMBER.—This and the two succeeding months will be found the dullest part of the year for gardening matters, and therefore it is necessary that the greater pains be taken with the glass portions of the *ménage*. In the first place the good arrangement of the plants occupies a foremost place in the necessary work, for the plants should be re-arranged frequently, so that the interest in the house may be maintained. Fresh arrangement of the plants, and the introduction of all new subjects to prominent notice, tends to keep up the interest in the house or houses to a far greater extent than is often supposed, and therefore particular attention should be paid to this point. Cleanliness is also an important part of the work in this department, for, unless it is carefully attended to, but little pleasure can be experienced in the examination of the plants; more attention being paid to the clothes, and in looking where to find a dry clean spot on which to stand, than to the plants. The destruction of insects and mildew, and the removal of all dead foliage and other matters which tend to cause fungoid growth or disease to the plants, should be rigidly attended to, and, in short, the house should be kept clear from all that is not of legitimate use. No empty pots, heaps of paper, tying material, flower sticks or *débris* of any kind should ever be found about the house, and therefore there should be no cause to advise their removal.

Ventilation must be closely attended to, but in damp weather some caution is requisite in admitting air, as, unless there is enough fire heat to dry the atmosphere, many of the plants will damp off, and therefore much attention must be paid to this point. In thick fogs it is not advisable to open the house at all, particularly if there are plants in bloom inside, as fog exercises a most deleterious effect on the blooms, and with some subjects causes the petals to fall off. Too great a fire heat must not be kept up for the next two months, or the plants will draw, and become too weak and sappy; but enough heat must be maintained to keep the place sufficiently dry. This result is best attained by abundant ventilation and warmth enough to keep the house at a temperature of 45°; but, of course, consideration will have to be given to the class of plants grown and their requirements.

The majority of plants will be at rest, but some will be blooming pretty freely, chrysanthemums being in strong force. Some re-potting will be found necessary, but except where really necessary it is not desirable to shift plants at this season. The last batch of Dutch bulbs should be got in, as well as some of the hardy plants that we have mentioned previously, but discretion must be used in the choice of subjects. In fact this is the slackest time of the year, and; as a rule, it is not advisable to do more than is absolutely necessary.

In some cases a root or two of rhubarb and a few pots of seakale can be brought in, and placed under the stage, and a very agreeable dish or two will be obtained with little trouble or expense; but too large a quantity should not be grown, as it tends to increase the dampness of the house.

Hardy plants in the frames should have as much air as possible, and be treated as hardy; but frost and excessive rain must be excluded, as plants of all kinds can stand more cold when in a comparatively dry state than when saturated with moisture and making a too sappy growth. Vines in the house should be pruned as soon as ripe, and all the foliage, dead bark, and prunings should be burnt up out of the way.

DECEMBER.—Except in such cases as is mentioned, the work this month is practically the same as last; cleanliness and freedom from insects being most necessary. Care in ventilation and applying fire heat is also necessary, but the rules have been given before. A further batch of hardy plants may be introduced. Practically, however, to the amateur work is at a minimum; all that is necessary should have been done last month.

JANUARY.—During the greater part of this month very little has to be done beyond the ordinary care of the plants; but towards the end of the month propagation of soft-wooded plants will demand attention, and the earlier the season the sooner will work in this direction commence. Before referring further to this matter we will take the earlier part of the month first. In the first place, it is necessary that due attention be paid to the individual plants composing the collection. All those plants which are showing bloom should be brought forward into the lightest and most prominent positions, while others can occupy places in positions not so conspicuous, but at the same time allowing each plant as nearly as possible the position most suitable to it. The previous directions as to cleanliness about the plants and house still hold good; and in the case of the destruction of insects, our remarks must be carefully attended to, as generally with the advent of the new year and brighter weather, the increase of insects is very rapid, particularly aphides, and perhaps they are the worst pests there are to contend with. How to destroy them has been previously described, so that there is no need to repeat the directions, but the remedies named must, as a rule, not lay idle. Great care is also necessary in watering, as too little or too much water is not calculated to keep the plants in the greatest health. A happy medium will have to be chosen, and this can only be learned by careful attention to the requirements. and nature of the plants, and no amount of book knowledge will ever teach this part of the work of the greenhouse. The heat of the house should also be kept at some point between 40° and 50°, according to the class of plants grown, but the temperature should not be such as to induce the plants to make premature and weakly growth. Ventilation must also be carefully attended to, as before explained, but, of course, in no case may a current of frosty air be carried over tender plants or plants in bloom. Hardy plants require the same treatment as previously described, and, except in cases mentioned further back, they should not. be induced to make any active growth yet. Ventilation must also be very strictly attended to.

In bad weather the preparation of the various soils and composts, getting ready a good store of crocks and labels, pot washing, and other necessary work, should be attended to, and everything got in readiness for active work so soon as it commences, as it is simply sheer waste of time to have these things to attend to when they are actually required for active use. Good heaps of compost should be kept under cover, as well as the other necessary articles for potting, and then they are always to hand when wanted. Tools of all kinds should be looked over, and all other odd work about the place should be done during the bad weather.

Towards the end of the month old plants of fuchsias, heliotropes, lobelias,. lantanas, verbenas, &c., should be put into a gentle bottom heat to induce them to throw up cuttings, which strike very freely on a gentle bottom heat. Some seeds can be sown in the end of the month, but of course due attention will have to be paid to the season in these matters, as the earlier the season the earlier their growth will commence. Some cinerarias may possibly be once again re-potted if extra large plants are required, and the young stuff must be brought forward as it is found necessary, but for the necessary information on these points see further back. Some more hardy plants and shrubs can be brought in to ensure a further supply of bloom, and hyacinths, &c., showing bloom should have a warm light position.

FEBRUARY.—This month is generally a very busy one in the greenhouse, and, in fact, it will be found difficult to keep pace with the work where large quantities of bedding plants have to be grown. First and foremost comes the preparation of the medium for supplying bottom heat, and unless regular propagating frames are at hand, it is well to use a good steady hotbed. As the heat required is not very high, but at the same time should be lasting, we give our method of making beds for this purpose when we find it necessary to do so. In the first place there should be a sufficient supply of leaves from hard-wooded trees or plants, and good horse manure that has been shaken out of a moderate shortness. These materials can either be shaken together or kept separate, but if well made, the bed will be practically as lasting whichever process is followed. The materials should be turned and shaken about twice, so that a proper state of moisture shall be attained, and should the materials appear too dry some water should be applied, but it is important that they should not be too wet, or a sudden violent heat will result, and the bed will be cold in a.

few days. The bed should be about 3ft. wider and longer than the frame to cover it, and it should be put together in small forkfuls, well shaking it about, and treading firmly as the work proceeds. When finished, the bed should be about 2½ft. high in front and 6in. or 9in. higher at the back, and should be 18in. wider than the frame on all sides; but if in a brick pit of course this will not be the case. Instead of having the materials mixed together, a layer of manure and a layer of leaves alternately may be used, in which case the leaves should be in layers about 3in. thick, and the manure treble the thickness, being careful that the bottom layer is manure and the top one leaves. When the frame is put on, about a couple of inches of soil, ashes, or sawdust should be put inside to keep down any rank steam or gases that may be emitted by the heating materials, and the outsides of the frame, or rather the material that projects beyond the frame, should be covered with boards, long litter, or other medium to keep off rain, as to get the outsides soaked with wet means a great diminution of the heat, besides removing a large quantity of the manurial value after the bed is cold. After about three days the bed will be in good fettle for the purposes desired, and the pots of cuttings may be placed in it; but it is necessary that just a chink, say of the thickness of a penny piece, at the back of the frame be left open, so that superfluous steam may escape, or it will condense on the foliage of the plants, and cause them to fog off. Great care is of course necessary that the covering of ashes or other material is not broken, as should this be the case, the rank steam from the bed will escape, and cause very undesirable results. Besides striking cuttings of the various bedding plants, this bed will be found useful for many purposes, starting seeds of lobelia, perilla, and other subjects, starting dahlia roots, and other jobs of a like nature, and many things that we have not space to enumerate here. As to the varieties of plants to be struck now, we must refer our readers back to the various articles on the subjects referred to, as a list would occupy too much space here. Where cuttings are not sufficiently numerous the old plants should be placed in heat as advised last month, and as a rule this will have the desired effect.

Soft-wooded plants generally will require attention, but there is not so much to be done in the way of re-potting, &c., as there will be next month, especially if the season is late, as the dull weather rather retards the plants, and it is not advisable to act too much against nature. It is, however, a good plan to select a few of the best fuchsias, petunias, zonale pelargoniums, &c., and give them a good shift, so as to obtain large plants for the various uses for which they are so often required. Cape pelargoniums should be trained, and in some instances re-potted as they require, and care must be taken that the foliage is dry before the sun reaches it, or the leaves will be scalded or spotted. A good batch of cuttings should be got in for autumn blooming, when they come in very useful. Continue to re-pot calceolarias as they fill their pots with roots, and, if necessary, more seed may be sown; but of course this must be left to the judgment of the grower.

Most of the hard-wooded plants are now making growth rapidly, that is if the season is early, needing careful looking over, and where such is required, should be top-dressed, and young plants that are growing forward for specimens should be re-potted where necessary. These latter must also be very carefully attended to in the way of training, &c., as the future appearance of the plants depends on the training they receive while young. The foliage must also be kept clean, and a rigid destruction of all insects must be carried out. As the house will now be getting gay with the display of bloom from the various subjects, it will be found more difficult to keep insects under, and fumigation will have to be done outside the house in a place provided for the purpose, as inside, the smoke would destroy the bloom.

More hardy subjects can be introduced from time to time, to keep up a good display, and nothing more will be necessary than to give the ordinary treatment afforded to the other occupants of the house. Hardy annuals, such as nemophila, collinsia, and similar subjects should be potted off carefully in 4in. or 6in. pots, according to the various habits of the plants, and should be replaced in the frame, care being taken that insects are kept under.

Great care must also be taken to afford a good ventilation to the house, and that the foliage of the plants is dry before the sun reaches it, or burnt or scalded foliage will result, and, to say the least, the appearance of the plants will not give credit to the grower.

MARCH.—If anything, the work this month is much more important than last, and the same amount of care must be given; but the results will be more marked, and the show of bloom will be largely increased. It is also very probable that the stock of green fly will be continually increased, and as the difficulties attending fumigation at this season are very great, recourse must be had to some insecticide, such as Fowler's or Pooley's tobacco powder, either of which is very effective if properly applied. Slugs and snails must also be sharply looked after, as should also woodlice, as these do much harm, especially among ferns and other plants of a similar nature. Staking and tying out the various plants, and removing dead leaves, must now be closely looked to, and it is also desirable that dead blooms should be removed ere they become too much decayed, as it is easier to introduce the germs of mildew into the house than it is to get rid of them. Ventilation, too, should be carefully attended to, especially where a fire is kept going, as a close, moist atmosphere at this season means plenty of mildew and insects, and should, therefore, be avoided. A free circulation of air is absolutely necessary, and must be varied according to the temperature outside, so that no blasts of cold air pass over the plants, especially in frosty weather. At the same time air must be admitted sufficiently early to dry the foliage, for the reasons stated in last month's directions.

The propagation of bedding plants of all kinds should be vigorously proceeded with, and so soon as rooted the plants should be potted off into small pots, and carefully hardened off to a certain extent to fit them for the greenhouse. All the autumn stores should be at once potted off if not already done, and, in fact, the work of propagating and preparing soft-wooded stock should be pushed on as quickly as possible. And here let us point out a wrinkle in growing young soft-wooded stuff : always use plenty of sharp silver sand, and do not pot too firmly, as the roots, being as a rule very tender, do not push very freely in heavy soil, and hard potting tends to break off the roots. It is also a good plan to retain as much soil as possible round the roots, as it protects them during potting, and also affords a means of the plants obtaining the necessary moisture and nourishment without receiving a violent check. Cuttings of dahlias and similar plants should be struck forthwith, and when rooted potted off and placed in heat until the roots have taken firm hold of their new quarters. Where room is scarce, towards the end of the month such things as scarlet pelargoniums, &c., can be placed in pits outside, provided frost and damp can be kept at bay. Many things that are nearly hardy can also be transferred to the frames at this season, and the space they occupied in the house can be profitably used for other subjects.

Hard-wooded plants will require increased attention to be paid them, and all young stock will have to be frequently looked to in the way of training and other matters. As, however, the matter is fully treated under the head of hard-wooded plants, no further remarks are necessary here, except that the plants shall be kept quite clean, both from dirt and insects.

In the cold frames things will be requiring attention generally, and perhaps the most important is the proper treatment of the plants. Watering, ventilation, and the destruction of insects are all important matters, and after these come the re-potting of those plants which require it. Many plants will have to be shifted into their blooming pots, calceolarias, picotees, carnations, &c., all requiring this to be done now. Training the various plants as found necessary, and potting off cuttings, will also form a part of the work. Nor must the sowing of the various half-hardy annuals, &c., be forgotten, as they make a grand display if treated properly. Indeed, it is necessary at this time to make the greatest efforts to supply the plants that are required for the decoration of both flower garden and greenhouse at a later season.

APRIL.—Arrears of work in the preparation of bedding plants must be made up forthwith, or the plants, as a rule, will not be large enough for any practical decorative use. There is no reason to repeat our directions about this part of the work, as it is practically the same as in previous months, except that a very great many of the plants can be propagated without fire heat, although the plants thus obtained will be late. The whole of the stock of zonale pelargoniums, and other nearly hardy plants of a like nature, should be in the frames, and where necessary should be repotted; but unless extra large plants are required, or the plants are to stand in pots, 3in. pots are large enough for the ordinary run of bedding plants. Great care must be taken in destroying insects, as they do a greater amount of mischief as the weather becomes warmer, particularly in the case of slugs and snails, which, if left unmolested, will soon defoliate the whole of the plants in a large frame, especially if the plants are of a soft, succulent nature. Where red spider or thrips are prevalent in the season, care should be taken that they are destroyed as soon as they appear, for a stitch in time saves nine in this direction.

Hard-wooded and other plants will now be in full bloom, and great care must be taken that no drip falls on the flowers, neither must too damp an atmosphere be maintained, so that water condenses on the blossoms or foliage, as such would do much harm to the appearance of the plants, but more particularly so if the sun reaches the plants ere the damp is dispelled, as in such case the plants will become spotted and scalded, giving them a very unsightly appearance. To this end it is advisable to open the top lights of the house early in the morning, not later than seven o'clock, and giving a thorough current of air a little later, according to the weather, and whether fire heat is, or is not employed. Anyway, it is necessary that the foliage be dry before the sun reaches it. For the special treatment of plants under this head see "Hard-wooded Plants."

The arrangement of the plants and training of roof climbers, &c., are in themselves very important portions of the work in this department, and must have especial attention paid them, as on the manner in which they are done very much depends, the appearance of the house at this season being one of its chief attractions; and it is generally admitted that, however fine the plants may be individually, unless well arranged, the effect they produce is only of a very medium quality.

In the frames there is still plenty to be done, many plants requiring to be re-potted, and many things have to be trained out in the way they should go, rather than as they desire to go. Various subjects will require liquid manure, and others top dressing, but for these items we must refer our readers to past directions. Cuttings of various plants must be got in, and in potting these a goodly quantity of sand must be used, both before and after they are rooted. Plenty of air must now be given, and insects must be kept at bay by the use of insecticides.

Vines must have great attention paid them where they are used instead of other roof plants; and it is scarcely needful to remark that they must not obstruct too much light, or the other plants will suffer. For treatment of vines see "Vine Culture for Amateurs," published at 170, Strand, price 1s.

MAY.—All the bedding plants should now be out of doors, and the house should only be occupied by such plants as are to be employed for the decoration of the house only. All the propagation of plants for outside work should have been finished by this time, and only the propagation of plants for indoor decoration should be in hand. The stock of bedding plants should be thoroughly hardened off, and, to afford room for the more tender plants, calceolarias and other nearly hardy plants and hardy annuals should be got into the beds and borders early in the month, if not done in April; and at the end of the month zonale pelargoniums, and the other plants of a like degree of hardiness, should be got into their summer quarters. Some of the best of these, however, should be put by and potted on for various decorative purposes in pots; and these reserved plants should be carefully tended, as they come in very usefully for many places which would otherwise be bare. The more tender varieties may remain until next month, and the space that is obtained by placing the hardier kinds out can be occupied by them.

Of course the same remarks about the destruction of insects, and the general cleanliness of both plants and the places they occupy, need not be further mentioned this month; but, as a rule, these are just the points that the amateur neglects, and consequently he has more or less ill-success with some of his plants, if not all.

Where it is desired that a few cucumbers should occupy the house or frames after the bedding plants are got out of the way, they should be sown at once on a brisk heat, choosing such as Rollison's Telegraph or Masters' Prolific, both of which are good and free bearers; or, if desired, plants can be purchased and put out at once.

As during the next two months the greater part of the present occupants of the house will be got into the frames, it is desirable that the plants that are to occupy their places should be pushed forward; and to this end fuchsias, balsams, celosias, begonias, lobelias, &c., should be got on so as to render the place as gay as possible for the time the plants are out, although where there is a good garden the bareness of the house will not much matter. At the same time a well-furnished conservatory is a nice place to spend a short time during rain or after the heat of the day is over.

Besides such plants as we have mentioned, there are plenty of subjects which can be prepared in the frames, and brought into the conservatory to bloom, and these will, of necessity, occupy some time. Seeds of primula, cineraria, and a few other plants will have to be sown for early work; and various other items of work only seen by the owner of the place will have to be done. Training and re-potting various plants, and the application of liquid manure where necessary, will also occupy time, and altogether this is a busy month, although not so much so as the preceding.

Ventilation must be carefully seen to, and while it is not altogether advisable to admit too much air on frosty mornings, still it is absolutely necessary that the foliage and bloom of the plants shall be quite dry ere the sun reaches them, or burnt and scalded foliage will greet the eyes, and in some cases the nose, of the amateur who allows this state of things to come about through neglect of the necessary precautions.

Vines being now in full bloom should be gently tapped or shaken a little before noon each day, so that the pollen shall be well diffused and a good crop of fruit set, as it is a comparatively easy matter to thin out superfluous berries, while it is a total impossibility to place in fresh ones where they may be deficient. The proper training of all roof climbers should be well attended to, and a good look-out kept for scale and other noxious insects which often infest them. Red spider and thrips must be particularly looked after, as they spread very rapidly in a dry atmosphere, but if care is taken they will not gain much head.

JUNE.—Early in the month, if the weather is at all propitious, the whole of the bedding plants will be got out, and the space thus left vacant will be required for the hard-wooded stock, which should now be transferred to the frames. Some of the hard-wooded plants require to be kept in the house for the whole season, but such things as oranges, camellias, azaleas, &c.,

are best out for part of the year. The best plan is to prepare beds of coal ashes in which to plunge the pots, as they are then not so liable to suffer from drought, or sudden changes, as when stood on the ground, and, besides, worms will not penetrate through the sharp ashes. Under the hole in each pot a piece of slate or tile should be laid as an additional safe-guard against the ingress of worms, as they do a vast amount of harm to the plants which they honour by their presence. Where it is necessary, plants should be re-potted, and some will be benefited by the application of clear liquid manure, but it is with the grower to state which plants do, or do not, require artificial aid. In fact, it is an open question as to the good or ill effects produced by the application of liquid manure of any kind; and, although we use it in many cases, still we consider that with hard-wooded plants it is far the better plan to re-pot rather than apply stimulants, as the effects produced are not really lasting. With large specimens the case is somewhat different, as it may not be desirable to give larger pots, and, therefore, stimulating manures are necessary to keep the plants in full vigour for some time; but this artificial stimulus tells on the constitution of the plants, and sooner or later they are sure to die off. The plants must be protected from heavy rains, but should have all the exposure possible consistent with their well-being. Due attention will have to be paid to watering and keeping clear of insects, and also to training the young stock, giving each plant sufficient room in which to develop itself.

In the house some care is requisite to keep the plants that occupy the places of the hard-wooded stock in good order, and plenty of light is of primary importance to all things but ferns. Watering must be carefully carried out, so that the foliage of the plants is not splashed when watering in the middle of the day, which will be necessary with some subjects which make a very gross growth. Ventilation must also be carefully attended to, the house being opened at six or half-past six every morning; in fact, air should be admitted all night, unless any special reasons exist for the contrary course to be pursued. The necessity of staking the plants, keeping down insects, &c., is too evident to need more than a passing note. Permanent trees and climbers will, of course, require due attention in the way of watering, keeping clear of insects, and other matters that will be readily seen, and, where such is required, the grosser shoots should be pinched back, so that the growth is equalised.

The various plants that are coming on for autumn decoration must be re-potted and trained as is necessary, and some cuttings of zonale pelargoniums and a few other subjects should be put in, so that in winter some good blooming plants shall be at hand. Primulas should be potted off, and more seeds sown.

Vines and climbers must have a fair share of attention, both in the way of training and the destruction of insects, and also in the way of giving a sufficient supply of moisture, as in too many cases this latter point is often much neglected. Thinning grapes, where there are any, is also an important job at this time, and much skill and judgment are required in this operation, it being necessary that the berries should only be left just thin enough to form a good bunch, but still that they shall not be over-thinned, as in the latter case the bunches will have an appearance not at all calculated to please the eye when placed on the table.

JULY.—The propagation of various plants will now be commenced, choice geraniums and other good plants of course taking the precedence of others of less value; but, as many plants, difficult to strike later on, now strike readily, choice should also be made of these. Seeds of various plants may yet be sown, and those seedlings which are of a sufficient size should be potted off, and older plants should be shifted on as they require. The various plants which are being grown on for autumn and winter use should be shifted on as necessary, and care should be taken that no neglect is allowed to befall them. Watering is a matter that needs especial attention, and previous remarks should be especially attended to in this respect.

The plants for decorative purposes in the house must not be neglected, and great care in watering, ventilation, &c., must be taken, especially with fine-foliaged plants. Previous remarks as to drip and watering the foliage must be carefully attended to, and full ventilation must be given by seven o'clock in the morning at the latest, as after this time any condensed moisture on the foliage will not have time to get away ere the sun comes on the plants with too severe force, and so cause severe disfiguration of the foliage. In fact, some ventilation should be given through the night. The destruction of insects must be attended to with unremitting care, and the house must be kept in a generally clean and tidy condition, both for the sake of the plants and the comfort of the visitors. Where necessary liquid manure should be applied, but as before explained, its use should be chiefly on short-lived subjects, and not on those of more permanent nature.

Hard-wooded plants should receive all necessary care and attendance; but the work is about similar to that of last month, and need not, therefore, be repeated. Suffice to say that the treatment for individual plants is given farther back. The treatment given should be such as will tend to cause a good sturdy growth of a floriferous nature, and to this end as much exposure as possible should be allowed, consistent with the habits of the plants. The earlier forced plants should be ripened off as soon as possible, so as to be ready to come into the house early next month. Care must be taken to keep all insects cleared off as soon as they appear, especially those which attack the foliage, as they damage the plants so very much in appearance.

Vines and roof climbers will still require some attention paid them in the way of training, &c. The final thinning should be given to grapes, and they should, after stoning, be well fed with liquid manure to cause them to grow apace, and become fine in the berry.

Repairs should be done at this season, and the outsides of the houses, frames, &c., should receive a good coat of paint, as this saves both the woodwork and putty, besides keeping the place watertight. (See also "August.")

FINIS.

INDEX

Catalogue

of

New & Practical Books.

LONDON : 170, Strand, W.C.

CATALOGUE.

HANDBOOKS ON ANIMALS, BIRDS, &c.

I.

Breaking and Training Dogs:
Being Concise Directions for the proper Education both for the Field and as Companions, of Retrievers, Pointers, Setters, Spaniels, Terriers, &c.
In cloth gilt, 5s.; by post, 5s. 4d.

II.

Diseases of Dogs:
Their Pathology, Diagnosis, and Treatment; to which is added a complete Dictionary of Canine Materia Medica. For the Use of Amateurs. By HUGH DALZIEL.
In paper, price 1s., by post 1s. 1d.; in cloth gilt 2s., by post 2s. 2d.

III.

Diseases of Horses:
Their Pathology, Diagnosis, and Treatment; to which is added a complete Dictionary of Equine Materia Medica. For the Use of Amateurs. By HUGH DALZIEL.
In paper, price, 1s. 6d.; post free, 1s. 8d.

IV.

Practical Dairy Farming:
A short Treatise on the Profitable Management of a Dairy Farm. Illustrated By G. SEAWARD WITCOMBE.
In paper, price 1s. 6d.; by post, 1d. 7d.

V.

Book of the Goat:
Containing Practical Directions for the Management of the Milch Goat in Health and Disease. Illustrated. By STEPHEN HOLMES.
Cheap edition, in paper, price 1s.; by post, 1s. 1d.

VI.

Rabbits for Prizes and Profit:
Containing Full Directions for the proper Management of Fancy Rabbits in Health and Disease, for Pets or the Market; and Descriptions of every known Variety, with Instructions for Breeding good specimens. Illustrated. By the late CHARLES RAYSON. Edited by LEONARD U. GILL.
In cloth gilt, price 2s. 6d.; by post, 2s. 9d.

VII.

General Management of Rabbits:
Containing Hutches, Breeding, Feeding, Diseases and their Treatment, Rabbits as a Food Supply, &c.
In paper, price 1s.; by post, 1s. 1d.

VIII.

Exhibition Rabbits:
Containing careful descriptions of Angora, Belgian Hare, Dutch, Himalayan, Lops, Patagonian, Polish, Siberian, Silver Grey and Silver Cream, Fancy Rabbits, with several full page portraits of prize specimens.
In paper, price 1s.; by paper, 1s. 1d.

IX.

Ferrets and Ferreting:
Containing Instructions for the Breeding, Management, and Working of Ferrets.
In paper, price 6d.; by post, 7d.

X.

Fancy Mice:

Their Varieties, Management, and Breeding. Illustrated.
In paper, price 6d.; by post, 6½d.

XI.

Foreign Cage Birds:

Containing Full Directions for Successfully Breeding, Rearing, and Managing the various Beautiful Cage Birds imported into this country. Beautifully Illustrated. By C. W. GEDNEY.

In cloth gilt, in two vols., price 8s. 6d.; by post, 9s.

Vol. I.—Parrakeets, Parrots, Cockatoos, Lories, and Macaws. In cloth gilt, price 3s. 6d.; by post, 3s. 9d.

Vol. II.—Waxbills, Finches, Weavers, Orioles, and other Aviary Birds. In cloth gilt, price 5s.; by post, 5s. 4d.

The vols. may be had separately.

XII.

Canary Book:

Containing Full Directions for the Breeding, Rearing, and Management of Canaries and Canary Mules; Formation of Canary Societies; Exhibition Canaries, their points and breeding; and all other matters connected with this fancy. Illustrated. By ROBERT L. WALLACE. In one vol., cloth gilt, price 5s., by post, 5s. 4d.

May also be had in parts as follows:
Part I.—General Management. } In paper, price 2s. each, by post, 2s. 2d.
Part II.—Exhibition Canaries.

XIII.

Poultry for Prizes and Profit:

Contains Breeding Poultry for Prizes, Exhibition Poultry, and Management of the Poultry Yard. Handsomely Illustrated. By JAMES LONG.
In cloth gilt, price 2s. 6d.; by post, 2s. 9d.

XIV.

Ducks and Geese:

Their Characteristics, Points, and Management. By VARIOUS BREEDERS. Splendidly illustrated.
In paper, price 1s. 6d.; by post, 1s. 7d.

XV.

Practical Bee-keeping:

Being Plain Instructions to the Amateur for the Successful Management of the Honey Bee. Illustrated. Re-written and Enlarged. By FRANK CHESHIRE.
In cloth gilt, price 2s. 6d.; by post, 2s. 9d.

XVI.

British Dogs:

Their Varieties, History, and Characteristics. Illustrated with numerous Portraits of Dogs of the Day. By HUGH DALZIEL.
Division I.—Dogs Used in Field Sports.
In Monthly Parts, price 6d., by post 6½d.

IN THE PRESS.

Rabbit Book:

Being a Complete Guide to the Successful Breeding and Rearing of every Variety of the Fancy Rabbit, both for the Exhibition Pen and the Table. Magnificently illustrated. This will be the most exhaustive work on Rabbits ever published.

Fancy Pigeons:

Containing full directions for the Breeding and Management of Fancy Pigeons, and Descriptions of every known variety, together with all other information of interest or use to Pigeon Fanciers. Illustrated. By J. C. LYELL.

MANUALS ON PRACTICAL MECHANICS.

I.

Patents, Trade Marks, and Designs :
A Practical Guide to Inventors and Manufacturers for Securing Protection under each of these heads. By ARCHIBALD CRAIG.
In cloth gilt, price 1s. 6d.; by post, 1s. 8d.   In paper, price 1s.; by post, 1s. 1d.

II.

Practical Architecture :
As applied to Farm Buildings of every description (Cow, Cattle and Calf Houses, Stables, Piggeries. Sheep Shelter Sheds, Root and other Stores, Poultry Houses), Dairies, and Country Houses and Cottages. Profusely Illustrated with Diagrams and Plans. By ROBERT SCOTT BURN.
In cloth gilt, price 5s.; by post, 5s. 4d.

III.

Art of Pyrotechny :
Being Comprehensive and Practical instructions for the Manufacture of Fire-works. specially designed for the use of Amateurs. Profusely Illustrated. By W. H. BROWNE, Ph.D. M.A., L.R.C.P. &c. Second Edition.
In cloth gilt, price 2s. 6d,, by post, 2s. 10d.

IV.

Minor Fireworks :
Containing Instructions for the Manufacture of the Common and Simple Varieties, of Fireworks. For the Use of Amateurs. Illustrated. By W. H. BROWNE, Ph.D., M.A., &c. (Author of "The Art of Pyrotechny").
In paper, price 1s.; by post, 1s. 1d.

V.

Practical Boat Building for Amateurs :
Containing full Instructions for Designing and Building Punts, Skiffs, Canoes, Sailing Boats, &c. Fully illustrated with working diagrams. By ADRIAN NEISON, C.E.
In cloth gilt, price 2s. 6d., by post 2s. 8d.

VI.

Printing for Amateurs :
A Practical Guide to the Art of Printing; containing Descriptions of Presses and Materials, together with Details of the Process employed, to which is added a Glossary of Technical Terms. Illustrated. By P. E. RAYNOR.
In paper, price 1s.; by post 1s. 2d.

VII.

Turning for Amateurs :
Containing full Description of the Lathe, with all its working parts and attach-ments, and minute instructions for the effective use of them on wood, metal, and ivory. Illustrated with 130 first class wood engravings. Second Edition.
In cloth gilt, price 2s. 6d.; by post, 2s. 9d.

VIII.

Carpentry and Joinery for Amateurs :
Contains full Descriptions of the various Tools required in the above Arts, together with Practical Instructions for their use. By the Author of "Turning for Amateurs," "Working in Sheet Metal." &c.
In cloth gilt, price 2s. 6d.; by post, 2s. 9d.

IX.

Working in Sheet Metal :

Being Practical Instructions for Making and Mending small Articles in Tin, Copper, Iron, Zinc, and Brass. Illustrated. Third Edition. By the Author of "Turning for Amateurs," &c.
In paper, price 6d.; by post, 6½d.

X.

Wood Carving for Amateurs :

Containing Descriptions of all the requisite Tools, and full Instructions for their use in producing different varieties of Carvings. Illustrated.
In paper, price 1s.; by post, 1s. 1d.

IN THE PRESS.

Organs and Organ Building :

Giving the History and Construction of the Modern Organ, and Descriptions of the most remarkable Instruments. By C. A. EDWARDS.

POPULAR NATURAL HISTORY.

I.

Practical Taxidermy :

A Manual of Instruction to the Amateur in Collecting, Preserving, and Setting-up Natural History Specimens of all kinds. Illustrated. By MONTAGU BROWNE.
In cloth gilt, price 3s. 6d; by post, 3s. 9d.

II.

Collecting Butterflies and Moths :

Being Directions for Capturing, Killing, and Preserving Lepidoptera and their Larvæ. Illustrated. Reprinted, with additions, from "Practical Taxidermy." By MONTAGU BROWNE, author of "Practical Taxidermy."
In paper, price 1s.; by post 1s. 1d.

III.

Popular British Fungi :

Containing Descriptions and Histories of the Principal Fungi, both Edible and Poisonous of our Country. Illustrated. By JAMES BRITTEN, F.L.S., &c.
In cloth gilt, price 3s. 6d.; by post, 3s. 9d.

IV.

British Marine Algæ :

Being a Popular Account of the Seaweeds of Great Britain, their Collection and Preservation. Magnificently Illustrated with 205 engravings. By W. H. GRATTANN.
In cloth gilt, price 5s. 6d.; by post, 5s. 10d.

IN THE PRESS.

Zoological Notes :

On the Structure, Affinities, Habits, and Faculties of Animals; with Adventures among and Anecdotes of them. By ARTHUR NICOLS, F.G.S., F.R.G.S. (Author of "The Puzzle of Life, and How it Has Been Put Together.")

PRACTICAL GUIDES TO GARDENING.

I.

The Hardy Fruit Book:

Consisting of a Series of Exhaustive Treatises on the various Hardy Fruits grown in this country; giving the History, the most desirable Sorts, and the best Methods of Cultivation of each. Illustrated. By D. T. FISH (Author of "Pruning, Grafting, and Budding Fruit Trees," "Bulbs and Bulb Culture" &c.

Vol. I.—"The Apple," "The Pear," "The Peach and Nectarine."

In cloth gilt, price 5s.; by post, 5s. 5d.

May also be had in parts as follow:

The Apple:

Its History, Varieties, and Cultivation.

In paper, price 1s.; by post, 1s. 1d.

The Pear:

Its History, Varieties, and Cultivation.

In paper, price 1s. 6d.; by post, 1s. 7d.

The Peach and Nectarine:

Their History, Varieties, and Cultivation.

In paper, price 1s. 6d.; by post, 1s. 7d.

II.

Orchids for Amateurs:

Containing Descriptions of Orchids suited to the requirements of the Amateur, ith full Instructions for their successful Cultivation. With numerous beautiful Illustrations. By JAMES BRITTEN, F.L.S. (of the British Museum), and W. H. GOWER.

In cloth gilt, price 7s. 6d.; by post, 7s. 10d.

III.

Rose Growing for Amateurs:

Being Practical Instructions for the successful Culture of Roses, with selections of the best varieties adapted to the requirements of the Amateur in Town or Country. By W. D. PRIOR.

In paper, price 1s. 6d.; by post, 1s. 8d.

IV.

Bulbs and Bulb Culture:

Being Descriptions, both historical and botanical, of the principal Bulbs and Bulbous Plants grown in this country, and their chief Varieties; with full and practical instructions for their successful Cultivation, both in and out of doors. Illustrated. By D. T. FISH.

Vol. I., in cloth gilt, price 2s. 6d.; by post, 2s. 9d.

May also be had in parts as follow:

Part I., Snowdrops, Bulbocodiums, Sternbergias, Crocus, Colchicums, Tulips, and Hyacinths.

Part II., Anemones, Narcissus, Lilies.

In paper, price 1s. each; by post 1s. 1d.

V.

Vine Culture for Amateurs:

Being Plain Directions for the successful growing of Grapes, with the means and appliances usually at the command of amateurs. Illustrated. By W. J. MAY (Author of "Greenhouse Management for Amateurs," &c.).

In paper, price 1s.; by post, 1s. 1d.

VI.

Pruning, Grafting, and Budding Fruit Trees:

Illustrated with ninety-three Diagrams. By D. T. FISH.

In paper, price 1s., by post, 1s. 1d.

VII.

Villa Gardening:

Being plain instructions for the proper Laying-out, Planting and Management of Small Gardens; with lists of Trees, Shrubs, and Plants most suitable, and thirteen Designs for small gardens. By W. J. MAY.

Cheap edition, in paper, price 1s.; by post, 1s. 1d.

VIII.

Rose Budding:

Containing full Instructions for the successful performance of this interesting operation. Illustrated. By D. T. FISH.

In paper, price 6d.; by post, 7d.

IX.

Greenhouse Management for Amateurs:

Descriptions of the best Greenhouses and Frames, with Instructions for Building them; Particulars of the various Methods of Heating; lists of the most suitable plants, with general and special cultural directions; and all necessary information for the Guidance of the Amateur. Illustrated. By W. J. MAY, Author of "Villa Gardening," "Vine Culture for Amateurs," &c.

In cloth gilt, price 3s. 6d.; by post, 3s. 9d.

IN THE PRESS.

The Apricot:

Its History, Varieties, and Cultivation.

Arboriculture for Amateurs:

Being Instructions for the Planting and Cultivation of Trees for Ornament or Use, and selections and descriptions of those suited to special requirements as to Soil, Situation, &c. By WILLIAM H. ABLETT.

SPORTS AND PASTIMES.

I.

Bicyclist's Pocket Book and Diary, 1879:

For Reference and Registration. Full of facts and forms of interest to Bicyclists. Contents: Bicycle Chart, with particulars of over 200 machines; Best known Amateur Performances; Bugle Calls: Attention, Assembly and Prepare to Mount, Mount, Dismount, Form Single File, Form Twos, Dinner Call, Bugle Marches, Calendar for 1879, with the Principal Events of Past Seasons; Cash Memoranda; Clubs, London and Provincial; Diaries: Cash, Engagements, Performances, Runs; List of Towns, with Inns and Distances in Miles from London; Monthly Review of 1878; Papers referring to Bicycling; Practical Bicycling Advice: Its Value as an Exercise, Choice of a Machine, Joining a Club, On Touring, On the Road, General Meetings, Things to be remembered, On Maps and Day Runs, Metropolitan Law affecting Bicycles and Riders; Racing Memoranda: The Amateur Champions of 1878, Oxford and Cambridge Annual Bicycle Contest, Times of Scratch Men worth noting, Probable open Amateur Events, Bicycle Races of 1878; Railway Charges for Carriage of Bicycles; Register of Performances.

Prices: morocco, 3s. 6d.; roan, 2s. 6d.; postage, 2d.

II.

Bicycles of the Year, 1878-79:

Being a Chronicle of the New Inventions and Improvements introduced each Season, and forming a Permanent Record of the progress in the manufacture of Bicycles; Designed also to assist intending purchasers in the choice of a machine. Illustrated. By HARRY HEWITT GRIFFIN.

In paper, price 6d.; by post, 7½d

III.

Practical Fisherman :

Dealing with the Natural History, the Legendary Lore, and the Capture of British Freshwater Fish. Illustrated.

In paper, in parts, price 6d. each ; by post, 6½d.

IV.

Camp Life on the Weser :

Being a graphic account of an autumn boating trip on the Weser ; pointing out where may still be had, within easy distance of London,' healthful recreation, combined with lovely scenery and old-world prices, without contact with the ubiquitous excursionist. By HARRY TOMLINSON and JAMES POWELL. Illustrated.

In cloth gilt, price 2s. 6d. ; by post, 2s. 7d.

V.

Country Pocket Book and Diary, 1879 :

For Reference and Registration. Full of facts and forms of the greatest value and interest to Country gentlemen and sportsmen. Contents ; Diaries—Engagements, Exhibitor's, Fishing, Shooting, Cricketing, Athletics, Bicycling, Football, Breeder's, Hunting, Cash ; Calendar ; Post Office Charges ; Close Time for Trout and Chard in England and Wales ; Weight of Trout ; Tolls on the Thames ; Sizes of Thames Fish that may be Killed ; Rainfall ; Amateur Aquatic Championship ; Bank Holidays ; Quarter Days ; Law Sittings and Terms ; Eclipses ; Phases of the Moon ; Close Time for Wild Birds ; Oxford and Cambridge Boat Races ; Swimming Amateur Championship ; Railway Carriage of Boats ; Dog Licences ; Game Licences ; Gun Licences ; Close Time for Game ; Winners of the Derby ; Gentlemen v. Players ; Winners of the Oaks ; Close Time for Salmon in England and Wales ; Size of Lea Fish that may be Killed ; Close Time for Fixed Engines for Eels ; Close Time for Oysters ; Winners of the St. Leger ; Winners of the Ascot Gold Cup ; Oxford and Cambridge Cricket ; Eton v. Harrow ; Close Time for Sea Birds ; Winners of the 2000 Guineas ; Inspectors of Salmon Fishing ; Newspapers relating to Sport ; Football Association Challenge Cup ; Papers devoted to Special Branches of Sport ; Magazines and Annuals relating to Sport ; Inter-Hospital Football Challenge Cup ; North v. South Football ; Oxford University Terms ; Close Time for the Thames ; Cambridge University Terms ; Close Time for Wildfowl ; Close Time for Salmon in Scotland ; Poultry and Pigeon Clubs ; Fire Insurance ; Barometrical Readings ; Railway Carriage of Dogs ; Dog Clubs ; Salmon Fisheries' Commissioners, Scotland ; Inspectors of Fisheries in Ireland ; Periods of Gestation ; Periods of Incubation ; Close Time for Rivers and Broads of Norfolk and Suffolk ; Acts of Parliament relating to sports and Rural Pursuits ; Locks on the Thames, and their distances from London and Oxford, and from each other ; High Water Variation in the Thames ; Weather Forecasts ; Thermometric Scales ; Close Time for Salmon and Trout in Ireland ; Coming Events ; Goodwood Cup Winners ; Winners of Waterloo Cup ; Railway Carriage of Bicycles ; Remarkable Performances ; Winners of the Grand Prix de Paris ; Liverpool Cup Winners ; English, Scotch, and Irish Miles ; English, Scotch, and Irish Acres ; Winners Middle Park Plate ; Thames Fishermen ; Close Time for Coarse Fish ; Australian Cricketers in England ; Parliamentary Papers and Reports on Subjects affecting Country Gentlemen and Sportsmen ; Acts of Parliament of last Session ; Notable Events ; High Water at London Bridge.

Prices ; In Russia leather, 5s. 6d. ; morocco, 4s. 6d. ; roan, 3s. 6d. ; postage, 2d.

VI.

Practical Photography :

Being the Science and Art of Photography, Developed for Amateurs and Beginners. Illustrated. By O. E. WHEELER.
Part I.—Wet Collodion Process.

In paper, price 1s. ; by post, 1s. 2d.

VII.

The Photographer's Pocket Book :

Containing Register for nearly 1000 Negatives. Compiled by O. E. WHEELER, author of " Practical Photography,"
Prices ; In cloth, 3s. ; in leather 3s. 6d. ; by post, 2d. extra.

VIII.

Photographer's Pocket Book Almanac :

Containing Monthly Calendar for noting state of weather and amount of work done ; Existing State of Photographic Progress ; Hints to Landscape Photographers ; Photographic Societies ; Every-day Formulæ ; Formulæ for Dry Plates, &c
Price, in paper, 6d. ; by post 6½d.

Practical Handbooks.—Sports and Pastimes (continued).

IX.

Leather Work Book :

Containing Full Instructions for Making and Ornamenting articles so as to successfully imitate Carved Oak ; specially written for the use of Amateurs. By ROSA BAUGHAN. Illustrated.
In cloth gilt, price 2s. 6d. ; by post, 2s. 9d.

X.

Cards and Card Tricks :

Containing a brief History of Playing Cards : Full Instructions, with Illustrated Hands, for playing nearly all known games of chance or skill, and directions for performing a number of amusing Tricks. Illustrated. By H. E. HEATHER.
In cloth gilt, price 5s. ; by post, 5s. 4d.

XI.

Sleight of Hand :

Being Minute Instructions by the Aid of which, with proper practice, the Neatest and most Intricate Tricks of Legerdemain can be successfully performed. Illustrated. By EDWIN SACHS.
In cloth gilt, price, 5s. ; by post, 5s. 4d.

XII.

Artistic Amusements :

Being Instructions for a variety of Art Work for Home Employment, and Suggestions for a number of Novel and Saleable Articles for Fancy Bazaars. Illustrated. Contents : Colouring Photographs, Imitation Stained Glass, Decalcomanie, Queen Shell Work, Painting on China, Japanese Lacquer Work, Stencilling, Painting Magic Lantern Slides, Menu and Guest Cards, Spatter Work, Picture and Scrap Screens, Frosted Silver Work, Picture Cleaning and Restoring, Illuminating and Symbolical Colouring.
In cloth gilt, price 2s. 6d. ; by post, 2s. 8d.

MISCELLANEOUS.

I.

English Pottery and Porcelain :

A Manual for Collectors. Being a Concise Account of the Development of the Potter's Art in England. Profusely Illustrated with Marks, Monograms, and Engravings of characteristic Specimens. New Edition.
In cloth gilt, price 3s. 6d. ; by post, 3s. 8d.

II.

English, Scotch, and Irish Coins :

A Manual for Collectors ; being a History and Description of the Coinage of Great Britain, from the Earliest Ages to the Present Time, with Tables of Approximate Values of Good Specimens. Profusely Illustrated.
In cloth gilt, price 5s. ; by post, 5s. 4d.

III.

Value of British Coins :

A Manual for Buyers, Sellers, and Exchangers, as giving the Approximate Values of good Specimens of English and Scotch Coins.
In paper, price 1s. ; by post, 1s. 1d.

IV.

Character Indicated by Handwriting :

With Illustrations in support of the Theories advanced, taken from Autograph Letters of Statesmen, Lawyers Soldiers, Ecclesiastics, Authors, Poets, Musicians, Actors, and other persons. By R. BAUGHAN.

In cloth gilt, price 2s. 6d.; by post 2s. 9d.

V.

Seaside Watering Places :

Being a Guide to Persons in Search of a Suitable Place in which to Spend their Holidays, on the English and Welsh Coasts. New and Revised Edition, with Descriptions of over 130 Places.

In paper, price 2s.; by post, 2s. 3d.

VI.

Stock and Share Investments :

Being Explanations for the General Reader of the Nature and Quality of the different Classes of Securities dealt in on the Stock Exchange. By ALBERT SHARWOOD.

In paper, price 1s.; by post, 1s. 1d.

VII.

Church Festival Decorations:

Comprising Directions and Designs for the Suitable Decoration of Churches for Christmas, Easter, Whitsuntide, and Harvest. Illustrated.

In paper, price 1s.; by post, 1s. 1d.

VIII.

Artistic Flower Decorations :

For Ball Rooms, Halls, Passages, Dinner and Supper Tables; with Directions for making Bouquets, Buttonholes, Hair Sprays, &c. Illustrated. By B. C. SAWARD.

In paper, price 2s.; by post, 2s. 2d.

IX.

Honiton Lace Book :

Containing Full and Practical Instructions for Making Honiton Lace. With Illustrations.

In cloth gilt, price 3s. 6d.; by post, 3s. 9d.

X.

Hints to Untrained Teachers :

Being Directions and Suggestions for the Assistance of Parents and others engaged in Home Education. By JANE ASCHAM.

In paper, price 6d.; by post 7d.

XI.

Practical Dressmaking :

Being Plain Directions for Taking Patterns, Fitting on, Cutting out, Making up, and Trimming Ladies' and Children's Dresses. By R. MUNROE.

In paper, price 1s.; by post, 1s. 1d.

THE COUNTRY,

A JOURNAL OF RURAL PURSUITS.

The Cheapest and Best Paper for Country Gentlemen.

"Like all grand conceptions, the process is remarkable for its simplicity."—
The Globe.

The Bazaar,

The Exchange and Mart,

AND JOURNAL OF THE HOUSEHOLD.

ILLUSTRATED.

Cut Paper Patterns.

To meet the demand for good and fashionable patterns of ladies' and children's garments at reasonable prices, there is issued in connection with THE BAZAAR a series of high-class patterns, each one of which has been specially designed and prepared for that paper, and ladies are invited to inspect the list before making other arrangements. This list is added to week by week, so that it contains the newest and most seasonable fashions. The list may be seen and orders given at any of the Local Agencies, or at the Head Office.

MUSICAL TUITION IN CLASSES.

C. ROYLANCE,

THE

Originator of Musical Tuition in Classes

(FOR VIOLIN, FLUTE, OR ENGLISH CONCERTINA,
AT 6s. PER QUARTER),

Has found it necessary to CAUTION intending PUPILS, or Purchasers of Musical Instruments, that his ONLY ADDRESS

IS

184, TOTTENHAM COURT ROAD,

Where instruments may be had on easy term of payment, and the
greatest advantage offered for cash payment.

A VIOLIN CLASS FOR LADIES MEETS EVERY SATURDAY
AT 6 O'CLOCK. TERMS 6s. PER QUARTER.

Price List and Prospectus Free.

184, TOTTENHAM COURT ROAD.

Large Size, Post Free, 24 Stamps

Small Size, Post Free, 14 Stamps.

STEVENS' SILICON
JEWELLERY REVIVER
TABLET.

THIS UNRIVALLED POLISH
(*Direct from Nature's Laboratory*)

Is not a manufactured article, but a very remarkable natural production, the best substance known for Cleaning and Polishing Gold, Silver, and Jewels without the least injury, and will prevent pearls becoming discoloured.

Sold in a handsome little box, with Brush, Leather, Directions for Use, an Analysis, and numerous Testimonials, price 1s.

A large size, containing also a Ring Cleaning Stick, and one for cleaning Studs and Buttons, price 2s.

The SILICON is also sold in Powder, for Plate Cleaning, at 6d. and 1s. per box, and in canisters at 2s. 6d.

To be had through all Chemists, Fancy Goods Dealers, and Jewellers throughout the kingdom, and Wholesale of all London Fancy Warehouses and Wholesale Druggists, and of the Proprietor,

GEORGE STEVENS,
376, STRAND, LONDON.

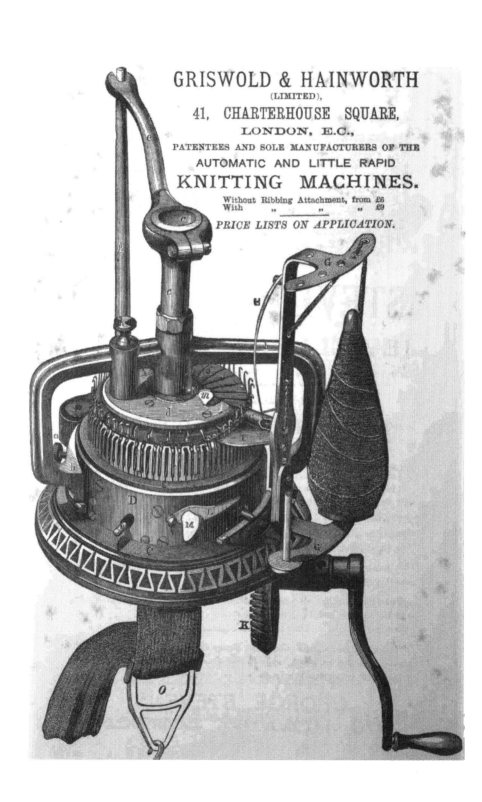

GRISWOLD & HAINWORTH
(LIMITED),
41, CHARTERHOUSE SQUARE,
LONDON, E.C.,
PATENTEES AND SOLE MANUFACTURERS OF THE
AUTOMATIC AND LITTLE RAPID
KNITTING MACHINES.
Without Ribbing Attachment, from £6
With   „   „   „ £9
PRICE LISTS ON APPLICATION.

Gentlemen wishing to Purchase or Exchange Machines are invited
to pay the

GREAT WESTERN

BICYCLE WORKS

a visit of inspection, where they will have an opportunity of seeing a
large variety of makes and sizes ranging from £7 10s. and upwards,
and the Proprietors will be happy to give advice as to the suitability of
machines for purchasers' requirements.

THE BICYCLES, TRICYCLES, &c.,

in stock are guaranteed to be of the Best Material and Workmanship,
and comprise Machines of the Best Makers, and also the latest
Improvements.

A TABULATED PRICE LIST POST FREE.

Photo of any machine, 3 stamps.

A NUMBER OF SOILED & SECONDHAND MACHINES ALWAYS IN STOCK.

Terms: 5 per cent. Discount for Cash, or

BICYCLES ARE SOLD ON

THE NEW HIRE SYSTEM.

FULL PARTICULARS ON APPLICATION.

SPECIAL TERMS TO SHIPPERS AND CLUBS.

REPAIRS are done on the premises by competent workmen, at a
moderate charge, quickly and well.

RIDING TAUGHT

by experienced instructors, and great care is taken to render pupils
quickly proficient, without allowing them to have unnecessary falls.

TERMS 2s. PER LESSON OF ONE HOUR.

Free to Purchasers.

Bicycle Sundries of every description.   Low prices and good value.

CROOKE AND CO.,

2, Praed Street, London, W.

Ingram Content Group UK Ltd.
Milton Keynes UK
UKHW020054100623
423210UK00005B/110